Praise for *Funding Forward*

As religious participation shifts in the United States, the economic model for churches is changing rapidly and significantly. In this moment of massive change and incredible opportunity, Grace Pomroy provides both inspiration and practical guidance for churches and denominations. Her research and insights are both appropriately realistic and deeply hopeful. This book is an essential read for church leaders who are finding their way forward.

—Mark Elsdon, editor of *Gone for Good? Negotiating the Coming Wave of Church Property Transition*, and author of *We Aren't Broke: Uncovering Hidden Resources for Mission and Ministry*

It is refreshing to see a book that operates from an abundance mentality. Grace Duddy Pomroy's *Funding Forward* inspires readers to reimagine how God is calling them to be innovative stewards of resources that go beyond traditional congregation functions.

—Rev. Martin Otto-Zimmann, PhD, senior director of Kindling Faith Ministry, United Lutheran Seminary

Facing the narrative of declining attendance, aging congregations, and budget shortfalls, in *Funding Forward* Grace Pomroy offers a transformative roadmap for congregations seeking to align with God's mission, revitalize community connections, and achieve sustainable ministry practices. This insightful guide navigates readers through the funding-forward process, equipping them with practical tools and strategies to discern their purpose, engage with their neighborhood, and embrace economic sustainability. With keen attention to leadership challenges and potential pitfalls, this book empowers ministries to embark on a journey of renewal and growth. A must-read for any congregation ready to embark on a path of purposeful transformation.

—Dave Harder, principal consultant, Trinity Centres Foundation, Montreal

Dire predictions for the future of congregations abound. Grace Pomroy describes a different, more hopeful pathway forward—one that grows from the congregation's mission, builds on its strengths, and serves its community. This is a book that provides pastors and lay leaders in every context with practical suggestions for faithfully and creatively funding the congregation into the future.

—Pastor Charles Lane, author of *Ask, Thank, Tell* and *Reflections on Faith and Finances*

The pandemic brought questions of alternative funding models and unused assets to the front of many clergy's minds. *Funding Forward* comprehensively addresses such issues and offers research, models, and examples of churches who have embraced both what God is calling them to do and innovative ways to fund that mission. While this isn't a path for all churches, every leadership team should read this book and consider this challenge of creating a sustainable model for ministry.

—Scott Thumma, director, Hartford Institute for Religion Research

Congregations are in uncharted waters right now, and their clergy have not been equipped to navigate them. Grace Pomeroy doesn't provide a life preserver, but more of a map for faith communities facing the challenges of dwindling numbers of people and dollars. She reframes the narrative from one of decline to one brimming with possibility and hope, and not through magical thinking. Rather, the myriad stories presented here are drawn from Pomeroy's research in real congregations who are creatively developing mission strategies that are contextual, faithful, and effective. Readers will find case studies with which they identify and action plans that resonate with their own situations. In surveying the assets in community and congregation to reimagine their future, church leaders can certainly count this book as an asset in that journey.

—Katie Day, Charles A. Schieren Professor Emerita of Church and Society, United Lutheran Seminary, Philadelphia

Finally! A book with practical applications that those of us out in the field can use to share our church space with the community we are grounded in! Grace Pomroy has given us a dynamic, thorough resource to use when we, as leaders in rural areas, are dreaming big and developing community engagement opportunities. By giving examples of how ministry can be community-minded and forward-moving, Pomroy has opened my eyes, and the eyes of congregations, to new and inventive ways to be church in the world. This book is a must-read for all congregations looking at the future and wanting to be creative with their current and future funding.

—Melissa Pickering, pastor, First Lutheran Church, Audubon, Minnesota

Funding Forward invites leaders to reflect on the ways money follows mission with such an approachable and grace-filled approach. From the wisdom that comes from both her research and years of practical experience, Pomroy offers congregations an on-ramp to discerning their future. Pomroy does not prescribe a one-size-fits-all plan, but readers will gain the tools to take first steps and the encouragement to continue on the journey.

—David P. King, Karen Lake Buttrey Director of the Lake Institute on Faith and Giving, Indiana University Lilly Family School of Philanthropy

The North American church faces critical decisions about how it will engage in mission in light of an uncertain economic future and increasingly precarious financial model. *Funding Forward* provides the church with a blueprint to ask critically important questions about mission and purpose that anchor church leaders as they seek to remain faithful to their calling. The straightforward process, practical tools, and vivid examples that Pomroy offers spur the reader's imagination and lay a foundation for the church to direct its attention toward a future filled with hope.

—Rev. Thad Austin, executive director, Common Table Collaborative; vice president, EveryAge Foundation; and author of *Congregational Social Entrepreneurship: A Field Guide for Lay and Clergy Leaders*

funding FORWARD

funding FORWARD

A Pathway to More Sustainable Models for Ministry

GRACE DUDDY POMROY

FORTRESS PRESS
MINNEAPOLIS

FUNDING FORWARD
A Pathway to More Sustainable Models for Ministry

29 28 27 26 25 24 1 2 3 4 5 6 7 8 9

Library of Congress Control Number: 2024935769

Cover design and illustration: Kristin Miller

Print ISBN: 978-1-5064-9333-6
eBook ISBN: 978-1-5064-9334-3

To my students whose questions have guided my work,
To the congregation leaders who are on the ground doing the work,
To my partner, Tyler, who has supported me and
created space for this work to flourish,
Thank you, this book is for you.

Contents

Foreword
by Dwight Zscheile

It is both a profoundly challenging time for churches and a profoundly auspicious time for the church to be the church. The world needs the saving, healing, reconciling love of God in Christ now as much as ever. Yet the predominant organizational model for American congregations for the past two centuries is unraveling amidst waves of social and cultural change.

Since the American Revolution, congregations have been organized primarily as voluntary associations that people join and support with their "time, talent, and treasure." The voluntary association model in American society also gave birth to service clubs like Rotary, veterans organizations, garden clubs, scouting troops, and countless other institutions in which people found belonging, meaning, and purpose.

Today, fewer people are joining and supporting voluntary associations of any kind as they seek individual self-expression. This institutional disembedding, particularly among younger generations, is wreaking havoc on the basic business models and operations of many congregations. You may be seeing its effects as you struggle to recruit members, secure volunteers, maintain buildings, and raise the budget.

It would be easy to succumb to despair about these trends. Yet this moment provides opportunities for reconnection and renewal, joining the triune God's life and movement in our surrounding communities, cultivating new relationships with neighbors, and discovering ways to organize and fund the church that fit more adequately with this cultural moment. This is a time of refocusing, letting go, and leaning in as we discover how to adapt the life of our churches so that people in our contexts may know the unconditional promise of God's love in Jesus Christ.

Funding Forward is a book full of hope grounded in a path-breaking research project into more sustainable business models for ministry in the United States and Canada. Grace Pomroy has discovered hundreds of congregations that are navigating the challenges and opportunities of this moment courageously and creatively. Their stories are not always neat and tidy, reflecting as they do the real-world ambiguities of taking the journey into an unknown future. Yet they offer rich practical wisdom and inspiration.

There are no quick fixes or easy technical solutions. What is required is deeper learning that invites us into a posture of humility, curiosity, openness, and experimentation. At Luther Seminary's Faith+Lead, we're committed to walking alongside churches and their leaders as they seek to respond faithfully to a changing world. This means clarifying and renewing who we are as the church (our identity), how we are gifted and called to join God's work in the world (our mission), and how our community's life can be shaped to embody that mission (our organization).

This book offers stories, insights, pathways, and practices to discover a more hopeful future in a time of stress and disruption. Read it with an open heart and mind for how God may be calling you into the adventure of discovering a new business model for your ministry.

Preface

In the fall of 2018, I led a preretirement seminar for Evangelical Lutheran Church in America (ELCA) pastors, deacons, ministry leaders, and their spouses in Chandler, Arizona. As I scanned the crowd, I was surprised to see a man in his late twenties in the audience that day. He was there to interpret the entire seminar for his father who was a Spanish-speaking ELCA pastor. It turns out that this son of an ELCA pastor was also a newly minted ELCA pastor himself. He had just received his "first call" to a congregation.[1] After months of waiting, when he finally had a chance to interview with a congregation, he was ready to do whatever it took to make the call work. He found out the congregation could only afford to pay for a three-quarter-time pastor, but they still hoped that he would complete all the duties of a full-time pastor (including being present every Sunday) despite being paid a three-quarter-time salary. They also asked that he go on his partner's health insurance to reduce the congregation's costs. While this new pastor accepted the call with enthusiasm, by the time I met him at this event, a few months later, I could tell his excitement was already waning. He knew that he had said "yes" too much during the interview process and had set himself up for resentment and burnout. What a way to begin his first role in ministry!

This story has haunted me for the last six years. What circumstances might bring this congregation to a place where they would ask the pastor to take on the congregation's financial burden in this way? This story is just one of numerous examples illustrating the financial constraints that so many congregations today are experiencing.

You may be weighed down by worry, grief, and fear about what the future might hold for your congregation. You care deeply about your congregation. You've seen how lives have been transformed through its ministry. And yet, you have seen the writing on the wall that your congregation's current financial situation is not (or soon will not be) sustainable. You believe God still has big dreams for your congregation but you're worried dwindling finances or a crumbling building may get in the way of making those dreams possible.

It was these experiences of financial constraint in the church today that inspired me to apply for the role of director of the Stewardship Leaders Program at Luther Seminary in early 2020. One of the key lines of the job description was to "equip students and other church leaders to innovate entrepreneurial, sustainable business models for Christian communities." I was eager to find out what those entrepreneurial, sustainable business models might look like and share those models with churches who are struggling financially, like the one I shared above. I knew the ever-popular narrative of church decline wasn't the end of the Christian story or even the church's story.

Exploring Funding Forward

In the spring of 2020, I was encouraged to get started right away with crafting a new course for seminary students titled "Funding Forward: Leading Organizations to Financial Sustainability."[2] There were many congregations who had engaged in this work, but not a lot had been written about it. I was so grateful to find two of Mark DeYmaz's books just days before my course syllabus was due: *Disruption: Repurposing the Church to Redeem the Community*[3] and the book he cowrote with his colleague, Harry Li, *The Coming Revolution in Church Economics: Why Tithes and Offerings Are No Longer Enough and What You Can Do About It.*[4] While these books created a spine for the course, the heartbeat of the course came from interviews I did with congregation leaders and practitioners who were engaged in this work.

I started by searching for a few "templates" for sustainable models that I could share with congregations. Yet, as I read articles about and interviewed leaders from congregations who were renting out their property, starting social enterprises, securing grants, and more, I realized that each congregation and its journey to sustainability was unique. There was no short list of templates that could work for every congregation. Instead, I began to realize the things that connected these congregations together weren't their denominational identity, their size, their financial situation, not even their desire for financial sustainability; instead, it was these four traits:

- **Mission:** A clear sense of what God was calling them to do and to be.
- **Community Connection:** The congregation had connected with its surrounding community and had a deep understanding of

the community's gifts, desires, and needs. Instead of creating a one-way relationship with the community where the church serviced the community's needs, they sought opportunities for mutual partnership.

- **Unique Assets:** An accounting of the unique assets God had entrusted to their congregation and community. This wasn't just about the building and the bank statements; they understood the often-intangible assets that made them unique. This might look like a group of entrepreneurial, previously incarcerated individuals who were struggling to find employment or a church staff member with a passion for baking.
- **Money+Mission:** They brought these three items together to live out God's mission for their congregation in a new way by using these unique assets to meet a need in their community. This isn't about giving more money away or sending more money overseas but rather making sure every line item of the church's budget connects to the mission God is inviting us to join.

I went into this process looking for cookie cutters. Instead, I found myself walking into a French patisserie where the only thing connecting the individual congregations was the yeast that caused their congregations to grow, expand, and blossom into beautiful new creations. That yeast is God's work—the mission and purpose God has placed in the heart of each of our congregations. The creations take different shapes based on the unique communities that we are called to serve and the assets God has called us to steward. Creating sustainable congregations is first and foremost God's work, not ours. As the ELCA would say, it's "God's work. Our hands."

In 2021, my colleagues in the Stewardship Leaders Program and I invited an ecumenical group of nine congregations who were interested in shifting their financial model into an online learning community. We learned:

- **Openness to change was a necessity:** We were clear in the application process that we were interested in engaging congregations who were ready to create change in their congregation's financial model. The pastors, staff, congregational leadership, and the congregation itself needed to be open to change for this process to be successful.

- **Most congregations don't have a clear sense of God's mission:** This isn't to say that congregations don't have a sense of the gospel. Instead, most congregations don't have a clear sense of God's mission or purpose for their particular congregation: What is God calling them to do and to be? What work is God already doing in their neighborhood that the Spirit is inviting them to join? If one of the keys to Funding Forward is finding money and mission alignment, you can't do this if you don't know your mission. This was often the first stumbling block congregations ran into while trying to do this work.
- **Congregation leaders had an abundance of ideas:** Brainstorming ideas was never the issue. Once the leaders in the learning community had heard some of the stories of what congregations were doing in this area, their brains lit up. They were filled with hope and excitement for how God might be calling them to use the assets God had entrusted to their care in new ways.
- **Congregation leaders struggled to get their broader congregational leadership team and the congregation on board:** While the pastoral and lay leaders that were involved in the learning community found the experience inspiring and invigorating, they faced numerous hurdles trying to translate their learnings to their church leadership teams and congregations as a whole. They wondered what practices they might use to help them as leaders, as well as the congregation, to navigate the change process.

In response to this experience in our learning community, I launched a two-phase research project to help us get to the bottom of these two questions: What conditions are necessary to help a congregation shift its financial model? And what practices might a congregation use to facilitate that shift?

Beginning in the summer of 2022, my research team and I assembled a list of two hundred churches[5] in the United States and Canada who had experimented with their financial model by using at least one consistent income source outside of tithes and offerings, intentionally reducing the congregation's budget to better align with mission, and/or creating an entirely self-sustaining individual church ministry. This experiment wasn't just financially motivated; it was also aligned with the congregation's mission. We quickly found out that there were congregations of all ages, denominations, sizes, financial positions, and geographic locations that were doing this work. While some had been recognized for it, most were doing this work in the shadows. They were eager to share their stories with others and connect with like-minded congregations who were engaged in the work. We sent a survey to each of these congregations in the fall of 2022 and received 101 responses.

In the winter and spring of 2023, we interviewed twelve of the surveyed congregations to wade deeper into their stories. Since the stories from these congregations are the lifeblood of this book, I wanted to introduce them to you from the outset:

7400 Woodlawn[6] in Seattle, Washington
Clarendon Presbyterian Church in Arlington, Virginia
Common Ground Church in Lodi, Wisconsin
Concordia Lutheran Church in Chicago, Illinois
The Emory Fellowship in Washington, District of Columbia
First Congregational Church of Kensington United Church of Christ (KCC) in Kensington, New Hampshire
First Presbyterian Church of Gulf Shores in Gulf Shores, Alabama
Galileo Christian Church in Fort Worth, Texas
Peace Lutheran Church in Tacoma, Washington
River Heights Vineyard Church and La Viña Inver in Inver Grove Heights, Minnesota
St. Andrew Lutheran Church in Eden Prairie, Minnesota
The Table UMC in Sacramento, California

What to Expect

What you will read in this book is a compilation of my conversations with congregational leaders and students as well as the findings of the research project. I hope to lift up and honor these stories in this book, bringing you as close to those who are doing this work as possible. It's important that the congregations be able to speak for themselves and tell their own stories. Every congregation is unique. Even if their stories, beliefs, and experiences are different from your congregation's, I hope they will help you think about your church's money and mission in new ways.

This book is broken down into chapters that can be read together as a church leadership team, stewardship team, finance committee, or even as a congregation. Or you may decide to pull together another group in your congregation focused specifically on this work.

Each chapter opens with a Scripture passage, some questions to drive conversation, and a brief prayer. This spiritual practice at the opening of each chapter is designed to ground us in God's word and remind us that no matter what financial minutiae might be discussed in this chapter, this is God's work, not ours. At the end of each chapter, you'll find a simple practice to help you engage one of the ideas from the chapter as well as some questions for reflection.

You may feel the push to rush through the book to find any quick tips to increase your cash flow. I can promise you that these quick tips will only get you so far if you are disconnected from your community and God's mission for your congregation. Taking the time to invest in this work will allow you to take bigger strides toward long-term sustainability and engage more deeply with God in the process. I hope that you leave with a deeper appreciation of the assets God has called your congregation to steward and the mission God is inviting you to join. I hope you leave brimming with ideas of new things to start and concrete steps you can take to make those dreams a reality. I hope that you leave with a deeper sense of hope as you face realities of decline, scarcity, and burnout.

And, now, let the journey begin.

PART 1

Building a Strong Foundation

Often congregation leaders come to me looking for the financial "silver bullet" that will relieve the pressure on their congregation's budget. They want a quick fix to get them back into the black. And yet, in most cases, the dip into the red is just one symptom of a few deeper issues: the congregation is disconnected from its community and unsure of how to participate in the work that God is already doing there. In this first part of the book, I will introduce you to the broader Funding Forward process, take a deeper look at these issues, and help you build a strong theological and missional foundation on which to do this creative funding work.

It may feel tempting to skip ahead to the funding-focused sections at the end of the book—especially if you are the "financially-minded" person in the congregation. While you may find some technical solutions in the later chapters, none are designed to be quick fixes. Without the deeper transformation work, these technical solutions are unlikely to work, and if they do, they will only provide temporary respite. Doing this difficult work on the front end, will give your funding ideas roots and ensure they not only help your congregation to create sustainability but live more deeply into what God is calling your congregation to do and to be. It's more about ministry than it is about money.

CHAPTER ONE

What Is Funding Forward?

John 6:1–14

"After this Jesus went to the other side of the Sea of Galilee, also called the Sea of Tiberias. A large crowd kept following him, because they saw the signs that he was doing for the sick. Jesus went up the mountain and sat down there with his disciples. Now the Passover, the festival of the Jews, was near. When he looked up and saw a large crowd coming towards him, Jesus said to Philip, 'Where are we to buy bread for these people to eat?' He said this to test him, for he himself knew what he was going to do. Philip answered him, 'Six months' wages would not buy enough bread for each of them to get a little.' One of his disciples, Andrew, Simon Peter's brother, said to him, 'There is a boy here who has five barley loaves and two fish. But what are they among so many people?' Jesus said, 'Make the people sit down.' Now there was a great deal of grass in the place; so they sat down, about five thousand in all. Then Jesus took the loaves, and when he had given thanks, he distributed them to those who were seated; so also the fish, as much as they wanted. When they were satisfied, he told his disciples, 'Gather up the fragments left over, so that nothing may be lost.' So they gathered them up, and from the fragments of the five barley loaves, left by those who had eaten, they filled twelve baskets. When the people saw the sign that he had done, they began to say, 'This is indeed the prophet who is to come into the world.' "

Dwelling Questions

1. What word or phrase jumped out at you as you read the passage?
2. Which character in this passage do you resonate with most?
3. Are there any tangible or intangible assets you or your congregation have that feel a bit like the boy's lunch?
4. What might God be saying to you or your congregation through this passage?

The Prayer of Good Courage

"Lord God, You have called your servants to ventures of which we cannot see the ending, by paths as yet untrodden, through perils unknown. Give us faith to go out with good courage, not knowing where we go but only that your hand is leading us and your love supporting us; through Jesus Christ our Lord. Amen."[1]

A few years ago, one of my students introduced me to the "miracle of sharing" interpretation of this passage.[2] What if the real miracle wasn't Jesus feeding five thousand people from a boy's meager lunch but instead that Jesus's sharing of the boy's lunch invited others to pull out what they had brought to share with others in the crowd. The miracle isn't that Jesus magically produced a catered feast in the wilderness but that a crowd of strangers were inspired to bring together their desperate collection of food to cobble together an abundant feast. Much has been written for and against this interpretation so I won't wade too much into the theological weeds, but I must say that there is a lot about this interpretation that both intrigues and inspires me.

During seminary, a college friend and I attended Christ Church Lutheran in Minneapolis, Minnesota. Walking in for the first time, it was easier to see what the congregation lacked than what it had. There were a hundred mostly gray-haired attendees on any given Sunday in a space designed to seat four hundred fifty. The congregation's vitality (or lack thereof) stood in stark contrast to its historic space. Immediately, I decided it was not the church for me but stayed for the service anyway.

What I experienced over the next two hours blew me away. I heard beautiful music and inspired preaching. But more than anything, there was a genuine sense of welcome that I had never experienced in a congregation before. As we walked up the aisle to meet the minister before leaving, I was shocked by how many people came up to us who not only gave us an obligatory "hello and handshake" but asked about where we worked, where we went to school, what we were studying, where we were from, and so on. Again and again, we were invited to come to the education building next door for fellowship and treats. While we hadn't planned to stay, we couldn't help but do so after all of those invitations. As we entered the education building, we were greeted by the scent of coffee and the sweet aroma of a buffet table full of sweet and savory treats. How could such a meager gathering create an abundant feast not just on one Sunday but week after week after week? Every person in that modest-sized congregation played a part in making that feast happen.

As I began to get to know the congregation, I also began to peel back the layers of their story. About a decade prior to my attendance, this congregation had nearly closed. The membership had dwindled, and they weren't sure how they would ever be able to maintain their beautiful space. As they discerned what to do next, they also began to realize how insular their congregation was. It was filled with older people of northern European descent who loved celebrating their traditions but didn't know how to open their doors to anyone else. They began to realize that in order to stay alive they needed to change. They needed to reach out beyond their doors, be a welcoming presence to those who came in, and embrace new traditions. They didn't want to bring in more members just for the sake of staying alive, they wanted to learn how to share Christ's love with their rapidly changing community.

At the same time, they needed to find a way to maintain their building that didn't put the burden on the congregation's limited resources. The Friends of Christ Church Lutheran (FCCL) nonprofit began in 2008 "with a primary mission to raise funds to help with capital projects the church could not undertake on its own, such as restoring the bell tower, upgrading the elevator to meet city code, replacing roofs, and rebuilding the court yard."[3] FCCL solicits individual donations, conducts fundraising events, leads tours, trains docents, and applies for grants the church alone may not be eligible for.

Like the disciples in the Bible story, Christ Church Lutheran faced a challenge that felt insurmountable. However, by uncovering and repurposing the assets God had already placed in their midst (historic building, deep liturgical tradition, membership open to change), focusing their orientation out toward the community and asking for their help, things slowly began to change. As a result of these changes, I and so many others were able to recognize God at work in this congregation and find a loving congregational home.

Funding Forward Defined

Funding Forward is the process of finding more economically sustainable models for ministry that emerge organically from the congregation's mission. What exactly does this mean? It means that we aren't just looking for any money-making opportunities in order to save the church. Instead, we're digging deeper into what God has called the congregation to do and to be and letting that experience of God's mission in our midst guide us as we seek out community partners, assess our assets, reshape our budgets, and solicit new forms of income.

Funding Forward requires a reorientation of your congregation's perspective. It's an opportunity to rediscover who God has called you to serve and the mission God has invited you to join. As I look at Christ Church Lutheran's story, I wonder what would have happened if they had just started FCCL and stuck to their northern European traditions and membership? What would have happened if the congregation had not changed? I have no doubt the building would still be standing today. It would likely be used as a concert venue or a vibrant art space, but it's unlikely it would still be a church. God had bigger plans in store for Christ Church Lutheran. Its worshiping community would grow and expand. Its space would be used throughout the week for community meetings, events, and concerts. It would be a place that both the congregation and the community could call home.

I will be breaking down the Funding Forward process one step at a time in the upcoming chapters of the book, beginning with chapter 3. I invite you to begin by assessing your congregation's assets. Then, take time to discern who God is calling you to serve and how God is inviting you to join what God is already doing in your community. Once you have a clear sense of your congregation's mission, you'll take the time to map out how your congregation's current use of these assets is aligned with this mission. After that, you'll consider how you might fund what God is calling you to do and, finally, how you might shift your congregation's financial model.

What assets has God entrusted to us?

Likely what immediately comes to mind for you are the physical assets: the property, the building, the supplies, even the staff. The things that you can see and touch. These are important—and it's good to take an inventory especially of those assets that might be hidden away that you don't see every day like an underutilized church gym, stacks of old hymnals, rows of old pews, and so on. Really, though, there are so many intangible assets that churches often neglect to consider, like the gifts and talents of your church's staff, lay leadership, members, or community that haven't yet been tapped. As my Faith+Lead colleague, the Rev. Jon Anderson shared with me, "The assets we have been given are a good place to start building hunches about what God is calling the congregation to do."

For instance, at Church of the Messiah in Detroit, Michigan, the Rev. Barry Randolph (Pastor Barry) has used a variety of church and community assets to share God's love in his neighborhood. As Pastor Barry began his ministry and started to get to know the people in his community, he realized that many of the young men they were reaching were formerly incarcerated and struggled to find work. As a former businessman, Pastor Barry began to help these men start businesses of their own using their God-given gifts and talents. Similarly, he has tapped people in his congregation to tithe their skills like law and accounting to help these entrepreneurs get their businesses off the ground.

The church has helped to launch countless businesses from a tea company to a media production company to a T-shirt company, and so much more. At the same time, the church has expanded the use of the property to include affordable housing, nonprofits, business offices, in addition to other uses. As Pastor Barry says,

> You can come to church to pay your rent, come to church to get a job, come to church to start a business, come to church to get the internet, come to church to see a doctor, come to church to see an attorney, come to church to get affordable housing, come to church to get transportation through the bike shop, come to church to be part of a band. So, you come to church for all these things. You eventually stop and say: let me go to church.[4]

It's easy to get so caught up in Pastor Barry's incredible ministry that you miss the simplicity of how this all got started. Pastor Barry heard the needs of his community and responded by using his own gifts as a businessman and inviting others to do the same. Similarly, he saw open space in the church that could be better used throughout the week, so he invited renters. At the time he started his ministry, his church had just forty members, but there were still untapped assets to be discovered and repurposed for the community to join God's mission in new ways.

How might we join what God is already doing in our community?

While some congregations may already have deep relationships with community members and a clear sense of where God is calling them, many congregations are disconnected from the communities they are called to serve. In one of my interviews with a congregation, they described another church who had sold their property to them. This church's mission was to be a retreat away from the world. They prided themselves on being separate from the community—so much so that they planted trees all the way around their building to hide themselves from their community. As the interview participant noted, it was no surprise that this church's membership dwindled, and it eventually closed. While I haven't heard of any other congregation going so far as building a forest around their congregation to hide from the community, it's no question that we have found many ways to keep our churches "safe" for those inside while locking out those on the outside.

If your church disappeared, would anyone, outside of the current members, notice? If so, what would they miss? Too often conversations about the mission in congregations have focused more on word-smithing a mission statement and less on creating relationships in the neighborhood and listening to the real needs and desires of the people we are called to serve. While this may feel like a big task to undertake, and it is, think of this less as something to check off your list before you can proceed with this process and more of a posture to cultivate in your congregation. Instead of trying to write the perfect mission statement, what if congregation members were invited to lean into the relationships in the community they already have and listen deeply to the needs of their neighbors? In chapter 4, I'll share with you some practices to help you listen to God and your neighbors so you can discern where God might be calling your congregation. This is a process for the whole congregation, not just its paid leaders.

Sometimes congregations have a clear sense of their mission that does not align with the needs of their community. Early in my career, I worked for a capital campaign consulting firm. One of the consultants was working with a congregation in Sun City, Arizona. Sun City was the first city in Arizona designated to be an active adult community just for those aged fifty-five and up. Residents must be nineteen years of age or older, and at least one member of the household must be fifty-five or older. There are no schools in Sun City. As the consultant was working with the congregation, he asked them what their mission was. They kept repeating again and again that they longed for a congregation filled with youth and young children and mourned that there were not any in the congregation. The consultant finally invited the congregation members to come with him to the front door of the church and to look out at their community. He said: "Who do you see?" This was the first moment the congregation realized that maybe God might be calling them to create a space for seniors, not youth.

How do our money and mission flow together?

Take the time to consider how the way your church is currently using its money and assets connects to its mission. Start by looking through your congregation's budget.

- How do the line items in the budget connect with the mission God is calling the congregation to join?
- How does it bring you closer to the people God has called you to serve?
- Looking at the numbers, are you investing in the right places?
- Do the percentages line up where you might expect?
- For instance, if you feel God calling you to serve the youth in your community, what is your investment in youth ministry?
- Might you be able to release some other congregational expenses to make a deeper investment there?

Too often, I see congregations move straight to income sources without considering how they might be able to realign their budgets and/or repurpose assets they already have. To be clear, I'm not talking about incrementally reducing your budget across the board but instead realigning the budget by dramatically reducing or eliminating certain line items entirely so the money can be used for other purposes. In chapter 5, I'll share tools to help you decide what should stay in your budget and what should go based on the mission you have discerned.

A great example of connecting money and mission in real and tangible ways is Common Ground Church in Lodi, Wisconsin (formerly First Lutheran Church). The congregation felt called to provide greater accessibility to people with disabilities, something their current building could not provide, as well as to connect with those disconnected from the church. They felt a tension, as many congregations today do, between preserving their familiar historic identity and serving those who lacked accessibility. After many years of discernment, they decided to step out in faith by dissolving First Lutheran Church and selling their building. They formed Common Ground Church and began meeting inside of the space of the nonprofit they had helped start years earlier, Reach Out Lodi. I'll dive into their story in more detail in chapter 5.

While this story of budget realignment may be dramatic, it illustrates the foundational nature of creating money and mission alignment in your current budget before considering other income sources. Letting go and/or pruning back certain ministries is an important practice to create space for new ministry to flourish. It's also important to stress that this change, like nearly all the changes I will discuss in this book, did not happen overnight. It was an iterative process of discernment that happened over many years with many small steps that created a larger change.

What might God be calling us to do?

Once you have a clearer sense of God's mission, your congregation's community, and the assets God has entrusted to your congregation's care, we'll look at what God might be calling you to do. I organized this section of the book (chapters six through eight) into three larger categories: property, enterprise, and staffing. Property is the most common way that congregations engage in this work, and it generally has the lowest barrier to entry—so it's a great place to start. We'll explore property rental, property sale, and property sharing. If your ministry does not currently own property, you may still find this section helpful as you consider what partnerships you might develop with other organizations through space rental and space sharing.

Next, we'll explore a variety of different forms of enterprise: forming nonprofits, starting a business, and selling products or services. While many of the ideas discussed will be income generating, I'll also be talking about creating and maintaining self-sustaining ministries. Too often we start ministries in a church with the assumption that the church should fund the ministry in perpetuity. What if the goal of the ministry was to sustain itself using its own streams of income? A great example of a self-sustaining ministry is Sustainable Renton, a 501c3 nonprofit that runs a free grocery store that takes place in the parking lot of St. Matthew's Lutheran Church in Renton, Washington, every Monday evening. While this ministry was not started by the church, the church is a vital part of making this ministry possible. The free grocery store is made possible by partnerships with grocery stores, community food banks, community gardens, and local businesses who provide the donations, a team of fifty to sixty volunteers who glean, sort, and distribute food, and St. Matthew's Lutheran Church who provides the parking lot, food storage, shipping containers, tents, and tables. This is a ministry the congregation could never sustain on its own, but through partnership with Sustainable Renton they can be one piece of the puzzle of addressing food insecurity in Renton in a sustainable way, both for the earth and the congregation.

Church staffing, like property, is a critical piece of the funding puzzle because it often makes up the majority of church budgets. Sadly, in some congregations, leadership refers to church staff as a negative budget expense rather than the central missional agents of their congregations. In so many churches, staff are ultimately the ones who make the ministry happen. While it may seem like a financial "no brainer" to incrementally slice down staff hours, salary, and benefits in an effort to keep the church budget in the black, there's often little thought put into how these actions might impact the broader ministry of the congregation. Instead, I will encourage you to think about the overall structure of your congregation's staffing. I will share ideas of creative staffing models from congregations that rely on a team of part-time, bi-vocational ministry staff to congregations that are primarily run by lay members and supported by clergy only a few hours per week. These models require not only some changes to the budget but an entire reorientation of a congregation's view of the roles of lay and clergy members. This is a fundamental change not only in how much money is needed to fund the ministry but also who is involved in making that ministry happen.

It's important to note, there will continue to be some churches with full-time pastors and/or staff members. However, given trends in attendance and affiliation, this will be less and less of a norm. Staff, similar to property, enterprises, and finances, should be tailored to the congregation's unique mission, assets, and community. The future of the church is a mixed ecology, where creatively staffed churches exist alongside traditionally staffed churches, not a one-size-fits-all.

How might we fund what God is calling us to do?

Many of the projects discussed above, including preparing church property for rental and starting a nonprofit, often require money up front. In chapter 9, we will think about where those startup funds might come from as well as other longer-term financing resources that might be available. In this section, we will take a closer look at where you might find funding both inside and outside of the congregation. Too often, I find congregation leaders tend to mistake short-term funding (like grants) for long-term solutions to their financial problems. We'll look at which projects these funding sources might be best used for and how much work might be involved in securing them so you can get a sense of which forms of financing might be the best fit for the ideas you have in mind.

How do we shift the congregation's financial model?

As I shared in the Preface, this is where the leaders from the Funding Forward learning community in 2021 struggled - when they started to put these ideas into action in their congregations. They struggled to discern what to let go of, what to keep doing, and how to shift expectations around the role of a pastor and lay leader in a congregation. They struggled with how to best get their congregation on board with all that they had learned over the past few months. But, most of all, they struggled with how to create change when there didn't seem to be much energy, interest, and "people power" to make that change happen.

It was precisely this experience that led my research team and me to survey over one hundred congregations and interview twelve so that we could listen deeply to their stories. In the final chapter, I will share with you the practices the congregations we interviewed used to shift their financial model. Practices that you can bring to your congregation, too.

In 2020, I had a conversation with another leader in a similar position at a different seminary. When I told her that one of the key focuses of my work would be to help congregations shift their financial model, she was quick to say, "Grace, that's great. But I don't know many seminary-trained leaders who can do this work. They were trained to be pastors, not entrepreneurs." Her statement stuck with me as I dived deeper and deeper into this work. On the one hand, she is correct. Most people who go to seminary aren't naturally entrepreneurs and they don't often learn much, if anything, about entrepreneurship in seminary. However, I do think she's wrong that most pastors can't do this work. One of the most exciting learnings from our research was that there are congregations all over the country doing this work. What unites this group isn't their denomination, their worship attendance size, their location (rural/urban/suburban), number of seminary-trained leaders, or even the amount of money they have, what unites them is their ear for what the Spirit is doing in their communities and their openness to try something new. One common thread you'll hear throughout these stories is that these congregations never did their work alone. There was always partnership between people inside the congregation and those outside of it. If you are a pastor reading this book thinking "I can't do this. I don't know how to start a social enterprise, rent out property, write grants. . ." you're not alone. There are people in your congregation and in your community who have the skills to do this work. And, in most instances, they will be so grateful you asked them to use these God-given abilities rather than inviting them to be a greeter, a reader, or a Sunday school teacher.

Will Funding Forward Be Required of All Churches?

It's a good question, and the simple answer is "no." There are some places where the twentieth-century model of church is still thriving today. They are continuing to attract more members and have more than enough money coming in through the offering plate to sustain their ministry. However, the number of churches who will be able to sustain themselves using this model alone will continue to dwindle over the next decade. That said, Funding Forward can be helpful for any church, whether they are struggling financially or not.

The congregations we interviewed engaged in this process for a variety of reasons: God's mission, community need, underutilized assets (i.e., building, land, staff, etc.), finances, and congregational need (i.e., building accessibility, decline in church attendance, etc.). However, there seemed to be a sweet spot

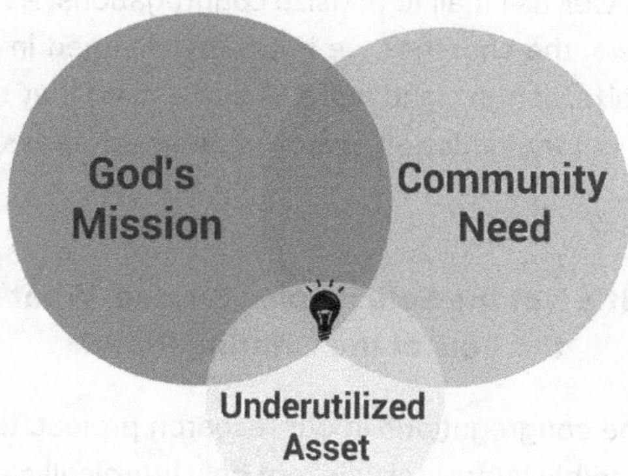

Figure 1. The sweet spot when a congregation finds alignment between God's mission, community need, and an underutilized asset.

when the congregation found alignment between God's mission, community need, and an underutilized asset, as figure 1 represents. While finances and congregational need may have been catalysts to get the conversation started, they were rarely the sole motivator. If financial motivations are not connected to God's mission for the congregation and the community's unique needs, it's unlikely to succeed over the long term.

St. Andrew Lutheran Church in Eden Prairie, Minnesota, was easily the largest and most resource-rich church in the interview dataset, and likely in the survey data set as well. St. Andrew Lutheran Church has an average Sunday worship attendance of nine hundred people and an annual budget of over 5 million dollars. It would be easy to believe that St. Andrew Lutheran Church didn't need to do this work, and yet, they saw a need in the broader church community that they were well positioned to fill. Their church began in the 1970s, experienced rapid growth over three decades, followed by a decade of deep decline and resurgence again under new leadership. They had learned something from this experience that they were eager to share with others, but they also knew they still had more to learn. Out of this idea came Church Anew: "a Spirit-led movement that nourishes Christian leaders and ignites communities of faith by setting an inclusive table of belonging and developing resources for a fresh, bold, and faithful witness in the world."[5] What began as an idea of putting on a few local conferences each year has grown into a thriving blog, event, and resourcing ministry serving over 300,000 people worldwide. This work has been transformative for the people inside and outside of St. Andrew Lutheran Church. The Funding Forward process works well in large congregations as well as small to midsize congregations. As you'll see in the upcoming chapters, the churches we interviewed varied in their congregation size, budget size, context, and more. The one thing they shared was their passion for living out their mission in more sustainable ways.

If It's Not the Sole Income Source, What's the Role of the Offering Plate?

In almost all of the congregations in our research project, the offering plate still plays an incredibly important role, not only liturgically and theologically but also financially for the congregation. Of the congregations we surveyed who are engaged in this work, about a third receive 80 percent or more of their revenue from donations, another third receive 60–79 percent from donations, and the last third receive 59 percent or less from the offering plate. Most congregations who are just getting started in this work do not receive a significant amount of revenue outside of the offering plate; the revenue tends to grow over time.

However, the "good news" of Funding Forward is that it can free the offering to return to what it was originally intended to be: an act of worship. In his book, *Giving to God*, Mark Allan Powell reminds us that the offering was first and foremost about our relationship with God. He writes,

> We are invited to put money in the offering plate on Sunday morning not because the church needs our money but because *we want and need to give it.* We have a spiritual need to worship God, and through our offerings we are able to express our love and devotion for God in a way that is simple and sincere. The motivation of the giver is what counts most, not the size of the gift or degree of benefit to the recipient.[6]

This reminds me of the worship services that I led as a camp counselor. The campers were not allowed to bring any money to camp, so we had to be very creative about the offering. We invited campers to offer each other hugs, affirmations, and prayer. We encouraged them to think about the strengths and assets God had entrusted to them and how they might use them to love their neighbors at camp and at home. While these offering experiences sometimes felt a bit hokey as we were putting them together, these were some of my favorite experiences of the offering I have ever had. They were sincere, concrete, and worshipful. They reminded the campers (and the counselors) of our relationship to God and our relationship to our neighbors—something the offering has done throughout history.

In many congregations, the offering time in worship has become more of a fundraising pitch than an act of worship. It often feels disconnected from the rest of the worship experience when, as Powell has said, it's meant to be one of the high points in the service. As someone who gives exclusively online, the offering portion of worship is incredibly uncomfortable for me. I feel guilty passing the mostly empty plate and not putting anything in it. I have a desire to engage more deeply in this part of worship, but there is rarely an opportunity to do so. Putting a laminated "I give online" card in the offering plate may help to quell my guilt but it does nothing to help me engage in this act of worship.

When I started attending Tree of Life Lutheran (Tree of Life) in Minneapolis, Minnesota, I was delighted to see that they did the offering differently. During the offering time, there were different stations set up. You could visit one or more of the stations in any order and return to your seat when you were done. There was a station to give using an iPad or put cash/checks in a basket. There was a station to light a candle and pray. There was a station to sign up to volunteer. And there was generally a more creative station that changed each week depending on the theme of the sermon. I loved this approach for so many reasons. First, it felt like an act of worship—a way to respond to what I had heard in the sermon. Second, if I didn't visit the iPad/basket station to give money no one cared and no one noticed. Third, most people in our congregation did not have much money to give and many of the people who came to our church had a lot of baggage around how money was talked about in other congregations. This offering format alleviated the pressure to give during worship, allowing people to do what they felt called to do without shame or judgment. Visitors, those who gave online, and those who didn't have the means to give could easily skip that station. Plus, we lifted up the multitude of other ways that God calls us to love and share with our neighbors—it's not just about the money! Taking the financial pressure off the offering plate can be a beautiful word of good news for the congregation's leaders and the congregation's members.

But Won't People Give Less to the Church if They Know Money Is Coming from Other Sources?

I would be lying if I told you this would not happen. In fact, it happened to a congregation who renovated their building to create affordable housing and open up space to local nonprofits. After they completed the project, they neglected to tell the congregation how much income was coming in from the housing and space rental as well as where the money was going. It's imperative that the congregation knows how much money is being earned through any of the entrepreneurial ventures discussed in this book and where the money is going. Often people in the pews will overestimate the money earned through these ventures, especially early on, and assume they are making enough to sustain the congregation.

If possible, I often suggest to congregations that money earned through these ventures go toward a specific line item of the budget rather than the general fund. For instance, money earned through building rental might go toward property expenses and maintenance. Have the money go toward a line item that's related to the venture but also not the congregation's favorite line item to support. For instance, in a congregation where many givers care deeply about the congregation's children, youth, and family programming, the money earned through the congregation's social enterprise shouldn't go to cover that segment of the budget. If your congregation has a practice where all income goes to support the entire budget, make sure you are even clearer about the amount coming in and the percentage of the overall budget it will cover.

This is a good opportunity to remind the congregation why their giving matters from both a spiritual and financial perspective. Let them know where their money is going and why the gift is needed both for the church and for them. Invite them deeper into your congregation's mission. Dream with them about the good work your congregation could do with an increase in the budget. Invite them to experience giving as an act of worship.

Permission to Try

At the beginning of my winter 2023 Funding Forward class at Luther Seminary, my students and I walked through a set of classroom agreements, a covenant that would set the tone for our time together. One of my last-minute additions to the list of agreements was "permission to try." I often find that the students who get the most out of my classes are the ones who come in with the least experience and are willing to try out new ideas, fail, and try again—bringing us all along on this vulnerable journey. I wanted to create a brave space for students to try on ideas or experiment with activities without fear of judgment, shame, or nonconstructive critiques.

Like my students, you will come across parts of this process that will challenge you because they seem outside of your realm of experience or expertise. As a leader in a congregation—whether lay or clergy—you may feel like you don't have permission to try out ideas and instead feel like you need to be an expert on every subject. I'm giving you a permission slip to release the need to be an expert and instead adopt a learner's posture. The best learning happens when we take the risk to test out an idea, even when it might fail. Stepping out and failing has so much more to teach us than staying inside our comfort zone.

Prior to taking on my current role at Luther Seminary, I had the privilege of working for Portico Benefit Services teaching pastors and other ministry leaders how to retire well. As I led preretirement seminars, I quickly learned that one of the most important things that I could do to build trust with the people in the room was to answer tough questions to which I didn't know the answer with "I don't know, but I'm happy to find out and get back to you." Every time I said "I don't know" I could sense a collective exhale in the room: "if the expert in the room doesn't know, it's okay that I don't know, too." For those of you feeling the pressure of being the expert in the room, I encourage you to test out the phrase, "I don't know, but I would love to find out together." In the words of Brené Brown, "Vulnerability is the birthplace of innovation, creativity and change."[7] I have often found that in classrooms and congregations vulnerability sparks vulnerability. If someone, particularly the leader in the room, is willing to share vulnerably, it sets the tone for the rest of the group.

♦ Practice: Create a Team ♦

None of this work is meant to be done in isolation. Take some time to gather a small team to read through the book and work through the process together. You might choose to work with an existing group like the congregational leadership, stewardship, or finance team. Or you might draw together a few ministry leaders or entrepreneurial members of your community.

After finding a regular time to meet, begin by putting together a brief covenant for your work together. I've put together some sample ideas below that you might use in your covenant:

- Discernment: Listen together for where God might be calling your congregation and share where you might be seeing God's direction. Let this leading shape and test each idea that is shared.
- Deep Listening: Suspend judgment and take the time to listen deeply to each other.
- Mutual Respect: Invite and honor diverse perspectives, ask clarifying questions, assume positive intent.

- Permission to Try: Create a brave space to try on ideas or experiment with activities without fear of judgment, shame, or nonconstructive critique.
- Expertise: Honor the knowledge and experience that we each bring to the table—none is more important than another.
- Celebrate: Take the time to acknowledge your efforts, both the wins and the failures.[8]

Reflection Questions

1. Which part of this process intrigues you most? Why?
2. Which part of this process do you believe will be most challenging? Why?
3. Who might you invite to join your Funding Forward team? Who might you invite to participate in a specific step of the process?

CHAPTER TWO

Why Isn't a Better Stewardship Program Enough?

Ezra 3:10–13

"When the builders laid the foundation of the temple of the Lord, the priests in their vestments were stationed to praise the Lord with trumpets, and the Levites, the sons of Asaph, with cymbals, according to the directions of King David of Israel; and they sang responsively, praising and giving thanks to the Lord,

'For he is good,
for his steadfast love endures for ever towards Israel.'

And all the people responded with a great shout when they praised the Lord, because the foundation of the house of the Lord was laid. But many of the priests and Levites and heads of families, old people who had seen the first house on its foundations, wept with a loud voice when they saw this house, though many shouted aloud for joy, so that the people could not distinguish the sound of the joyful shout from the sound of the people's weeping, for the people shouted so loudly that the sound was heard far away."

Dwelling Questions

1. What word or phrase jumped out at you as you read the passage?
2. Have you ever witnessed an event that provoked a response of both joy and weeping?

3. What emotions does your church's current financial situation evoke?
4. What might God be saying to you or your congregation through this passage?

Prayer

Author of love, we give thanks that your love does indeed endure forever. We give thanks for all of the resources you have entrusted to our care to aid in funding your mission in the world. Grant us wisdom as we examine the ways we have funded your church in the past and how you might be calling us to fund it moving forward. Accompany us as we hold together grief and joy as we walk into the future you have prepared for us. Amen.

When my husband and I decided to sell our suburban home and move to downtown Minneapolis in the summer of 2019, I was hoping to find a new church within walking distance of our new apartment. A few weeks before we moved, a friend introduced me to Tree of Life: a new ELCA worshiping community. At that time, Tree of Life was meeting for evening prayer in a wedding venue just a few blocks from our new apartment.

I'll never forget the first Sunday evening I came to evening prayer at Tree of Life in November 2019. I walked in off the chilly streets to find a small, warm community of about thirty people who met for worship and shared a meal together afterwards. Unlike most of the churches I had attended over the past seven years since I graduated from seminary, it was a place where I immediately felt like I belonged. It was a community created for millennials and Gen Zers who had been burned by the church. It was a place where anyone could bring their questions, their curiosities, their full selves. It was a place where nerdy Dr. Who references and nerdy Bible questions could coexist. It was a breath of fresh air. This church became my home over the next three years of pandemic, racial reckoning, and social upheaval. It was the community where I grieved, questioned, confronted, grew, and encountered God anew. It was a beacon of hope during a dark time.

However, as I began to get to know the community, my church finance brain started whirring. Prior to the pandemic, anywhere from ten to thirty people attended each congregational event and, while the numbers were slowly growing, I was concerned about sustainability. In January of 2020, we had a congregational gathering where we got a chance to see and discuss the budget together. This was the first time I had seen the church's financial statements. As a new start congregation, we were almost entirely reliant on denominational funding, regional church funding, and funding from another neighboring church in Minneapolis. We agreed that to become more sustainable we had to grow our membership, and we had lots of ideas to do so. Unfortunately, the pandemic set in just as many of those ideas were getting off the ground.

The more time I spent with the people at Tree of Life, both in person and online, the more I began to think about the demographics of the congregation. This was the youngest church I had ever attended (both by age of the church and age of membership.) We drew people from local campus ministries, recent college grads, and many people who were still in the beginning of their career. We had many artists, musicians, and people starting their own businesses. I began to realize that even if we did get our member numbers up, it was still unlikely that a congregation with this audience would ever be able to support a more traditional model of church with a full-time pastor, paid musicians, and its own congregational building, due to the congregation's demographic. Like the people in our reading from Ezra, I was filled with hope because of the grace, love, and gospel I and so many others had experienced at Tree of Life. However, I was also weighed down by grief. How long could a community like this last without substantial outside funding? Were we existing on borrowed time?

You may also be coming to this book with a posture of grief and hope. Dr. Cameron Howard first introduced me to the connection between this Bible passage from Ezra and the work of innovation in the church today. In this passage, as in the church today, "God's people had to find a 'new normal'—a way to flourish in their culture and their faith amid the particular demands of a singular power."[1] Like in our world today, this was a time of political, social, and religious upheaval. As Howard writes,

> The fall of Jerusalem shook the foundations of Israel's faith. God's promises to David of an eternal kingdom seemed broken, and the ruins of the temple—understood to be God's dwelling place—led even the most faithful Israelites to question whether God had abandoned God's people altogether. But then, in 539 B.C.E. King Cyrus of Persia defeated Babylon and instructed the exiles to return to Judah and rebuild the Jerusalem temple. Hope surged.[2]

Like the Israelites after the fall of Jerusalem, many congregations find themselves at a turning point. They too wonder if God may have abandoned them in the midst of this season of scarcity as the values of our culture shift away from congregational engagement. They too wait impatiently for God's action. In this chapter, I'll get to the root of this problem and answer the question of why "a better stewardship program" won't be enough to solve this problem for most congregations.

For Most Churches, the Offering Plate Won't Be Enough

I have watched as more and more congregations have closed their doors, and for those who have kept their doors open the question of "How do we raise enough money to pay the bills?" has become more and more urgent. While many congregations have several expense lines in their budget, most congregations have just one income line: donations. For many faith communities, it has or will become less and less feasible to fund their missions on tithes and offerings alone. This isn't to say that tithes and offerings are no longer needed or no longer important from a spiritual, theological, or biblical standpoint. Rather, if churches continue to rely on them as their only source of income, it's likely they will see a decline in overall income.

According to the National Study of Congregations' Economic Practices by Lake Institute on Faith and Giving, 81 percent of congregations' revenue comes from individual donations and "in fact, 40% of congregations receive essentially their entire annual revenue from individual donations."[3] The vast majority of these individual donations are given during a worship service (78 percent).[4] This means that for most congregations their financial stability hinges upon the offering received during worship.

This was most clearly seen during the pandemic. At the start of the pandemic after churches closed their doors and moved to online worship, many congregation leaders who had never thought much about online giving in the past decided to start or reinvigorate their church's online giving program. They knew that the financial sustainability of the congregation hinged upon their ability to continue to receive donations during the worship service. According to the Lake Institute's COVID-19 Congregational Study, many congregations (73 percent) had online giving options available pre-pandemic, 39 percent of those who did not scrambled to add them shortly after the pandemic set in.[5]

By the summer of 2020, almost all congregations (94 percent) with a hundred or more participants had an online giving option available.[6] This trend has made giving more accessible and expanded the congregation's pool of givers to include people who attend online as well as those who may have been previously affiliated with the congregation but no longer attend regularly. While this trend buoyed many congregations' budgets during the pandemic, this expanded pool of donations is still not large enough to support many congregations' financial needs over the long term.

With the reduction in church membership and attendance, particularly in mainline churches, income from individual donations has become (and will continue to be) less and less reliable. As you've likely seen, church members are attending church less and less frequently.[7] Most people who attend church these days attend once or twice a month, and those who do attend more consistently are more likely to be older members.[8] The ELCA's Office of Research and Evaluation looked at the trends in baptized membership and average worship attendance in 2017. If nothing changed, they projected that in less than forty years, baptized membership would decrease by 98 percent to just 2 percent of its original size.[9] They saw a similar pattern with average weekly worship attendance, except they projected those decreases to take place in less than thirty years.[10] Such a stark decrease will likely lead not only to fewer people in the pews to give on a Sunday morning but also less people affiliated with a congregation who might give online, even if they are not physically present.

If churches continue to rely on the weekly offering as their only source of income and attendance trends continue, it's very likely that they will also see a decline in overall income. I frequently hear from congregations whose declines in attendance have led to a decline in donations, particularly post-COVID. However, I have also heard from congregations who have experienced declines in attendance but have not also experienced a decline in donations. Generally, in these cases, their offering income has not declined yet because a small pool of aging donors are keeping the budget afloat with their funding. When the donations from this small pool run dry, these congregations will likely be in for a big wake-up call.

While I would be the first to say that congregational stewardship matters, the offering plate is an essential part of worship, and most churches have much they could do to improve their internal fundraising practices, given the precipitous declines in attendance anticipated over the next few decades, I am not sure even the best stewardship appeal would yield enough income to support a traditional congregation's budget—particularly with the sparse number of people left in many mainline congregations on a given Sunday morning. Unless the affiliation and attendance trends are reversed, the numbers simply won't be enough to keep most churches afloat.

There's More to the Story

While the decline in tithes and offerings may be a major cause of grief in the church today, it's often only part of the story. Most churches are not stewarding the assets they already have well, and they don't have a clear sense of their mission. These two problems need to be addressed before we can even think about what funding model might be right for them.

Stewardship of assets

The amount of tithes and offerings a congregation brings in is not a measure of how well these churches are stewarding the assets God has entrusted into their care. Many churches have assets that are sorely underutilized, like buildings that remain vacant except for a few hours on Sunday and Wednesday, savings the church is afraid of spending, pastors who long to be more present in their community but are stuck focusing on administrative tasks, and entrepreneurial members who long to engage in ministry using their God-given talents, but are reduced to the role of greeter, reader, or Sunday school teacher. As we've focused on raising more money, we've often neglected a bigger question: *How is the church called to steward the assets God has already entrusted to our care?*

Instead of focusing on stewardship, we have focused on building bigger barns. We have often viewed any additional money coming in as a sign that we should build more buildings and create more staffing infrastructure rather than giving more money away or, heaven forbid, letting people know that more than enough money had been given (Exodus 36:5–7). In his seminal book, *We Aren't Broke: Uncovering Hidden Resources for Mission and Ministry*, Mark Elsdon uses the parable of the rich fool in Luke 12 to talk about the mode many churches have operated in since the mid-twentieth century. The rich man, like churches today, has taken ownership of what he has, rather than remembering that it all belongs to God. Similarly, when the rich fool "experiences success, the rich man can only see the *problem* of storing his riches for himself rather than the *responsibility* he has to steward his excess differently."[11] While preparing for the future in some ways is not a bad thing, might there be more of a balance between building an endowment for tomorrow's needs and meeting the needs of the community today?

The boom in attendance and money that many churches experienced throughout the mid- to late-twentieth century led many churches to focus on their own needs, rather than toward the needs of their community. While the creation of more buildings was necessary to house the boom in attendance, it also created more debt and maintenance on buildings that now remain vacant most of the week. For many church leadership and finance teams, the building costs and labor consume the conversations, causing these discussions to turn even more inward toward the church's needs. *How might God have us use, share, care for—and even, in some cases, release—these spaces to be used for God's mission?* A mindset of scarcity keeps us from seeing the assets that God has already entrusted to our care. We'll talk more about these assets in chapter 3.

Participation in God's mission

This leads to the biggest problem of all. Most congregations today don't know how they are called to join God's mission in their community. They may have a dusty old mission statement that hangs on a beautifully embroidered quilt in their fellowship hall or a statement that adorns the top of the congregation's annual report, but does anyone in the congregation, outside of its leadership, know or understand it? For the congregations that do have some understanding of their mission, it's very generic: "share the gospel in our community" or "love God, love people" or "be church." What does that mean? What does that look like? How are we called to live into that mission together?

Throughout the boom of Christianity in the twentieth century, congregations were so busy caring for the people coming through their doors that they didn't take the time to discern how they might be called to participate in God's mission. As the boom has stopped and decline has stepped in, the fear of closure and scarcity of resources has caused churches more often to have an inward focus and become increasingly disconnected from the communities they are called to serve. For many churches, the unspoken mission statement has often become "keep the doors open, and by doing so, keep the church alive." This mission statement drives church leadership meetings to focus on how they might fund deferred maintenance and church stewardship teams to focus on asking people for more money just to keep the church going. I constantly hear from seminary students, pastors, and lay leaders in congregations who have creative ideas for their churches to follow God's lead to meet the needs of their communities who struggle to get congregation leaders to listen. When they do get a hearing, they are often turned down because "we need to make the church more stable before we can do anything creative." And yet, this obsession with stability, constraint, and maintenance is exactly what turns people away from the church and keeps people from giving to it. In chapter 4 of this book, I'll invite you to consider how the Spirit might be leading your congregation to join in God's mission in your community.

And Yet, There Is Hope

The offering plate may not be enough to fund congregations today, and maybe that's okay. This isn't the first time the church has had to pivot to a new financial model. Too often in the Western church today, we assume that the first and only model for church funding is the offering plate. However, throughout biblical and church history a variety of different income sources were used to fund God's work.

Often the Old Testament is looked to as the foundation for the donation-based financial system. However, as we look through the Old Testament, we see a variety of different income sources were used to fund God's work—in particular, tithes, taxes, and gifts.[12] While some of these sources of income were given voluntarily by the people, many were seen as mandatory, more similar to a "tax" than a "free-will offering" system as we know it today. Similarly, this income came in the form of money. But it also came in the form of "in-kind gifts" such as animals, land, building materials, and precious stones, as well as the use of artisanal skills. Most importantly, the Israelites were not the only ones to fund the temple system; various political officials also supported the temple's work. The temple was not funded by tithes and offerings alone.

Similarly, in the New Testament we see a few different models for funding Jesus's ministry, the apostles' ministry, and the early church. While Jesus talked about money a lot, he wasn't asking for money for his ministry directly. Jesus and his disciples were bi-vocational: they participated in Jesus's ministry in addition to their secular jobs. Jesus invited his followers to "take nothing" for their journey and rely on the hospitality of others. Asking for money does not appear to be part of the instruction. Jesus sets up a different financial system, asking both his disciples and those who contribute to the ministry to go beyond tithes and offerings to host and be hosted as they share the gospel.

This radical sharing is taken even further in the book of Acts: "All who believed were together and had all things in common; they would sell their possessions and goods and distribute the proceeds to all, as any had need." (Acts 2:44–45) While some biblical scholars have debated the historical accuracy of this idealistic depiction of the early church, this text has inspired many throughout Christian history to create intentional Christian communities where all possessions are held in common, so that everyone in the community is provided for. In contrast to the Old Testament model and Jesus's model of radical poverty and hospitality, this model invites believers to bring all of who they are (and all that they possess) to the table to be shared with others.

Paul continues in the pattern of Jesus by serving as a bi-vocational minister. This approach to ministry became common until the reign of Constantine.[13] That being said, Paul also argued for the right to ask for and receive money for his apostolic work using a particular pattern:

> He did not ask for or accept money from a community in which he was actively working to establish a church. The basic reason he gives for this is his concern about hindering the forward movement of the gospel, whether by giving offense or by burdening fledgling churches. Once a church was established, however, he expected it to finance his travel to the next town.[14]

When this support was not available, he went back to funding his ministry through his work as a tentmaker. Paul was very flexible so that he could best serve the churches under his care.[15]

While Paul was often reluctant to ask for his own support, he was tireless in asking for support "for the poor among the saints at Jerusalem" (Romans 15:26). While this collection originally began in Antioch, Paul widened out "the ask" for this collection to all non-Jewish believers. This collection was a way for these believers to not only support the Jews in Jerusalem but also to repay something they owed to them: "for if the Gentiles have come to share in their spiritual blessings, they ought also to be of service to them in material things." (Romans 15:27) While Paul does seem to reintroduce the idea of donations, these offerings seem to be for other communities and for Paul's ministry rather than supporting their own faith communities. For Paul, donations were a way to partner in the broader mission and ministry of the church.

Similarly, throughout early, medieval, and modern church history, we also see a variety of economic models. The church used government support, wealthy patronage, donation of land, sale of products, and more to fund its mission. The focus on the offering plate as we know it today emerged in the late nineteenth century when churches were no longer funded by the state and needed to find a new way to fund their missions. Like today, this period was a frightening turning point in the church's ministry. Many wondered how churches could survive without governmental support. The church used a variety of different funding methods, including "renting or selling pew space, subscription lists, church suppers, church socials, raffles and lotteries."[16] However as church leaders increasingly began to look for biblical support for their fundraising, they rediscovered the biblical concept of tithes and offerings.

People began "to see giving as a biblical mandate, a spiritual matter, and an act of worship. Therefore, it made sense to incorporate the collection of offerings into Sunday morning worship alongside preaching, singing, and prayer. By 1900, most American churches took up weekly offerings."[17] This was the beginning of envelope giving and the depiction of tithing that most of us know today. The religious, financial, and baby boom following the Second World War only helped to solidify this model. As church attendance grew exponentially, so did church wealth. Most churches could easily fund their missions and more on tithes and offerings alone.

However, it is important to note that many congregations struggled financially, even during this mid-twentieth-century attendance boom. Congregations that served people in marginalized communities had no choice but to diversify their economic models, as the people they served could never donate enough on their own to fund the church's mission. These churches led additional fundraisers, started nonprofits, created businesses, rented property, and/or hired bi-vocational or even unpaid ministers. They did this out of necessity and were often shamed by other booming congregations and denominational bodies for doing so. There is a lot that can be learned from these communities who have employed these methods for decades. There is hope that expanding a congregation's income sources outside of the offering plate can be a faithful next step to not only find greater financial stability but also live more deeply into God's mission for the congregation.

Did We Fail?

As we look this season of decline in the eye, it's likely to bring up feelings of failure. We may wonder: *Did we fail? Did we let down the people of faith who came before us?* Instead of thinking about it as a failure, think about it as being ushered into a new season of ministry. Just as technology changes, so does the church. We may be excellent at making CDs, but if everyone is streaming music it won't really matter. The Spirit is inviting us into a new season of being church that requires different practices and plays by different rules. That does not make our old ways bad. In fact, there is a lot we learned in this previous era of church that we can bring with us into this new season.

A few months ago, a student asked me: "Where are you seeing hope in the church today?" It can be so hard to see hope amid the pain, heartache, and deficits in the church today. But I can honestly tell you that I have seen hope and new life springing from the hundred plus congregations who participated in our survey as well as the twelve that we had the chance to talk with more closely. I hear the Spirit singing in their stories, proclaiming God's love to a broken world in real and tangible ways. I see them being the hands and feet of Jesus bringing healing and restoration. I see God creating an abundant feast from what might look like meager ingredients. This work has brought God to life for me in ways I never expected.

I appreciate the way that one of our research participants, the Rev. G. Jeffrey MacDonald, put it:

> When I read scripture and church history, I see God working through adversity so often and calling people to abide in faith when outcomes are not certain and when the winds of the world feel like there's no way forward. . . . I believe that God is using constraint in churches all over. That financial constraint is compelling congregations to pick up their feet and do more of what they've been called to do all along. . . . Could God not use financial constraint to generate creativity? When you have a power outage and everything in the refrigerator goes bad, you

> start getting creative about what's in the pantry and discover you can make some pretty great things. That's when the creativity happens, not when you can just go to the refrigerator any time you want and pull out something that's ready to eat. And so I feel like economic constraint is moving our historic mainline churches into an era of greater faithfulness and creativity.

Maybe the grief and the hope are tied together? Maybe it is this death of the way we've always known things to be done that will lead to new life? Thanks be to God that God is with us through it all, breathing life into our dry bones.

♦ Practice: Back to the Future ♦

Take some time to look back through your congregation's history. How was its ministry funded? Were there any other income streams outside of the offering plate like land sales, special fundraisers, pew rentals/sales, grants, nonprofits, funding from other churches, or something else? How was the money raised to start your church? Are there any ministries in your congregation, for instance the youth ministry, that are funded using multiple income streams?

Are you part of a new ministry? Discuss how other congregations you have been connected to have been funded.

Reflection Questions

1. Is the income from the offering plate enough to fund your congregation's ministry today? Why or why not? When might this funding not be sufficient?
2. If the offering plate income is not currently enough for your congregation, which of the factors discussed in this chapter (decrease in attendance, serving marginalized populations, etc.) might be contributing to it?
3. Where do you see grief and/or hope amid these realities for your congregation?

CHAPTER THREE

What Has God Entrusted to Our Care?

Exodus 35:4–9, 20–21; 36:2–7

"Moses said to all the congregation of the Israelites: This is the thing that the Lord has commanded: Take from among you an offering to the Lord; let whoever is of a generous heart bring the Lord's offering: gold, silver, and bronze; blue, purple, and crimson yarns, and fine linen; goats' hair, tanned rams' skins, and fine leather; acacia wood, oil for the light, spices for the anointing-oil and for the fragrant incense, and onyx stones and gems to be set in the ephod and the breastpiece . . .

Then all the congregation of the Israelites withdrew from the presence of Moses. And they came, everyone whose heart was stirred, and everyone whose spirit was willing, and brought the Lord's offering to be used for the tent of meeting, and for all its service, and for the sacred vestments . . .

Moses then called Bezalel and Oholiab and everyone skillful to whom the Lord had given skill, everyone whose heart was stirred to come to do the work; and they received from Moses all the freewill-offerings that the Israelites had brought for doing the work on the sanctuary. They still kept bringing him freewill-offerings every morning, so that all the artisans who were doing every sort of task on the sanctuary came, each from the task being performed, and said to Moses, 'The people are bringing much more than enough for doing the work that the Lord has commanded us to do.' So Moses gave command, and word was proclaimed throughout the camp: 'No man or woman is to make anything else as an offering for the sanctuary.' So the people were restrained from bringing; for what they had already brought was more than enough to do all the work."

Dwelling Questions

1. What word or phrase jumped out at you as you read the passage?
2. When was the last time your "heart was stirred" to give to a cause?
3. Have you ever been in a situation where you were overwhelmed by generosity? If so, when?
4. What might God be saying to you or your congregation through this passage?

Prayer

God of abundance, we give thanks that even in the desert you provide more than enough to do your work. Help us to see the abundance you have entrusted to us in the midst of scarce situations. Guide us to use those resources that have been underutilized, discarded, or even forgotten. Through this process, may we learn to trust your provision even more deeply. Amen.

In my Funding Forward seminary class, we play Rooted Good's "Mission Possible" game. This game is designed to teach the process of design thinking through play. Players are invited to solve a large world problem like homelessness or climate change, and they are given what seems like an impossibly small amount of time and resources with which to do it. There are four types of resources in the game: facility, human assets (volunteers, skills, etc.), equipment, and finances, but each team only gets three resources (one card each from three of the resource categories). There is an intentional constraint built in.

The resources you receive may not be the ones that you expect. They could be grandiose, like one hour of time from a pop star or three days' use of a sports arena, but they might also be something you would easily disregard like ten thousand paper cups. Every time I've distributed the resources, I've remarked on the confused faces of my students who wonder why they didn't get all four and how they could ever use that random set of resources to solve such a complex problem. And yet, I've seen some pretty amazing ideas emerge after just twenty minutes of ideation. For example, those ten thousand paper cups could be given to a hundred local artists who are commissioned to create art pieces about climate change that will be showcased and auctioned off at a three-day environmental educational event. As you read through this chapter, I encourage you to consider all your congregation's resources, even the small and seemingly insignificant ones, like those paper cups, that you might easily forget.

I find a lot of parallels between the "Mission Possible" game and the passage from Exodus 35–36. The people of Israel were given a seemingly impossible task: building a dwelling place for God while they were wandering in the desert. Everyone brought what they could from what they carried with them. I imagine a tabernacle built from family heirlooms, fine cloths saved for a special occasion, and spices purchased just before leaving Egypt. These were precious, meaningful possessions they had carried with them for decades. I can imagine when the people heard the work God had called them to do, they might have felt discouraged. How could they create a dwelling place worthy of God's presence when they each had so little? And yet, together they brought more than enough to do God's work.

I love the outpouring of abundance in this passage. The people brought so much that they had to be restrained from giving. What a vision of enough! *Has a congregation ever told you to stop giving because enough had been given to fulfill a specific project?* It goes against all traditional fundraising advice. If this project is fulfilled, we should move on to the next one, bigger and better than before. And yet, the leaders found themselves overwhelmed by the generosity of the people. Together, they had more than enough.

I'm also struck by what God called them to do. God called them to build a tabernacle, a dwelling place that they could carry through the desert. This was not a temple or a cathedral. Had they tried to build anything else, they likely would have come up empty, but because they responded to exactly what God called them to do, there was a match between the resources and the project, the money and the mission.

Asset Mapping

Create an inventory of the things your congregation holds collectively (building, staff, property, etc.) as well as the things individuals connected to the congregation hold (time, talents, relationships, money, etc.). I have organized these assets into four categories: financial, skills, time, and network. You may find some items fit in more than one category. Write these assets (big and small) in the margins as you think of them. We will put these to good use in the practice at the end of the chapter.

Financial assets

Financial assets are likely the easiest to quantify. They include not only your congregation's cash and investments, but also its physical assets like property. Begin by considering all your congregation's finances: tithes and offerings, checking and savings accounts, endowment funds, grant funding, and any other streams of income for the congregation. Then, take a look at your congregation's physical assets: church buildings, church furniture, office supplies, art, audio-visual equipment, musical instruments, books in the church library, and even some seemingly inconsequential church junk like ten thousand paper cups, five hundred old chairs, or a room stacked full of hymnals. *What are the physical assets that make your church unique?*

One of my favorite stories about the use of financial assets comes from The Emory Fellowship in Washington, DC. When the congregation first discovered the need for affordable housing in their community, they never considered using their own church property for the project because it was landlocked. Their church was up on a hill with a grassy area they used for events on one side and a parking lot on the other. While the parking lot only had twenty-two spaces, the congregation needed those spaces because DC street parking was at a premium. Next to the parking lot was an old parsonage, which had been renovated and rented out for a transitional housing program through a partnership with the city. There just wasn't any space to put up houses. They began looking for other property on their street but kept coming up short. It wasn't until a member suggested using their own property that they began investigating this option. They realized that while they didn't have space to build houses, they did have space to build rental units, since they had air rights to the space above their building. This started them down the path of renovating their entire church campus to create the Beacon Center, which includes ninety-nine units of state-of-the-art affordable housing, a gymnasium, classrooms, a food pantry, immigration clinics, and small business services.

As they began to raise funding for the Beacon Center project, they started with their own congregation. They raised $1.4 million dollars through a capital campaign. As The Emory Fellowship's lead pastor, the Rev. Joe Daniels, described it to me, this was one of the greatest miracles of the whole process:

a four-hundred-member working-class congregation raising over a million dollars. In addition to the money raised from the congregation, the church was able to take advantage of housing production trust fund monies from the city, a variety of tax credits, other low-income housing monies, and denominational support to make this $58 million dollar project possible. The Emory Fellowship tapped into a variety of financial assets to make this vision a reality.

Skill assets

Take a look at what skills or talents might be present in the pastors and staff as well as the members and friends of your congregation. I've seen many congregations use "Time & Talent Inventories" and yet the only talents listed are ones that connect to current roles within the church. *What skills might be present in your community that you have not tapped yet?*

In January 2020, Tree of Life discerned that we wanted to write our own evening prayer service together. This was a great way for us to tap into the skills of our entire congregation. Our pastor had a heart for writing liturgies and our lead musician was a songwriter. Similarly, we were a community full of people who appreciated church liturgy, good music, and the process of creating art and music together. During COVID, we created our own evening prayer service together, "Brightness and Shadows." It was a deeply communal effort: some wrote prayers, some made art, some listened to the early stages of the liturgy and contributed their feedback, and some composed new music. It tapped into skills that most of our members had never brought to our community before, and it tapped into skills that our paid leaders often didn't get the chance to bring to their regular roles. Just about every member of the Tree of Life community was involved in making this project happen.

As you consider what skills might be untapped, I encourage you to pay special attention to the skills that your congregation's paid leaders may not get the chance to bring to their regular roles in the congregation.

- Does your pastor have a background in business?
- Is your bookkeeper also a master gardener?
- Similarly, what skills might members of the congregation have that they have never thought to bring to the congregation because it doesn't neatly align with the list of volunteer roles?

This is your opportunity to consider as many skills as you can think of, even if you aren't sure how God might want to use those skills.

Time assets

In January 2022, Faith+Lead had the privilege of publishing a piece by the Rev. Keith Anderson on the stewardship of our attention.[1] Anderson begins by talking about the attention economy and particularly technology's focus on capturing and holding our attention. He writes, "While information is everywhere, our attention is still limited, and it is in high demand. There is enormous competition to capture and keep it."[2] Anderson calls us to consider how we might be good stewards of our attention. He writes, "In the Reign of God, the attention economy is not about the attention we receive, it is about the attention we give."[3]

Often, stewardship of time and talents is rolled together and for good reason: it takes time to offer a skill. However, in this section, I would invite you to think specifically about opportunities to offer time without a particular skill attached to it. While we all have time to share, there are some who may have more than others. My 94-year-old grandmother is a great example of this. Many of the gifts that she used to offer to her congregation, like her beautiful singing voice, she is no longer able to share due to her age. However, she has more time available to her than she has ever had before. She has used this time wisely to care for others by praying, writing cards, sending texts, and calling people on the phone. When I was recovering from surgery, I could feel her holding me in prayer each day and it made a big difference for me.

Consider the time that might be available to children, youth, young adults, and teachers who are off school during the summer or school breaks. You might also consider seasons of life where people naturally have more time: college students waiting for a job, those who have been furloughed or laid off, or those in retirement. How might God be inviting these individuals to use this time and attention?

Two of the interview sites shared stories of using time exceptionally well. The Emory Fellowship's pastor, the Rev. Joe Daniels, invited his congregation to pray for the Beacon Center project at 6:10 a.m. and 6:10 p.m. every day. They choose 6:10 because their address number is 6100 Georgia Avenue. Many people in the congregation would set alarms on their phones and watches as a reminder to pray. During evening meetings, a series of alarms would go off at 6:10 p.m. and together they would stop and pray. This project took eleven years to complete. One of the key things that kept the congregation moving together through this journey was consistent prayer, which reminded them of their mission and encouraged them to look for ways God was present at every point in the process. While we may not feel like we have a lot of time in the day, taking two minutes each day to pray is feasible for just about anyone.

Time assets were also an important factor in the story of Church Anew, mentioned in chapter 1. After the pandemic hit, they weren't sure how to proceed, since up until that point they were leading in-person events. They wondered if they should just put this ministry "on pause" until the pandemic was over. However, one of the team members had a "hare-brained idea": What if they started a blog? The team member explained that many of the speakers with whom they were connected for their in-person events had recently lost work due to the pandemic. As the Rev. Matthew Fleming put it,

> These speakers were out of work. So all of the things that they had counted on weren't going to happen. And that has a financial impact, but it also has a "what-do-I-do-in-this-time" impact. They had more time in their schedule than they'd ever had before.

What a unique opportunity to invite people, who might normally be much too busy, to use blog writing to share their voice during this devastating season. The first three blog posts Church Anew published were by Diana Butler Bass, Walter Brueggemann, and Michael Curry. Those blog posts went viral, introducing Church Anew's ministry to a whole new audience and magnifying its impact.

Network assets

Along with time assets, I think network assets are one of the most underutilized assets a congregation has at its disposal. Network assets refers to the web of relationships between people in the congregation to other people, associations, and institutions in the community. One of the key findings from our research was that for congregations to lean into new forms of generating income they had to reach outside themselves to partner with others in the community. Too often congregations don't consider partnerships until they are desperate. What if we sought them out when we were still in a position to bring something to the partnership?

For each of the congregations I've used as examples in the preceding sections, network assets were also a key part of their story. For The Emory Fellowship to finance its project, they needed to partner with the city to get access to housing production trust fund monies, new market tax credits, 9 percent tax credits along with other low-income housing monies. For Church Anew, while the blog idea certainly relied on the writers having enough time to commit to the project, it was also important that someone on the team had preexisting trusted relationships with these writers and speakers in order to help get them on board. For Tree of Life, they received grant funding from another congregation that gave them the startup funding to make "Brightness and Shadows" possible.

However, I was really pleased to see the ways network assets played a role in the shift in First Congregational Church of Kensington United Church of Christ's (KCC's) ministry—a small, rural congregation in Kensington, NH. While their relationships with the broader community, particularly the local school, had once been seen as a deficit, they were now being seen as an asset. As one lay member put it,

> We shouldn't look at the other parts of the community as competition. We should look at it as, "How can we all work together to make our town whole?" Everybody has gifts, each different organization has a different gift, and our Jesus has given us all gifts. So why can't we combine those gifts?

Together, we can make a bigger impact than we could on our own.

As you consider the network assets in your midst, think about the partners your congregation is currently connected with, like places where your congregation has donated time or money. You might also consider other organizations or community partners that individuals in your congregations are connected to through their work, hobbies, volunteer service, and/or generosity.

Are These Assets Really Ours?

No, these assets belong to God. God has entrusted us as stewards, or managers, of all these assets. While this may seem like a small detail, it has the potential to transform the way we view our individual and communal assets. *How might we use them differently if we believed they belonged to God and not to us?*

That said, I always find it a bit sticky to talk about what God has entrusted to our care because that language can allow us to hide behind God's blessing without naming other socioeconomic, governmental, cultural, and political forces that govern the distribution of wealth in our world today. This is true of us as individuals as well as our congregations and communities. While this is certainly a time to celebrate all that God has entrusted to our care, it is also a good time to consider whether all this wealth is really ours and the ways some of this wealth may have come into our possession. We can't begin to "fund forward" unless we have done the work to repair the past.

It's important to consider how these assets, particularly the financial ones, came into your congregation's hands.

- Is your education wing sitting on native land?
- Was your chapel built by the hands of enslaved people?
- How much did economic inequality factor into the creation of your congregation's financial wealth?

These are not easy questions to answer. It can take time to sift through your congregation's history and learn the true story behind how these resources came into your possession.

Once you know the stories, it can also be challenging to know how to handle these assets that continue to be in your possession, even if they don't truly belong there. I have no easy answers to share with you because there are no easy answers to give. This work of repair is best done in relationship with and under the leadership of those who were harmed. It's an ongoing process, not a "one and done" experience. But I would urge you, as you consider the different opportunities for generating income that are described in this book, to take the time to consider how you might utilize some or all of what you've earned to begin the process of repair.

A Beautiful Constraint

I hope as you read this chapter you were reminded of the abundance that God has entrusted to your congregation's care, but it may still feel like God has invited you to feed five thousand people with just one boy's lunch. While it may seem like endless assets would make creativity and innovation easier, the opposite is true. As Amy Blaschka put it in a 2020 Forbes article: "Though most people think that unlimited resources are what fuel innovation, the best ideas are born from creative constraints."[4] As I saw with my students playing "Mission Possible," the limitation on their resources unleashed greater creativity. It caused them to focus on the uniqueness of their individual resources and use them in unexpected ways because they had no other choice. Constraints invite us to ask new questions like "What if?" and "Why not?" They also help to limit our focus and direction in constructive ways. As Blaschka writes,

> Without restrictions, the research suggests, we'd remain stuck in our old ways of thinking. Constraints create an environment that demands that we unleash that which would otherwise remain untapped, which fuels innovation. Instead of resisting constraints and seeing them as inhibitors to your success, reframe them as creative challenges essential for innovation.[5]

One surprising finding from our research project was the way that COVID, a monumental and grievous constraint, helped many congregations to shift their model for ministry. Over half of the congregations we interviewed noted that COVID played a significant role in creating new pathways for them to live out God's mission in their community. In many of these congregations, COVID freed up the congregation to think in new ways. It released them from the routine of doing ministry and invited a season of flexibility. The congregations we studied would never "give thanks" for COVID. It was a time of deep grief and trauma that will never be forgotten. And yet, it was also a place where God met them and there was enough space for the Spirit to move in new and different ways.

One of the key questions we asked in all of our interviews was about the congregation's openness to change. For many of the congregations we interviewed, the pandemic created a liminal space where the congregation was more open to change. It was a time where congregations became more intimately connected with the needs of its community and were invited to participate in God's mission in new ways. While they certainly could have gone back to business as usual post-pandemic, many of these congregations used this moment as a catalyst to step forward with changes they had been discerning for a long time.

As we see in the dwelling text at the beginning of this chapter, and time and time again throughout the Bible and Christian history, it is in these times of constraint, these times where we are called into the desert wilderness, that God meets us and does a new thing in us. Amid their wilderness wandering, God called the Israelites to create a tabernacle and provided more than what they needed to do the work. During COVID, God entrusted to these congregations exactly what they needed to do God's work, whether it was starting a farming ministry for youth, moving their event ministry online to reach even more people, or renting out their education wing to businesspeople in need of office space. God redeemed even this grievous constraint to share God's love and grace with the world in new ways using resources that had often been untapped prior to the pandemic.

♦ Practice: Create Your Congregation's Inventory ♦

Take some time on your own after reading this chapter to create a list of at least ten assets God has entrusted to your congregation's care for each of the four asset areas. Be sure to go back and add any notes you put in the margin to your lists. Then, come together as a group to share your lists and put together a larger inventory that you can add to over time.

Reflection Questions

1. Which type(s) of assets do you think your congregation is utilizing well right now? Why?
2. Which type(s) of assets do you think your congregation is underutilizing? Why?
3. How will you lift up these underutilized assets moving forward?
4. What's one unique congregational asset that came to mind as you were reading this chapter that you hadn't considered before?

CHAPTER FOUR

How Might Our Congregation Join God's Mission?

Matthew 25:31–45

"When the Son of Man comes in his glory, and all the angels with him, then he will sit on the throne of his glory. All the nations will be gathered before him, and he will separate people one from another as a shepherd separates the sheep from the goats, and he will put the sheep at his right hand and the goats at the left. Then the king will say to those at his right hand, 'Come, you that are blessed by my Father, inherit the kingdom prepared for you from the foundation of the world; for I was hungry and you gave me food, I was thirsty and you gave me something to drink, I was a stranger and you welcomed me, I was naked and you gave me clothing, I was sick and you took care of me, I was in prison and you visited me.' Then the righteous will answer him, 'Lord, when was it that we saw you hungry and gave you food, or thirsty and gave you something to drink? And when was it that we saw you a stranger and welcomed you, or naked and gave you clothing? And when was it that we saw you sick or in prison and visited you?' And the king will answer them, 'Truly I tell you, just as you did it to one of the least of these who are members of my family, you did it to me.' Then he will say to those at his left hand, 'You that are accursed, depart from me into the eternal fire prepared for the devil and his angels; for I was hungry and you gave me no food, I was thirsty and you gave me nothing to drink, I was a stranger and you did not welcome me, naked and you did not give me clothing, sick and in prison and you did not visit me.' Then they also will answer, 'Lord, when was it that we saw you hungry or thirsty or a stranger or naked or sick or in prison, and did not take care of you?' Then he will answer them, 'Truly I tell you, just as you did not do it to one of the least of these, you did not do it to me.'"

Dwelling Questions

1. What word or phrase jumped out at you as you read the passage?
2. What's one way your congregation tends to one of the needs mentioned in this passage? How have you seen God in this work?
3. What's one tangible need in your community that you think God might be calling your congregation to address?
4. What might God be saying to you or your congregation through this passage?

Prayer

Ever present God, you lived among us and understand the pain of hunger, thirst, sickness, and loneliness. We give thanks that you know all our needs and are near to those who are crying out for help. Grant us courage as we venture into our neighborhoods and communities to listen deeply to those you have called us to serve. Invite us into trusted relationships as we partner with you and our neighbors to do your work in our communities. Amen.

One of the things that shocked my research assistants and I as we conducted our interviews was that every congregation we talked to in this study had a very clear sense of mission. In most cases they could rattle it off without even thinking too much about it. While I expected this from the pastors we talked to, I was amazed to see the lay members were able to do the same thing. Mission was at the heart of every interview we conducted. They couldn't talk about the money moves they had made without also talking to us about the mission.

For some, living out their mission was the reason they had stumbled into new sources of funding. Funding was just one tool in completing the work God had called them to do. For others, their financial situation drove them to discern who God was calling them to be in this stage of their congregation's life and get out into the neighborhood to see how the community's longings and the church's assets might align. Often, it was a mix of both reasons. But it was amazing to see how even those who had initially started out with a purely financial motivation quickly shifted gears to focus on mission and could honestly say that these new financial opportunities were a ministry, not just a funding source.

I saw this clearly in the story of the small-town congregation First Presbyterian Church of Gulf Shores in Gulf Shores, Alabama. They were initially drawn into Funding Forward work because of the church's financial situation. When the Rev. Chrisy Ennen finally received a current financial statement in the fall of 2021, nearly nine months after she had arrived as minister of the congregation, she realized they had a problem. Prior to COVID, the congregation had received a large investment gift. When the stock market plummeted during COVID, they took this money out of the stock market and began to use it to pay for staff salaries. When the Rev. Ennen was hired, they only had enough money left to pay her salary for two years, and by the time she saw the financial statements even less was available. Something had to change.

So, the Rev. Ennen took two steps. First, she pulled together a group of congregation leaders to brainstorm ideas. The congregation realized that the biggest asset that they could use to create change was their building, which remained vacant for most of the week. Second, she began asking people in the community, "What's needed?" She heard two themes emerge from the community: a need for childcare and a need for affordable office space. After running the numbers on childcare and realizing it was unlikely to be an income-generating venture for them, they decided to lean into creating affordable office space. They have now rented out six classrooms, a library, a larger room, and staff office space. Their previously vacant education wing is now the "Hand-in-Hand Business Center." Curious to learn more? I will be discussing property rental and any tax implications in detail in chapter 6.

While the business center originally began as a solution to the congregation's financial problems, it has become so much more. As the Rev. Ennen put it, there is a line in First Presbyterian Church of Gulf Shores's mission statement: " 'To perpetuate hope for our community and world by being consistently mindful of the indescribable gifts God has bestowed upon us and to express gratitude for such.' We believe that one of the gifts that God has given us is this facility. And by using that in a way that supports our community, that aligns our mission to . . . [gratefully share] what we have been given." The congregation's leadership team now sees this business center as a central part of its mission and ministry. It has helped them use the assets God had entrusted to their care to meet the tangible needs of their community in an entirely new way. Like in the Matthew 25 passage, they were providing offices for those in need and ended up encountering God in the process through these new relationships with their neighbors.

"But, I'm Just the Finance Person"

I realize some of you reading this book, whether you are the bookkeeper on the church staff or you are the volunteer church treasurer, may be tempted to skim this chapter. After all, you're just responsible for making sure the "business" side of the church stays running, the pastor and other leaders are responsible for worrying about this "spiritual" stuff. But the truth is, for the church, and really any organization, the business and the mission can't be separated from one another. The mission should guide every element of the church's life, including the more "business-y" elements. And, if we aren't attentive to seeking God's mission and intentionally aligning the way we use our money with the mission, the money will dictate our mission. As Jesus says in Luke chapter 12: "where your treasure is, there your heart will be also." The good news is that anyone in the congregation, not just the pastor, can engage in the work discussed in this chapter. While you may not be the one who leads it, your congregation's engagement in this work will have a tremendous impact on what funding opportunities your congregation decides to pursue. Who knows? Maybe you are just the person God is calling to get this conversation started.

Why Mission Matters

Our call to stewardship as individuals and as congregations can be summed up in this statement from Luke 10: "You shall love the Lord your God with all your heart, and with all your soul, and with all your strength, and with all your mind; and your neighbor as yourself." We are called to use all the assets that God has entrusted to our care to love God and our neighbors, especially our neighbors in need, as Matthew 25 reminds us. Throughout the Bible we see the importance of not just one or the other but both commands. And they often go together, as we see in Matthew 25 where, in loving the neighbor, these people were unwittingly also loving God, whether they knew it or not.

Too often, I think congregations have confused loving God and loving neighbor with loving their buildings and their fellowship with other members. They have sustained the church for the sake of those inside the building on Sunday morning rather than those who aren't there yet. While simply having a church might have been mission enough in the boom of church growth, that's just not the case anymore. Most "nones" (those with no religious affiliation) and "dones" (those who have stopped attending church) do not see a church building as a beacon of hope in the community; rather, they are suspicious of churches as they wonder whether religion has done more harm than good. In the words of Jonny Baker, Britain Hub mission director at Church Mission Society, "You've got to be good news, if you want to talk about good news in that context."[1] *Is your church good news to its neighborhood?*

The goal isn't to sustain our church but to be lights of God's love in our communities. No one wants to partner with an organization whose sole purpose is its own survival—it's neither practical nor biblical. Funding Forward provides a unique opportunity for churches to not only generate additional revenue but live into their mission in new ways.

At the beginning of the "Mission Possible" game I mentioned in chapter 3, players are given an impossibly large problem to solve, like homelessness or climate change. This challenge can feel very overwhelming. How could a small group with limited time and resources ever present a solution to such a large problem? After taking some time to understand the problem, the groups are invited to "get specific" about which part of the problem they will try to solve. As the instructions say, "If you know of lots already happening to address the issue, is anyone currently 'missing a trick'? Are you going to tackle a symptom or a cause or something in between."[2] The greatest commandment to love God and neighbor and the great commission to bring the gospel to all nations can often feel like the challenge distributed at the beginning of "Mission Possible"—so big it leads to despair not action. That's why it's important to get clear on specifically what God is inviting your congregation to do to join God's mission in your community. As the Rev. Mark DeYmaz declares in his book *Disruption*, "while you may not be able to change the world, you just might be able to transform a zip code, a neighborhood, or an apartment complex when your vision is more precise."[3] Mission helps to clarify what God is inviting us to focus on. Mission is a beautiful constraint that helps to shape innovation in our congregations.

To be clear, the mission I have in mind isn't a beautifully crafted, long-winded statement that no one can remember. This isn't something that just emerges a few times a year during the congregation's annual meetings and leadership gatherings; this is something that guides the congregation's work every day. It's something that members know by heart and can explain.

I was struck by the simplicity of many of the mission statements that were shared during the interview process. The mission of St. Andrew Lutheran Church in Eden Prairie, Minnesota is "living out our faith in daily life." This mission statement has led them to start an early learning center, a camp, and now Church Anew. For River Heights Vineyard Church in Inver Grove Heights, Minnesota, it is "love God, love people, and change the world." This purpose statement has led them to sell one part of their building so it could be used for affordable housing and to start a Spanish-speaking congregation, La Viña Inver, in another part of their building. The Emory Fellowship in Washington, DC, seeks to "inspire people to LEARN from Jesus, LOVE like Jesus, and LEAD others to Jesus so that we can LIVE a WHOLE life." They have taken this mission statement to the next level by creating an acronym of what it means to live a WHOLE life that serves as their vision statement:

> God's vision for us is to offer a WHOLE life to every broken-hearted person from Georgia Avenue to across the globe. (Psalm 34:18; John 10:10)

WHOLE is an acronym for us, based on Jesus statement in John 10:10, and stands for being:

- **W**ell physically
- **H**ealed emotionally
- **O**bedient spiritually
- **L**oved unconditionally
- **E**mpowered financially[4]

The mission and vision infuse every part of their life as a congregation, but I could hear it clearly as they talked about the decades of ministry the congregation has done with the unhoused in their community and the new opportunities made possible through the Beacon Center.

A church's mission is its "why," while a church's vision explains "how" this "why" is lived out. In this chapter, I'll be focusing mainly on the "why," with the hope that the remaining chapters of the book (particularly chapters five through eight) will help you flesh out "how" you will bring the mission to life.

Where Is God at Work?

I grew up in an Assemblies of God church, part of the Pentecostal and evangelical traditions. We had no trouble naming God's agency in the world. Sometimes I think we were a little too quick to name something as "God's work" without first taking time to discern God's action. I'm not sure getting a good parking spot at Target is necessarily a sign of God at work. That being said, the words "Spirit," "Jesus," and "God" were used all the time in my church growing up. We were eager to talk about where we saw God at work in our lives, the lives of others, and in our world today.

As I tiptoed into ELCA churches in college and seminary, and slowly found a home there, one of the first differences that stood out to me was that people in the ELCA, and as I found out later in other, mainline traditions, were more hesitant to name God's agency in the world. We read about God in the Bible, heard the word of God preached, experienced God through the sacraments, but outside of these experiences we were pretty hesitant to name God's presence.

The mission we are called to follow is God's, not ours. It would be easy for a group of well-meaning Christians to sit in a room and decide what their mission should be, and yet what makes the church different from secular nonprofits is we believe God is active in the world and that this mission ultimately belongs to God and not to us. Jesus is the restorer, redeemer, and savior—not us. As the ELCA tagline says, it's "God's work. Our hands."

Discerning where God is at work in our lives and communities is some of the most difficult work the church is called to do, and yet it is also some of the most important. At first, it may feel awkward, weird, or counterculture. You might be accustomed to relying on Scripture to know God's character and using this experience of God to interpret how we as Christians, and our churches, are called to live as Christ's light in the present. You might believe

God is present in the world today but be unaccustomed to talking about God's action in the present tense or even naming God's action. The practices in this section are going to help you take that approach a step further.

So, how do we discern what God is doing and how we are invited to join in this work? During the pandemic, I was struggling to see God's activity in the world in a way that I never had before. It felt like grief, destruction, and injustice were closing in and I began to wonder where God was. I wanted God to show up like a burning bush, to part the sea, to heal the sick. I was looking for big signs of God in the world and coming up empty. I finally reached out to my pastor who invited me to look for the small ways God was showing up every day.

I started to practice a simplified version of the Ignatian Prayer of Examen. In the evening, I walk back through my day in my mind and ask myself four questions:

- Where did I see God today?
- What barriers got in the way of me experiencing God today?
- What will I pray for from today?
- What prayer do I have for tomorrow?

This practice encourages me to see God's presence in small moments of the day: the smell of a spring flower, a perfectly timed encouraging word from a friend, a smile from a stranger. On the days when I struggle to see God's presence, I ask myself, "When did I experience love today?" because God is love (1 John 4:8). My Luther Seminary colleague, Michael Binder, often invites people to look for hope: "Where did you experience hope today?" Between hope and love I find I can often come up with at least one way, if not more, that God has shown up during my day. I find that the more consistent I am with my practice, the longer my list is each day and the more likely I am to notice God in the moment and not just during the practice.

One of the most astonishing and uplifting parts of this research was getting to hear from both the survey and interview participants where they are seeing God at work. I can still remember looking at the survey data for the first time in December 2022 and weeping while I read the responses to the "Where have you seen God in this process?" question near the end of the survey. As we put the survey together that fall, I wondered how many people might skip this question simply due to survey fatigue, but the responses were astounding. I have shared a complete list of these responses in Appendix A. I share a few of my favorites below just to give you a taste (emphasis added by me):

> In our newest venture that serves Christian leaders, God has been present blazing a trail of relationship and community . . . And has even blazed a trail for our congregation to support and celebrate this vibrant ministry, whose impact goes far beyond the walls of our congregation to every continent on the globe and countless expressions of Christian witness. **It has felt more like following and riding the Spirit's wave than leading it at times.** God continues to show up now as we reach toward financial sustainability in connecting us with the right partners and organizations who are providing capacity building support and catching the vision for our mission.

> **There have been so many 'God winks' in this process**—everything from unexpected financial gifts just when they were needed most, to doors being opened to find the perfect renters for the business center, to relationships being built with various people and organizations in the community, to a sense of purpose and anticipation about how God is leading and providing for the church. Last year at this time, **I wasn't sure we would even be here, and the ways God is providing is amazing.**

> This has all been A LOT of work for us. **The leadership of our church is burned out. And yet, God still finds a way to energize us with curiosity at what is next.** We also continue to experience a sense of peace. Though [it] surpasses all our understanding at times, peace at the edge of a financial and ecclesial cliff is like feeling calm and content on hospice care. **We don't yet know if death is the next journey for our church, but in that uncertainty, God's peace abounds.**

> Grants have been a life-giving source of inspiration and experimentation for our congregation. Since this is a new way of being church that I introduced, **I give God 100% of the credit for easing the conflict that this [paradigm] shift would have caused.** Grants take up a lot of my time. The congregation just seemed to accept that there would be fewer staff working here due to budgetary constraints, and the rector would be less available to do other church duties.

> **From the beginning we have recognized that this ministry belongs primarily to God, and we are invited into it (rather than us owning it and bearing the full burden of responsibility).** This has freed us to take courageous moves in adding serving days, hiring staff, etc. God is present every time someone comes to volunteer or share lunch. The relationships we have in the kitchen and at the serving window are God's presence among us.

I wish I could tell you that there was a short, magic formula you could follow to discern what God is up to. But it's a lot more like forecasting the weather than completing a math problem. We can look back at what God has done in Scripture and in our own lives, we can share where we experience God in the moment, and we can do our best to follow God's lead into what comes next. It's something best done in community, so we can listen, learn, course correct, and see what themes emerge. Listening for God, like the Prayer of Examen, is a practice.

I appreciate the way my Luther Seminary colleagues Dwight Zscheile, Michael Binder, and Tessa Pinkstaff framed this in their recent book, *Leading Faithful Innovation*:

> Often, the direction of God's leadership is not easy to determine ahead of time . . . it more commonly unfolds through experiences of encounters with neighbors, conversations among believers, life-giving connections, and trial and error. It is not linear. The inherent ambiguity in discerning God's leading (and the real risk we can get it wrong) pushes us deeper into scripture, deeper into prayer, deeper into reflection in community (especially across cultural differences), and deeper into experimentation.[5]

As we listen to where God is leading, we also need to be open to pivot and change direction as the Spirit prompts us. There is no end to the discernment process—it is a process of continual learning and growth.

We can discern God's presence through individual practices like the Prayer of Examen, but we can also make it communal by asking one another, *Where have you seen God this week?* and sharing the places where God has shown up for you. This practice can feel intimidating if your congregation does not have a history of talking about where they see God active in their lives. However, paired with the Prayer of Examen, this can give congregation members an opportunity to share what they have seen in their individual practices, listen to what others have seen, and notice what themes emerge through that conversation.

Similarly, Dwelling in the Word can also help us notice God's presence together. This is an ancient practice of listening to God's word together with a group of people. Generally, the text is read twice, by two different people, then each person is invited to pair up with a "reasonably friendly looking stranger" and reflect on what they heard using a few simple guiding questions. Often these questions are used: What catches your imagination in this passage? What questions does it bring up for you? What might God be saying to you through this passage?[6] Then, everyone is invited to share what they heard from their partner.

When you dwell in the word together, as we have at the beginning of each chapter, we put the gospel at the center of our conversation. The biblical text can help us to hear God's voice in new ways and interpret God's action. We use this practice often in our meetings at Luther Seminary. When we start with dwelling together, it's amazing how themes from the text begin to weave their way into the meeting. It also grounds us and reminds us why this work really matters: It's not about us, it's about the gospel. We have also used the practice of "calling for the text," which means at any time during the meeting someone can "call for the text," so we go back and read the text together before continuing our conversation. This practice can be a great way to recenter conversations that have gone astray.

While these practices are designed to be used all the time, they can be particularly helpful when discerning the congregation's mission and/or making a critical decision. I appreciated the community discernment practices that the Rev. Peter Benedict from River Heights Vineyard Church in Inver Grove Heights, Minnesota, shared with me following my interview with him:

> First, [the pastoral staff] pray (sometimes with fasting from food) for the issue, often for weeks, individually and together. Issues we've prayed through this way range from primary leadership transition after 24 years with our founding pastors, to how we can pray together for a friend with a longtime hindrance to worship, etc.
>
> Second, after we have reached unity we present the results to our leaders. At roughly 350 [per] week attendance our leader circle was

usually 45 people or so. We've presented results we were pretty sure we'd heard clearly from God, and generally the leaders have been on board. We've also shared with the leaders when we feel there are multiple options and we're unsure, and we've shared when we had no idea yet what God was doing. We usually have people pray together around tables, choosing a volunteer to record what people are hearing or sharing. We collect and assemble everything that is presented as coming from God.

Third, we have several times called whole-church meetings for discernment. This has involved sharing the results of the first two steps, and inviting everyone to pray, and then having an open mic or breaking down into table discussions and collection. We normally have a pastor stand next to people who are sharing, and if someone starts to ramble off topic, we'll help them to finish or get back on track.[7]

They also have a monthly prayer meeting that has a similar tenor:

We have a monthly meeting (called CHANGED) where we worship for perhaps 45 minutes, share a shorter message (10 minutes or so), make space for gratitude and/or group spiritual direction, and have prayer ministry.

Our prayer ministry takes two forms: First, we always give people a chance to pray for one another. Second, we often have the community wait on God together, and give people the chance to share whatever God might be giving them. Often this is after a message about where God has been leading the community, and what God might ask of us, and/or where God might want to take us next.

My experience is that in most churches these issues are decided by staff and/or leaders, separately from the congregation. At River Heights Vineyard Church when we ask everyone to pray into these things, we believe God speaks, and that His guidance comes even through community members with mental health issues, addictions, etc. When someone shares a prayer/vision/etc. that starts with "I think . . ." we treat that as an opinion, but when someone shares "I believe God is saying" or "I hear God saying" we treat that much more seriously, regardless of the source. We often record this kind of feedback, and thank people for sharing what they hear God saying.

I'd normally qualify this process by saying something like: "Of course if someone shares something crazy or counter to [scripture,] we know that's problematic," but in my experience this doesn't really happen. Our congregation is largely working class, every month we have people present with substantial challenges to mental health, "moral living," addictions, etc., and to a [shocking] degree the guidance we get from the Holy Spirit during these times is consistent, helpful, scriptural, and leads to church health as we put it into practice. Over the years I have grown less and less attached to the "worthiness" of the speaker, and more and more focused on whether they're presenting their own opinions or whether they believe God is speaking. Feedback from the latter category has been so helpful.[8]

Context matters in discernment conversations. The pastors at River Heights Vineyard have invested a lot of time in creating a culture of discernment where everyone has a clear sense of what it means to hear God's voice and to share a personal opinion. This culture takes time and energy to cultivate; it does not happen overnight. Even with this cultural development, it is still possible that someone could use a phrase like "I heard God say" to manipulate others into following their opinion. That is a risk that we take in participating in this process together as a community. However, I think this risk is well worth taking compared with the risk of not voicing the ways we hear God speaking to us. As you try this practice, and other practices in this chapter with your congregation, the word "might" can be a helpful disclaimer: "I think God might be saying" or "I think I heard God say" gives us permission to try while also acknowledging our humanity.

You may also wonder, *What happens if we aren't sure what God is saying to us?* As much as we might want this process to be simple and efficient, it often isn't. A lack of clarity should not be an invitation to decide for ourselves or rush the process but instead an invitation to pause and seek God's guidance. Wait on the Lord by wading deeper into Scripture, leaning into spiritual practices, and focusing on prayer. This is incredibly difficult, but it is the only way forward.

Listening Outside the Four Walls of the Congregation

While all this discernment work is imperative, it is not complete unless we are able to get outside of the four walls of our congregations to be in conversation with the people God has called us to serve. While a secular resource, sustainable economic development expert, Ernesto Sirolli, captures the importance of listening well in his TED Talk: "Want to help someone? Shut up and listen!"[9] Sirolli begins his TED Talk by describing his early work in Africa for an Italian NGO. Every single one of their projects failed. As he puts it, "I thought, [at] age 21, that we Italians were good people and we were doing good work in Africa. Instead, everything we touched we killed."[10] In his first project, they decided to teach the Zambian people how to grow Italian food. They used Italian seeds to grow tomatoes and zucchinis in a magnificent valley near the Zambezi River. They were amazed that the local people wouldn't use this valley for agriculture, especially since everything the Italians planted grew beautifully. However, when the tomatoes were perfectly ripe, about 200 hippos came out of the river and ate them all: "And we said to the Zambians, 'My God, the hippos!' And the Zambians said, 'Yes, that's why we have no agriculture here.' 'Why didn't you tell us?' 'You never asked.'"[11]

You never asked.

After this experience, he has taken a different approach: "I do something very, very, very difficult. I shut up, and listen."[12] Instead of arriving in a community with his own ideas, he sits with the local people where they already are: in cafes and pubs. He listens to what they are passionate about. Instead of giving them ideas, he comes around these people to connect them with the support they need to make their own ideas a reality. He serves as a connector.

How often has your congregation listened to the people in your community? I've seen so many congregations with very good intentions try to go out and "serve their community" without any sense of what is really needed. They have offered food to those who weren't hungry, water to those who weren't thirsty, and clothes to those who were fine with what they were already wearing. Instead of doing the hard work of listening to others and championing their ideas, we have done what was easiest for us to do (often what we saw worked for other congregations) and called it "good." As well-intentioned as these projects may have been, like the development work Sirolli described in the TED talk, they have often done much more harm than good, creating distrust and skepticism about the church's role in today's world.

You may wonder why listening matters so much to Funding Forward work. Particularly those of you in financial straits may wish to focus on bringing more money in before you lean out to create relationships in your community. But our efforts to generate income in our community are destined to fail if we aren't partnering with those we are called to serve. More importantly, saving the church as an institution is not, and has never been, our calling. Our church does not exist solely for the purpose of keeping its doors open. We exist to love God and love our neighbors. We live out the great commission by sharing the good news of God's love, grace, and mercy with all people. We are called to make disciples. *As Matthew 25 says, we serve God by serving our community, we love God by loving our neighbors, and how can we do that if we don't know them?*

Here is the good news: This listening work is often a lot easier than we make it out to be. As you heard earlier in this chapter in First Presbyterian Church of Gulf Shores's story, the Rev. Chrisy Ennen took the time to listen to people in her local community, and particularly people in the organizations she was already connected with, like the local Chamber of Commerce. She asked over and over again, "What's needed?" Similarly, in The Emory Fellowship's story they listened to and created deeper relationships with people they were already serving through their homeless and transitional housing ministry. They began to realize that the needs of this community went far beyond what they were currently addressing. They started with people they were already connected with and moved out from there.

Think of someone who is peripherally connected to your church already. Maybe it's a partner who rents church space, a regular at your church's food pantry, a neighbor who lives close to the church, a local business owner, or someone who just started attending your church online. Start by listening to just one person.

Not sure who you should connect with? You might start by taking a prayer walk. This isn't about proselytizing; instead, it's about paying attention to what God is already up to in your neighborhood. Zscheile, Binder, and Pinkstaff describe how to take one in *Leading Faithful Innovation*:

> First, determine a time and place to walk, and invite people to walk with you. Consider printing a map of the area or having one ready on your phone. Make a plan for how far you will walk and in which direction you will go. Begin with a reminder of the goals of the Prayer Walk—paying

> attention to your surroundings and asking God to help you see what God sees. Be ready to pray for things as you encounter them. . . . You can stop and pray aloud together, pray silently as you continue to walk, and pray for people you come across. . . . When you are done with your walk, stop and pray a closing prayer with your group. Ask those with you if anything from your walk seems particularly important. Consider together if there is anything you noticed that God might be inviting you to spend more time learning about in the future. Thank God for being with you on your walk.[13]

As you go on your prayer walk, you might ask God to show you who you should connect with either during or after the prayer walk. When you have the chance to talk with someone, keep the conversation simple. Make the person you are speaking to, not your congregation, the focus of the conversation. The goal is not to get them to come to your church, but to learn from their wisdom and experience. Here are some questions you might use during the conversation:

- What are your hopes for our community?
- What are a few of the most pressing needs in our community right now?
- What assets does our community have that are currently being underutilized or even untapped?
- What gifts do the people in our community have that are currently underutilized or untapped?
- Prior to this conversation, what was the first thing that came to mind for you when you thought about [your church name]?
- If you had a chance to tell the church where they should direct their energies, what would you wish they would focus on?[14]
- Who else in the neighborhood should we be listening to?

Including that last question about who else you should be listening to allows you to find a pathway from this first conversation to the next one.

Listening shouldn't be a "one and done" or even an activity that your congregation engages in just for a specific period of time. Rather, listening should be a practice your congregation is engaging in all the time. It's an important practice not just for the pastors, staff, and leadership of the congregation but for the congregation as a whole to participate in together.

Listening is the important first step in the Faithful Innovation process.[15] We "listen" to God, one another, and our neighbors. Then we "act" on what we heard by trying something new based on God's leading. Then, we take time to "reflect" on what we tried, share what we learned, and name where God might be inviting us next. This time of sharing ultimately leads us back to listening again. Listening is the springboard that shapes the action we choose to take. This applies not only to our church programming but also to our church funding. And the good news is that we don't have to wait until the listening is "complete" to act because it's an ongoing process that will never be complete.

Listening to who God has called us to serve paired with the practices of discerning what God is up to can help us hone in on where God is calling us to go. As Zscheile, Binder, and Pinkstaff put it,

> You might see God doing something unexpected, in an unusual place or through an unusual person. . . . Sometimes, the things God shows you are an invitation for you—and for the members of your congregation—to personally or collectively join God in that work. What you hear and observe might press you to consider whether you and the people you serve are ready to trust God by stepping out in faith and trying something new.[16]

What I love about this process is that it often leads to new ideas and partnerships that the church could never have created by staying inside "its four walls." Instead of doing work "for" or even "on behalf of" the community, the church is now partnering with the community. This work breaks down walls.

What Is Your Congregation's Mission?

After listening to God and to others, it's important to name the particular way(s) that God is calling your congregation to participate in God's work in the world. Creating a mission statement, and potentially a vision statement for how you might live this mission out, is a great place to start. Too often mission statements are seen as the conclusion of the listening and the discernment process, when they are really just one signpost along the way. Listening and discernment should be ongoing practices. Keeping these practices alive will help us to reshape this statement over time as we continue to engage in the work God has called us to do. Again, this mission is ultimately God's, not ours.

Looking back at the interviews, while each of the congregations was guided by its mission, the congregations who seemed to find most alignment between their mission and their funding were the ones with the most memorable mission statements. They seemed much more like taglines than traditional church mission statements. Plus, they were much more memorable! Both the pastors and congregation members could share them without having to look at their congregation's website, bulletin, or archived materials.

Too often mission statements focus more on "what we do" rather than "why we matter." The "what" of our work as a church rarely motivates people, but the "why" of our church can be a rallying cry that creates genuine change, both for individuals and communities, particularly if it's stated in non-churchy language. While a more robust statement of your congregation's mission and purpose may be important, for the sake of the funding work, I'm going to encourage you to create a tagline: a short and pithy articulation of your congregation's "why." If your church already has one, after you've done some intentional listening to God and neighbor, I encourage you to come back to it and ask the following questions: *Is this who God is calling us to be in this time and place? Does this reflect what we have heard? If not, what changes need to be made?*

If you have a mission statement, but don't have a tagline, is there a way to shorten it into an actionable tagline? For instance, a church in my local community has the mission statement, "Gather in Grace. Grow in Faith. Go in Service." While that may already seem short, they might make a tagline of "gather, grow, and go." Similarly, another Lutheran church in my community has this mission statement: "Growing a Christ-centered community who welcomes gladly, sings joyfully and serves boldly!" While I can appreciate that this speaks to their character as a church, I'm not sure what good news this brings to those outside of the church. That's why I was so moved by their tagline: "Where grace meets life." That tagline is not only more memorable and life-giving than the mission statement, but it also offers a litmus test through which they can view every area of the congregation's work. As you can see, the tagline might reuse words from the mission statement, or it might capture the spirit of the statement.

Don't have a tagline or mission statement to work with? Here is a simple process to help you get started. After doing some of the listening and discernment work listed above, invite members of your congregation to answer these four questions:

1. Why does our congregation matter to you?
2. Why does our congregation matter to our community?
3. What work is God calling us to join?
4. What three words best describe our congregation's mission?

You could put sheets of paper up in a high-traffic space in your congregation and invite people to put up their responses on sticky notes before, after, or even during worship over the course of a few weeks. You could also bring these questions to small groups, adult education hours, or even send out a brief survey. Since people may have a tendency to wax prolific on the first three questions, I suggest creating a character limit. If you're gathering this information in person, sticky notes can help people to keep it brief. You'll be amazed at the stories that can be told in that little space!

Once you have this data, gather a few skilled writers, researchers, and/or journalists from your congregation. Invite them to create a brief list of common themes and a few possible taglines. If they need a hint in identifying key themes, it can be helpful to use an online tool to create a word cloud with all of the responses. These taglines should be anchored by action words. They should also be simple and memorable—no more than ten words. Depending on your congregation's leadership structure, these themes and taglines could then be shared back with the congregation as a whole and/or the congregation's leadership team for final selection and approval.

Finally, developing the tagline isn't the end of the journey. Now, it needs to be shared. Yes, put it on your congregation's website and in your congregation's leadership team minutes, but it needs to move from being a statement of purpose to a congregational rallying cry. Incorporate the tagline into your worship liturgy by saying it together as the sending at the end of worship. Bring it into sermons and prayers. If you can, put it up in your congregation's sanctuary and gathering spaces. Make it the theme for adult education and small groups so people can internalize it and gain a deeper understanding of what it means for them, the community, and the congregation. Remember, the average person needs to hear something seven times before they remember it. And, since most people aren't at worship every week or participating in every ministry, you'll need to repeat it.

The tagline and mission statement are just two small steps we can take in discerning how God is inviting us to participate in what God is up to in our community; they are not the end of the road. These are signposts on our broader journey of discernment. In other words, having a tagline and mission statement do not excuse us from the process of listening to God and our neighbors. They can assist us in finding direction, but they shouldn't be the last word. For many congregations, listening to God and neighbors requires not only a change in mission but a change in culture as we reorient ourselves away from the church's needs and toward participating in God's mission for the sake of our neighbors.

♦ Practice: Listening to God and Neighbor ♦

Agree that each of you on the Funding Forward team will have a conversation with a neighbor this week using the questions listed in this chapter. Then, come together and discuss these conversations. Begin by dwelling in the word together using the text and questions at the beginning of this chapter. Then, share a summary of what you heard and, at the end, share your responses to these two questions:

- Where did you see God in these conversations?
- Based on these conversations, where do you think God might be leading our congregation?

Take the time to walk through this chapter and note the different practices and tasks that your congregation needs to tend to before proceeding with creating its Funding Forward plan. Put together a calendar for getting this work completed over the next month or two. This is a place where many congregations get stalled. Don't let that happen!

The point is to create a regular practice of listening to God and community that can happen through everyday conversations with neighbors and by introducing consistent congregational practices to talk about what you hear and where God might be leading you. If this feels like too daunting of a task right now, focus on using some of these practices in your small group and slowly inviting others in the congregation to try out some of your favorites. Remember this is a practice, not a "one and done."

Reflection Questions

1. If you had to describe the current mission of your congregation in your own words, what would you say?
2. Does your congregation currently have a mission statement and/or tagline? Does this align with where you think God is currently leading your congregation?
3. What processes does your congregation currently have in place to listen to those God is calling them to serve? How might you introduce your congregation to one or more of the practices outlined in this chapter?

CHAPTER FIVE

How Does Our Congregation's Budget Align with the Mission?

Luke 12:22–34

"He said to his disciples, 'Therefore I tell you, do not worry about your life, what you will eat, or about your body, what you will wear. For life is more than food, and the body more than clothing. Consider the ravens: they neither sow nor reap, they have neither storehouse nor barn, and yet God feeds them. Of how much more value are you than the birds! And can any of you by worrying add a single hour to your span of life? If then you are not able to do so small a thing as that, why do you worry about the rest? Consider the lilies, how they grow: they neither toil nor spin; yet I tell you, even Solomon in all his glory was not clothed like one of these. But if God so clothes the grass of the field, which is alive today and tomorrow is thrown into the oven, how much more will he clothe you—you of little faith! And do not keep striving for what you are to eat and what you are to drink, and do not keep worrying. For it is the nations of the world that strive after all these things, and your Father knows that you need them. Instead, strive for his kingdom, and these things will be given to you as well.

'Do not be afraid, little flock, for it is your Father's good pleasure to give you the kingdom. Sell your possessions, and give alms. Make purses for yourselves that do not wear out, an unfailing treasure in heaven, where no thief comes near and no moth destroys. For where your treasure is, there your heart will be also.' "

Dwelling Questions

1. What word or phrase jumped out at you as you read the passage?
2. What's one worry that you or your congregation is holding on to?
3. Where is your congregation's treasure?
4. What might God be saying to you or your congregation through this passage?

Prayer

Creator God, we give thanks for all that you have made: ravens, lilies, grass, and our very selves. You have created each of us with care and provide for all of our needs. You know how easy it is for us to get tangled in webs of worry that keep us from seeing your provision. Guide us as we take a closer look at where we are investing all of the assets you have entrusted to our care. Remind us that where our treasure is, our hearts follow. Amen.

For many congregation leaders, the pandemic gave them an opportunity to look at their congregation's budget with a new set of eyes. Suddenly, so many of the things that churches spend money on—buildings, office space, food, supplies, in-person events, and more—no longer mattered in the same way they used to. Congregations quickly began to pivot in 2020 and 2021 to allocate money toward technology, benevolence (giving to mission and ministries outside of the congregation), and more as their church and community needs changed. Similarly, the length of the pandemic and the amount of time that many congregations were out of their buildings gave leaders the time to reflect on where their money was going and where it might be redirected in the future.

This was true for Tree of Life as well. During the pandemic, as we began to look more closely at our budget, we realized how much money we had been spending on renting space for our evening worship services. We had been renting a wedding venue in the North Loop area of downtown Minneapolis. A prime spot with even more prime prices. And while the space was beautiful, we realized it wasn't working as well as we would have liked. There wasn't a working kitchen that could be used to prepare meals or wash dishes after dinner church services. It was difficult for guests to find and parking was tough to come by. When I visited Tree of Life for the first time in the fall of 2019,

I nearly didn't find it. I was afraid I had stumbled across a small wedding, not a church. While everyone was very welcoming once I made my way into the worship space, it gave me, as a first-time visitor, the impression that this church was secretive and exclusive, caring more about the people inside the church than those outside of it. This is the exact opposite of Tree of Life's values, and yet that was the message being conveyed.

We realized that even though Tree of Life had been planted in Minneapolis for over three years, it still wasn't attracting many people from the North Loop neighborhood. Most people drove downtown just to attend Tree of Life. These rental fees were taking up a significant portion of Tree of Life's budget (it was the biggest line item after staffing) and in many ways it was getting in the way of Tree of Life's mission. So, we decided to look for another space.

Together, the congregation brainstormed different ideas for places to meet. The pastor and intern gathered these ideas, visited the sites, negotiated the pricing, and landed on a few different sites for the community to test out together. Over the course of summer 2021, the congregation visited each site and held a worship service there. We paid attention to how easy it was for someone new to find it and park as well as how usable the space was for dinner church. However, we also took it a step further. Instead of just looking for a place to meet, our pastor encouraged us to look for a community and a place where we felt called to invest. Is this a place where we could get connected with the neighborhood and see ourselves serving our neighbors? Could we partner with the work this host organization was already doing? Where might God be calling us?

We ended up moving just across the river to the Northeast neighborhood in Minneapolis and meeting at Twin Ignition Start-Up Garage, a tech start-up coworking space. The space itself was flexible—with chairs, desks, and tables that were all on wheels—to allow us to make the space into what we needed it to be. It had a small parking lot, kitchen, and prominent signage. But, more than anything, their values aligned with ours. We were a church made up of many geeky entrepreneurs, college students, and people just starting out in their careers—it seemed to make sense that we would all share the same space. We could also see options for embedding ourselves more deeply in the neighborhood. Plus, we ended up saving quite a bit of money in the process.

Too often, I see congregations focus on small-budget moves, like shaving just a small amount off each program's line item or cutting down a pastor's benefits in order to balance their budget. Instead of looking at where the money is going and having a bigger conversation about how to better use the assets God has entrusted to our care, we nickel and dime beloved church pastors, staff, and programs. Undoubtedly making big changes like moving to a new space, selling church property, and letting go of a beloved program that no longer aligns with the church's mission is a big deal. It takes more time, more communication, and much more commitment, but I believe this is the brave work God is calling us to do.

In Luke 12, Jesus explicitly tells us that the places where we invest our treasure will take our hearts with them. This applies not only to individuals but also to our congregations. As I look back at the Tree of Life example, investing in the wedding venue space rental not only took away money that could have been spent on other areas of the budget or given away to our community, it took away so much more that we never noticed until after the pandemic hit. Our pastor began to realize how much time she was spending each week we met for dinner church to arrange a catered meal, put out the church signage, make sure the meal stayed hot during worship, and clean up all the paper plates and utensils after worship was over. This space forced her to spend a lot of time acting as an event planner that she could have spent on pastoral duties.

What Story is Your Church's Budget Telling?

In their seminal book *Ministry and Money: A Practical Guide for Pastors*, Janet T. and Philip D. Jamieson make a provocative statement about church budgeting. They write,

> Each year churches make a statement of faith in which they reveal that which is most important to them. This statement of faith usually is not declared on a Sunday morning, and quite possibly the majority of the church members never see or hear it. Nevertheless, this confession reveals the mission and everything else the congregation values most. It is not a historic document or creed; this statement of faith is the annual operating budget.[1]

Have you ever thought of your church's budget as a statement of faith? The budget is one of the clearest places that our congregations name what we value and put a price tag on how much we value them. While this might seem a bit crass, that is what we are doing. We are giving some pieces of the church's ministry more resources than others. While money is certainly not the only asset, as we discussed in chapter 3, it is a key one, and it can serve as a great litmus test. In the words of Lynne Twist, "One of the greatest dynamics of money is that it grounds us, and when we put money behind our commitments it grounds them too, making them real in the world. . . . Money is a great translator of intention to reality, vision to fulfillment."[2] As Jesus says in our dwelling passage, money has the power to take our hearts with it. It is one of the unique places where we can put our faith into concrete, meaningful action.

One of my favorite class activities to do with my students is to invite them to consider what story their congregation's budget is telling. First, I invite them to find an image that describes their church's mission. I usually direct them to a website like Unsplash where they can find provocative, high quality, and freely usable images.[3] Then, I invite them to look at the numbers in their church's budget as if they had never been to their church and choose a second image that describes their church's values as solely reflected in this budget. I have done this activity now with hundreds of students, and I can only remember one instance where the images were the same.

For instance, using Tree of Life as an example, I might first choose an image of a woman blowing bubbles across a crowded square. Like the woman in the square, this community is small, and yet the work it is doing has a broad impact on the church and the world. We are called to experiment with ways to engage those who have been burned by church so we can share what we have learned with other congregations. Similarly, we are called to meet those we serve in the places they already are, like bars, restaurants, public parks, and coworking spaces. You won't find us inside of a traditional congregation. The image is vibrant, capturing joy and motion—just like our congregation, which is always ready to experiment, innovate, laugh, and welcome someone new to our community.

For my second image, I might choose a black and white picture of three ballerinas moving in sync. Looking at our budget, you see a distinct focus on staff with almost all of the budget being spent on those inside of the church. Similarly, only 14 percent of Tree of Life's budget was coming from member giving, with the rest coming from the ELCA, its regional church body (Minneapolis Area Synod), funding from other congregations, grants, or cash on hand. While the leadership in the congregation is dynamic and innovative, the budget shows how much of this mission is currently resting on their shoulders with limited investment from the community members. Instead of participating in blowing the bubbles, we too often find ourselves in the audience watching our leaders on stage doing this dynamic work.

After discussing the images in small groups, I ask my students to make this even more concrete by answering this question: *If your church's budget could tweet, what would it say?*[4] I find that even within a small character limit, you can still make a profound statement:

- More money, more problems.
- Love God. Love Neighbor. LOVE BUILDING.
- Take only what we need and give away the rest.

Here is my slightly less creative tweet for Tree of Life: "Church experiment with equitably paid staff, worship, and food funded by the wider church." While many of the responses in this activity are often a bit on the snarky side, it shows how much our budgets really have to say about how we are living out God's mission.

An activity like this, no matter how silly it may seem, can be a really helpful way to open up the conversation about budget realignment. This activity can be more revealing than you might think, upon first glance. When done with people from the same congregation, it can start a conversation around the variety of ways that the congregation's mission has been interpreted and lived out. Without a clear sense of alignment around the congregation's mission and what it looks like in practice, it can be really challenging to realign the budget around this mission.

Budget Realignment

Depending on the size, leadership, and structure of the congregation, this practice is likely best completed by the congregation's leadership team. No matter your congregation's size, it's important to have ministers, staff, and lay members at the table for the conversation. Lay members often have a different perspective on the mission and the congregation's investment in its mission than the paid ministry staff.

While many congregational budget conversations begin with, *What small things can we cut to make the budget line up?* I encourage you to start with where you are aligned and release the rest. *Where do you see real alignment between money and God's mission?* For Tree of Life, I saw that alignment in our move to the new location, but I also saw it on our staffing. We took pride in the fact that we were able to pay our pastoral staff and musicians equitably. We also knew that we were called to serve not only millennials but also Gen Z; adding a part-time pastoral intern who was Gen Z was an important step in that direction. Instead of bringing on the intern full-time, we partnered with a larger congregation to give our intern a more well-rounded internship experience and to share in the costs as well.

These places of alignment are the roots of your congregational budget. They are the foundation for how God's mission is being lived out in your congregation's ministry. I encourage you to put a box around each of these items on your congregation's budget. Then, instead of looking at the remaining numbers, I encourage you to look at the remaining categories. *Are there any categories that aren't aligned with the mission God is calling your congregation to join in this time and place?* These might be things that were very aligned in another era of the church's history, but now are no longer in alignment. For instance, Tree of Life had previously paid for our pastor to have a desk at a local coworking space. We thought it might be a great way for the pastor to be more rooted in the neighborhood and connect with people who lived and worked there. She let this desk go during the pandemic and since we decided to move the church to a new neighborhood and she had adapted to a new office setup during the pandemic, we realized that this was no longer an investment we needed to make. In your congregation, this may look like a church program that is past its prime or no longer aligned with the direction of the congregation, or it may be an investment in maintaining a part of the building that is rarely used.

As you walk through expenses that aren't in alignment, keep an eye out for any expenses that could be funded in another way outside of the congregation's budget. For instance, Tree of Life had a line item for food we had usually used to purchase catered meals for the congregation to eat during dinner church. Since we were in a new space that had a working kitchen, we had a member of the congregation approach us and offer to purchase the ingredients and cook the meal for at least some of the dinner church services, which produced a large budget savings. This was also a deeply missional move as we sought to get more members of the congregation to invest their time and talents.

It's important to note that these misalignments can appear on the income side of a church's budget as well. I know many congregations that have gifts that are sitting in a church bank account that they can't use because the gift was given for a purpose the congregation will never be able to complete. For instance, a congregation where $20,000 was given by a member of the congregation to create a church bell. The congregation never desired to build a bell and it isn't aligned with where God is calling them to invest today. Often these types of gifts are left on the church books because it feels too difficult to talk to the member and discuss a new purpose for the gift. In these cases, I often encourage congregations to think of the original intention for the gift (if they know). In this case, the member might be passionate about music and using the bell to bless the community and create more awareness of the church's presence. The good news is that those particular goals can be accomplished in a variety of ways. Maybe your church feels called to create an after-school music program? It would be well worth it to take the time to talk about this idea with the donor so these funds could be released to start the program.

Similarly, one of the sites we interviewed, Galileo Christian Church in Fort Worth, Texas, found that renting out their building was no longer aligned with their mission, even though it was generating income. As the Rev. Katie Hays put it in the survey: "we just hated doing it, and started resenting the renters, and realized it was not contributing to our love of humanity or our near neighbors." Just because something generates income, does not mean it is mission aligned.

Once you have identified the categories that are no longer aligned with your congregation's mission, cross them out. Then, for the remaining sections of the budget that are not crossed out, look at the percentages of the budget that go toward those particular categories. *Are the percentages of money aligned with the mission? Do they need to increase or decrease? Are there other mission-aligned categories that need to be added?* For instance, if a key part of your mission is passing on the gospel to younger generations and there is minimal or no investment in children, youth, or young adult ministry, that is a problem.

This is not just about investing more money in benevolence. Every part of your congregation's budget should play a part in bringing God's mission for your congregation to life. Benevolence is just one way that your congregation participates in God's work in your community.

The Grief and Grace of Letting Go

Letting go of beloved buildings, programs, and staff is very difficult work to do. This was a theme that came up in many of the interviews we conducted. Letting go was what created the space (and assets) for new life to flourish. River Heights Vineyard Church in Inver Grove Heights, Minnesota, sold a portion of their property to create affordable housing and the sale of this piece of property miraculously covered the renovation costs for the other side of their property so they could live out God's call to start a Spanish-speaking congregation in that space. Seattle, Washington's 7400 Woodlawn, Center for Community, Arts, and Spirituality, only exists today because Bethany Lutheran Church made the courageous decision to close its doors and leave its building to its regional church body (Northwest Washington Synod) to be used for a new mission start. St. Andrew Lutheran Church in Eden Prairie, Minnesota, closed a campus to focus on what God was calling them to do on their main campus, creating space for Church Anew to be born.

There can be immense grief in letting go. This theme came across clearly in the story of Common Ground Church in Lodi, Wisconsin. Common Ground Church not only let go of a beloved church building, they also closed their former congregation and started a new one in order to focus on an entirely new mission. This was a mired and painful process that took place over the course of five years. While the leadership of the congregation could say without a doubt that the process was worth it, I'm sure there were many times during those years when the change felt just too hard and they would have rather just stuck to the status quo.

The process began because the historic building, First Lutheran Church in Lodi, Wisconsin, had limited accessibility. The building had several layers and no elevator. This accessibility concern became very apparent during funerals when loved ones with mobility challenges couldn't partake in the fellowship and lunch afterwards, as they couldn't get to that area of the building. In an effort to afford greater accessibility to people with disabilities and those disconnected from church, a task force of lay leadership was formed. This task force discerned that the congregation would need to move to a new property. In the process, they also unearthed a deep, painful tension that existed between those who wanted to preserve the congregation's historic presence and those who wanted to serve those who lacked accessibility.

For nearly two years, the congregation wrestled through this tension. The congregation's leadership invited its members to pray and reflect: Was God calling the congregation to move to a new location or transform its current location? Eventually, it was discerned that God was calling First Lutheran Church to not only change its location but also to transform its mission through a process of death and resurrection. Practically, this meant that they needed to dissolve First Lutheran Church, sell the building, and use the proceeds as well as new mission partnerships to launch a new missional community, Common Ground Church. With support from their regional church body, the congregation then spent the next two years bringing this new vision to life.

Because of the tension, the congregation lost some valuable leaders who could not tolerate the stress of it any longer. Even though the majority of members of First Lutheran Church agreed with this pathway forward, particularly after the long and thorough period of discernment, there was a vocal minority who did not. As one of the leaders of Common Ground Church put it, "It has not been, in any way, a light, easy situation. When we talk about dying and rising, I mean, it's real . . . it's totally visceral, real-life stuff. It cuts right into your very soul." The experience was not just tense but traumatic at times. And yet, in the midst of tension and trauma, God was at work. As a lay member put it,

> The whole sale of the building . . . took away that aspect of clinging and fixation on . . . "Oh, we need a building to be a church," and put it back into . . . "Well, this group of people can be the church." And gave us really more opportunity to focus on . . . What is our mission in this community? What are we working towards? And we've definitely solidified that over . . . the past two and a half years since making the transition to Common Ground.

This conversation, that started with accessibility, led to a realignment of the budget and deeper clarity about how God was calling this church to join God's work in Lodi and around the world. First Lutheran Church experienced the ways in which our treasure can take our hearts with it and can, at times, distract us from the opportunities that God is calling us to. In this case, the building became a beloved idol that got in the way of the congregation living out its mission to serve people in its community who would never feel comfortable entering their church, whether for reasons of physical accessibility or because they had been previously hurt by the church.

In his Faith+Leadership article, "Pruning for sustainable design," L. Gregory Jones says, "to enable growth, a leader needs to understand an institution's 'soul' and be willing to prune anything that doesn't contribute to its thriving."[5] He shares examples of organizations whose leaders have made tough decisions, saying "no" to good things in order to reorient the organization to focus more deeply on its mission. Jones suggests that, "This reallocation of resources was based on discerning the 'soul' of the organization—the heart of its mission—and clearly identifying the needs of its primary constituents and community."[6] To do this pruning work well, you need to understand the organization's mission/soul, have a clear view of where its resources are currently being allocated, and have a leadership team with authority who can speak to the different aspects of the organization's life and work without being beholden to it.[7] Jones reminds us of Jesus's images of pruning: "We may need to remove some things that are otherwise healthy for the sake of even greater faithfulness and effectiveness. Healthy rosebushes need to be pruned for the sake of even greater growth, beauty and creativity. So also with institutions."[8] Too often, I see congregations holding on to programs, buildings, and sometimes even staff long past their period of being useful for the congregation's mission. *What might it look like to let go of beloved programs, buildings, and staff while they are still viable so they might experience new life somewhere else?* Isn't this at its core what death and resurrection are about? Letting go of what is good with the promise that something better might spring from it. Similarly, could a program or committee take a year's sabbatical and then come back at the end to see, *Was it missed? Can it be released? What might need to remain?*

Depending on what you need to let go of, this process of pruning may take time, as it did for Common Ground Church. It takes time to discern what God is up to, to get the rest of the congregation on board, to grieve what is lost, to celebrate what was, and to say a proper "goodbye" before moving into your new future. Too often I see congregations skip past this section because they would rather add more income sources than deal with letting go of something they are currently doing that is no longer serving them. And yet, it is often only by releasing the old that we can begin to make space for the new.

Communicating these changes to the congregation can be challenging. If there is any way to include the congregation at large in the realignment process so they can feel they have some ownership in the decision, that is ideal. Let the congregation know about the budget realignment process in advance and give them appropriate spaces to offer feedback or even participate at points along the way. This will allow them to see the conversation unfold and have more understanding of the final decisions, even if they aren't the ones they would have chosen on their own. Similarly, providing updates to the congregation as you move through the process is essential, so that any final decisions don't feel like they come out of left field but are an outcome of a multi-step process. While this will not eliminate all grief, it can soften the blow. Making the process more public can also serve as a reminder that even good things come to an end. We grieve, prune, and God brings new growth.

Are There Any Underutilized Assets?

Your congregation's budget only represents some of the assets God has entrusted to your congregation's care. Go back to the inventory you created in chapter 3 and consider how the other types of assets (skills, time, and network) are being used. *Are there any resources that are untapped? Might all the assets be headed toward a few activities that aren't very aligned with the mission?*

This is a great time to consider how church staff and pastors' time is aligned with the mission. This might also be a great time to do a time audit so that the church staff, pastors, and leadership can get a clearer sense of where the time is actually going. I heard from the pastors who participated in our Funding Forward Learning Community in 2021 that they struggled to figure out where they would find the time to commit to this work. The congregation already had so many expectations of them, they couldn't imagine adding one more thing to their already too-full plates. At one of the learning community gatherings, Michael Binder shared the "Expectations Analysis Tool" (Appendix B) designed to help congregations name their current expectations of leaders and members, as well as how they might reflect on and reframe these expectations. In the tool, leaders are encouraged to consider what their members expect from them vs. what they expect from themselves. One of the biggest learnings Binder shared was that leaders often expect more from themselves than their people expect from them. It was often their own expectations, not members' expectations, that got in the way of doing the work God was calling them to do. While this may not be true in every congregation, this activity can still help members and paid clergy/staff leaders to get on the same page.

Similarly, the tool also invites you to look at what the congregation expects from members and what they expect from themselves. There was an enormous chasm between what was expected from the members and what was expected from the leaders. Often the biggest key to freeing up more space for leaders to participate in this work is to invite more members to take on some of the roles traditionally fulfilled by the leader. We'll talk more about how you might do this in chapter 8 on staffing.

Take an inventory of the volunteer roles that are currently being filled in your congregation. *Do these volunteer roles contribute to making the mission happen? Are there other volunteer roles that might be needed?* I realize it may feel challenging to add any volunteer roles when you may already have trouble filling the roles that are in place. As one pastor told me recently, "How will I ever get congregation members to join in starting a new ministry at the church when I can't get enough volunteers as it is to help in the sacristy on Sunday morning?" I said, "I can understand that. Which do you think people might be more eager to volunteer for?" And we agreed, "The new ministry."

While some of these roles may still need to exist, might it be possible to shift the responsibilities for other roles to free up space for new opportunities? Instead of making people sign up in advance to read, serve communion, usher, etc. and risk them not coming, could you ask for volunteers at the beginning of the service? It feels like much less of a commitment to read the benediction or pour the wine during communion when you get to say "yes" in the moment. *Instead of asking someone to sign up for a three-year commitment to serve on a committee, could you invite them to serve for a season or run it like a task force?* People appreciate it when they are invited for their specific skills rather than just filling in a role.

For those teams, like the congregational council, session, vestry, or board, where you have specific rules and bylaws to follow,

- How might you lower the barrier to entry to participate?
- Could you allow people to join online?
- Might you meet before or after worship when people are already at church and there may already be childcare available?
- Could you begin the practice of sending out the materials that everyone is expected to read at least three days in advance and keep the conversations to one hour?

Most of our volunteer roles in congregations haven't changed in decades, and yet so much of our lives has changed.

The best news is that these new mission opportunities are likely to be of interest to a new group of people who never felt like a good fit for the traditional list of roles. Michael Binder shared a story of meeting an entrepreneur who was new to his congregation. So often this man had been invited by other congregations to serve as a greeter or as a Sunday school teacher. Yet he didn't have the skills, personality, or desire to participate in either of these roles. The church was trying hard to fit him into a box based on the roles they needed to fill, not his gifts. *What might happen if the church invited him to use his entrepreneurship skills for the good of God's mission?*

Don't Skip Ahead!

I realize this work is neither fun nor flashy. It requires us to take a clear look at who we are and how we are using our assets before we can move ahead to start something new. That said, this is deeply spiritual work. If we don't tend to where our treasure is going, our hearts may be taken away from the mission God is calling us to join. I like to think of this step as creating a solid financial foundation for all that is to come, and hopefully, through the process, creating space for something new to emerge.

I'm reminded of the words at the beginning of the dwelling text for this chapter. Jesus tells us not to worry and reminds us that God will provide for us. Often it is fear that holds us back from engaging in this difficult and courageous work. Fear that we don't have enough. Fear that something we have invested in may have run its course. Fear of the unknown future God may be calling us into. It feels safer to keep things the same in the hope that things will just get better. If only more people would just come to church, then we would have enough money to keep things going as it is. And yet, this passage reminds us that food, drink, and dollars in the offering plate have never been the end goal. Jesus calls us to "instead, strive for his kingdom, and these things will be given to [us] as well."[9]

In his address to the 2023 Luther Seminary graduating class, the Rev. Dr. Rolf Jacobson reminded the class that they are not now all that God will call them to be in the future. Today God has equipped them with spiritual gifts to do God's work, but in their lives in ministry they will receive new calls with new challenges and God will equip them with new gifts to complete this work. God will never call us into work God has not equipped us to do.

Numerous times during the interviews we heard miraculous stories of God's provision just at the moment it was needed. However, this provision generally came when people were seeking God's direction and boldly following God's call into the unknown. We are not today all that we will be. There are different eras in a church's ministry. Instead of marking the past as "bad" and the future as "good", we are reminded that God equips us for different calls at different times. Letting go of something that no longer aligns with God's mission doesn't mean this thing was not mission aligned when it began. We can grieve and celebrate what was, while also letting it go to make space for the new.

♦ Practice: What Story Is Your Church's Budget Telling? ♦

Engage in the activity discussed in the beginning of this chapter:

- Choose an image that describes the mission God is inviting your church to join—use a site like Google or Unsplash to spark your imagination.[10]
- Choose an image that describes what your church values as it is reflected in the budget.

Discuss the images together as a group. Then, walk through these questions together with your church's budget in hand. Give yourselves the freedom to work through the activity without needing to make any final decisions in the moment:

- What are places of real alignment between money and mission? Put a box around these items.
- Are there any categories that aren't aligned with the mission God is calling your congregation to join in this time and place? If so, cross them out.
- Are there any expenses that could be funded in another way outside of the congregation's budget? If so, cross them out.
- Are the percentages of money allocated to the remaining categories aligned with the mission? Do they need to increase or decrease?
- Are there other mission-aligned categories that need to be added?

Reflection Questions

- Where do you experience grief and/or hope as you realign the budget?
- How will you sunset and celebrate the budget categories you will be releasing? How will you create space for people to process their grief?
- What work needs to be done to find funding for those expenses that could be funded outside of the congregation's budget?
- What other assets need to be adjusted to align with the mission God is calling you to join?

PART 2

What Might God Be Calling Us to Do?

The work you've done in the last five chapters has set the stage for you to consider how you might fund the work God is calling you to do. Over the next three chapters I will be sharing three different possibilities: property, social enterprise, and staffing. Think of this as a "choose your own adventure" section. The goal is to get your creative juices flowing and move you to ideation and collaboration. Some of the ideas will spark your imagination, others might challenge you. Take what's helpful, leave what isn't. Don't attempt to "copy and paste" any of the ideas from another context into your own. It doesn't work that way! Every congregation's context, assets, and mission are entirely different.

Go into these chapters with a learner's posture. You will hear stories of congregations like yours and ones far different from yours—resist the urge to judge any of the congregations in this section and instead see what kernels of wisdom you might be able to pick up from them. Similarly, I also encourage you to not "play the comparison" game. God has something special in mind for your congregation and community. It may not look like the stories you see in the upcoming chapters, but that does not mean it's any less valuable or necessary.

Given the complexity of some of the ideas in these chapters (i.e., selling church property), I will not be giving you a start-to-finish guide on how to complete this work. Instead, I will be sharing stories, and I will invite you to use the resources in the appendixes to get started.

As you read through this section, I encourage you to use the Money & Mission Matrix[1] below, created by Mark Elsdon from Rooted Good, to evaluate your ideas. The gray areas are where you should focus your energy. Notice those areas are the ones with positive mission impact, not the most financial impact. There will always be part of a church's ministry that has a positive impact but comes at a cost. We will not stop doing this work. However, we ought to also consider opportunities with positive missional impact that either break even or generate money. Most people are surprised when they see that Elsdon encourages congregations to proceed with caution when it comes to income-generating opportunities that are "mission neutral." If God's mission is to lead the way, we ought to hold out for those opportunities that have both a positive financial and missional impact.

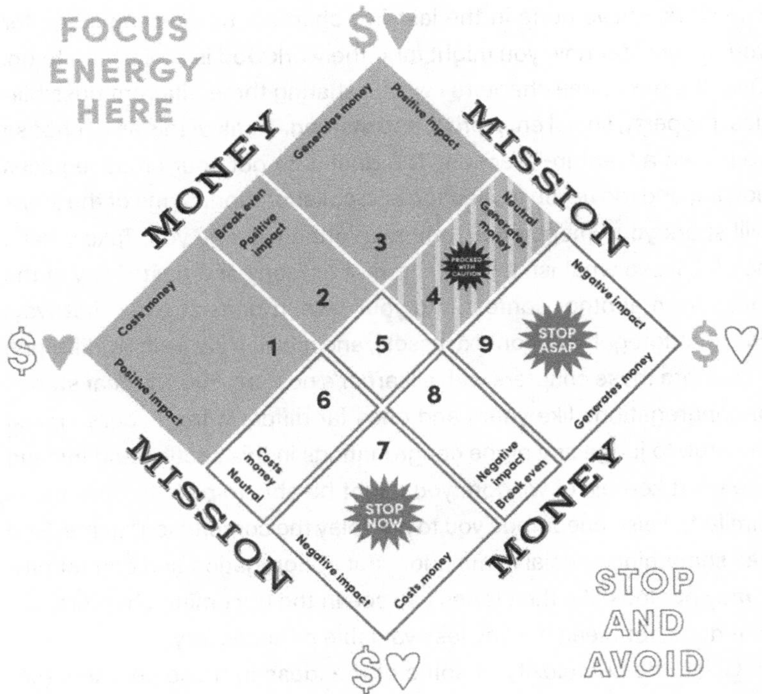

Figure 2. Money & Mission Matrix, by Mark Elsdon.

For instance, one congregation from the learning community was approached by a company that wanted to put Electric Vehicle (EV) charging stations in their parking lot. Initially the congregation was poised to say "yes" to this opportunity. It seemed like a low-risk way to generate some income for the congregation. However, as they began talking with the EV charging station company and others in their community who had charging stations, they realized that this opportunity was likely to generate a little income but not nearly as much as they thought. It was more likely to "break even" (at least at the outset) than generate income. As they ventured deeper into the Funding Forward work, I encouraged them to consider the mission impact, not just the money impact of this idea. While they had initially not been sure if the project was connected to their mission, as they talked together with their congregation's leadership team, they realized that this project aligned with their congregation's mission to care for creation and that this might be an opportunity for deeper relationship with people in the neighborhood as they waited for their cars to be charged in the parking lot. In the end, they decided to say "yes" to this opportunity more for the mission impact than the financial impact. While this opportunity was right for this congregation, it's possible your congregation could receive the same opportunity and decide it isn't right for you based on your mission, your community, and the assets God has entrusted to your care.

While the mission component is likely the most important, that doesn't mean that the financial elements of these decisions should be disregarded. For so long we have worked with the assumption that all ministry should come at a cost to the church's budget and donations were expected to foot the bill. This shift in model invites us to shift our perspective to think about the economics at play in individual elements of our ministries. It requires us to do the appropriate research to have a clearer picture of the full cost before starting a new ministry. The goal of this process is to find a balance between mission-aligned work that costs money, mission-aligned work that is self-sustaining, and mission-aligned work that generates income.

CHAPTER SIX

Property

Acts 2:1–4

"When the day of Pentecost had come, they were all together in one place. And suddenly from heaven there came a sound like the rush of a violent wind, and it filled the entire house where they were sitting. Divided tongues, as of fire, appeared among them, and a tongue rested on each of them. All of them were filled with the Holy Spirit and began to speak in other languages, as the Spirit gave them ability."

A Reflection from the Rev. Natalia Terfa

Pentecost isn't just one day.

Well, it is, but what happens on Pentecost doesn't last just one day.

Sometimes I think that because the Holy Spirit is a complicated thing to understand, we just move on after the wind and fire day and get back to Jesus. Or God.

The spirit is, after all, hard to define.

And as soon as we try, it seems like we're trying to contain something pretty uncontainable.

Wind and fire?

The characteristics of the Spirit are destructive and unpredictable?

Or wild?

Renewing?

Refining?

Really?

If that's the case, then I don't know if I want anything to do with her.

Hard pass. I'd like baby Jesus back please.

It's much easier to think of the Spirit being an advocate (which comes from Jesus), or a friend. That seems more palatable, and nicer, than a mighty wind and fire.

But what if we stayed with our uncomfort a bit longer?

What if we asked ourselves—when is wind good? When is fire helpful?

We don't get to control the spirit, just as we can't control the wind or a fire (think of wildfire here, not a bonfire pit).

And maybe that's the point.

When the spirit comes, we don't get to control what stays and what blows away.

But the spirit doesn't just come and ruin everything and leave.

Because the Spirit doesn't just show up on Pentecost and leave.

The Spirit remains.

Stays.

Renews.

Rebuilds with us.

And this happens every day.

The Spirit stays.

And she continues to blow through our lives and mess things up just when we thought we had it all put together. It's frustrating.

It is scary and painful that some things are not going to make it.

The Spirit is blowing in our lives and world and churches right now.

I don't like when things don't look like they used to.

When my relationships change, when the world changes, when I change.

But I trust God. I trust that renewal and redemption and reconciliation are a part of the work of the Spirit too . . .

God has come, and God stays.

Spirit come. Spirit stay.[1]

Dwelling Questions

1. What word or phrase jumped out at you as you read the passage and reflection?
2. Which description of the Spirit used in the passage and/or reflection sticks out to you?

3. Are there assets that your congregation is holding on to tightly that you wish the Spirit wouldn't touch?
4. What might God's Spirit be saying to you or your congregation through the passage and reflection?

Prayer

Spirit come, Spirit stay. Refine, renew, redeem, and restore. Accompany us as we examine how we might be called to use the property you have entrusted to us in new ways. Release what is holding us back. Guide us as we walk with our congregations into the new future God has prepared for us. Amen.

The Rev. Peter Benedict (Pastor Pete) and his congregation, River Heights Vineyard Church in Inver Grove Heights, Minnesota, know well the Spirit's power to renew, rebuild, reconcile, and restore. Their building is a concrete testimony of the Spirit's work. River Heights Vineyard Church sold the property on one side of their building to create long-term homeless housing so they could generate income to expand the other side of their property to house the Spanish-speaking congregation they had helped to birth, La Viña Inver.

As Pastor Pete explained to me during the interview, he received a vision while jogging about how they might use their property in a new way. They originally purchased land to the north of the church because they thought they might need it for a building expansion; however, it turned out their current property might be just enough to do what God had in mind:

> At the time, we were looking at expanding our building. And in the building expansion process, we discovered that an easement was 25 feet more generous to us than we had been told . . . it turns out we might never need the space to the north. And we were needing to raise funds [for the building expansion]. And so, I thought, what if we could sell [the land to the north] at like 75% of its value to something that furthers our mission?

Pastor Pete began conversations with the housing commission and the Metropolitan Interfaith Council on Affordable Housing (MICAH), and after a year of conversations, it became evident that the greatest need in their community was for long-term housing for housing insecure families who had failed out of all other Minnesota supportive housing options. They were then paired with a developer who had done a few other projects like this in the state. After a period of discernment with the congregation, as well as four years of obstacles, roadblocks, and false starts on the development side, they were finally able to make this vision a reality.

While this building sale alone makes for a beautiful mission story—it's a tangible expression of their purpose statement to "love God, love people, and change the world." There is also a beautiful mission story behind what they did with the money. While they had initially received a low estimate on their building expansion, it turned out in the end that they needed every dollar from the building sale to make it happen. The money from this property sale made it possible for the congregation to expand its food ministry by building a commercial kitchen; create space for children, youth, and family ministries to take place in the same space as the adult ministries (previously these ministries had taken place across the street); and to make room for the budding Spanish-speaking La Viña Inver congregation they had helped birth, who had been meeting in their space in the evenings, to have a sanctuary of their own.

Because of the building expansion, they now have two congregations (one English- and one Spanish-speaking) meeting at the same time on Sunday mornings, and the children and youth from both congregations have a chance to meet together. This has been a unique ministry opportunity that mainly started because the congregation didn't have the space, staff, or volunteers to create separate offerings in Spanish and English.

As one of the pastors at River Heights Vineyard Church put it in the interview,

> Our kids are doing this in school. . . . [They don't have] segregated classrooms. . . . They are together. And if they can do this in public school, then we can do this here. And we can do it really well. And I think it's grown into something that represents to me the final kingdom, the kingdom of God, when there are all these races and tribes and kingdoms together, worshiping together and celebrated and not asked to conform or be apart to make things easy. So I think it started out of necessity, and it's grown into something that I feel is pretty beautiful.

What began with putting up PowerPoint slides of the words to worship songs in English and Spanish has expanded to incorporating bilingual songs, creating different circles to read Bible stories together in Spanish and English, and expanding the leadership team to reflect the cultural diversity of the children and youth involved in the ministry. Usually congregations who share space don't have the opportunity to meet at the same time, but the building expansion has made this possible. It has brought new opportunities for learning, fellowship, and connection for the kids, youth, and adults that would never have happened otherwise.

How might God be calling your congregation to use its space?

For so many of us, our church spaces are storehouses of memories. The space is sacred—not just because it is a church but because of the way that it has shaped our faith. These tender memories can make it difficult for us to imagine these sacred spaces being used for anything else.

- If we let go of the space, will it take our memories with it?
- If someone else uses it, will they treat it with just as much reverence?
- Does releasing the space mean future generations will not have access to the same transformative experiences we have had?

And yet, for so many of our congregations, our spaces no longer fit. They are too large for the current body of Christ. Looking across the interview data, property was often mentioned as the congregation's primary underutilized asset. It was their "five loaves and two fish" that God used, beyond their wildest imagination, to feed a multitude.

Is your congregation called to property rental, property sale, or property sharing?

Tales of Renting Church Property

As I shared in chapter 4, in the fall of 2021, the Rev. Chrisy Ennen realized that her congregation, First Presbyterian Church of Gulf Shores in Gulf Shores, Alabama, was in financial hot water. After weathering COVID, thanks to grants and Paycheck Protection Program (PPP) loans, she realized that her congregation had been pulling consistently from a substantial donor gift to fund her position. If they did not make a change soon, they would no longer be able to fund her position by August of 2022. As the Rev. Ennen put it, "I remember standing for our congregational meeting in January [2022] and saying, 'We're presenting you this budget that the [congregation's leadership team] has approved and you can see that we feel confident we can fund about half of it. So, we're going to have to do something different.'" And doing something different is exactly what they did.

After deciding to create affordable office space, the Rev. Ennen had conversations with the small business development center, Chamber of Commerce, and entrepreneurs in her area beginning to move this idea forward, when someone came to them out of the blue and asked to rent a room in their building. Even though they didn't have all of the details figured out, they decided to take a step forward and rent their space. As of the date of my research team's interview with the Rev. Ennen in February 2023, less than a year after the first person asked to rent their space, their church building is entirely full of renters.

What I love so much about this story is that it's not just about finding a path to sustainability but about joining God's mission in their community. This isn't just space rental, it's a ministry called the "Hand-in-Hand Business Center." The church hopes the business center will serve entrepreneurs striving to launch their businesses, while meeting the need in the business community for affordable space. As I listened to both the lay and pastor interviews, the vibrancy this project has brought to their space was palpable. A space that had once felt overly large, empty, and even lonely, now bustles with new life. The business renters share the church's kitchen and fellowship hall with the church staff—giving them new opportunities for collaboration and conversation. One of the renters is an artist and she asked if she could decorate the halls with her art—bringing even more brightness and beauty to the space. It's now a space that both the church and the renters can feel proud of. And the renters are talking about this space in the community, giving the church a whole new reputation in the neighborhood, bringing new people from the community into the church not only throughout the work week but also on Sunday morning for worship.

One of the things that continues to impress me about this story is the way that the congregation dived right into a sustainable vision of property rental. They did their homework to build a business model that was both affordable to the renters and income generating for the congregation. They used their network to make connections in their community and said "yes" when the first opportunity presented itself, even though they didn't know if they were quite ready yet.

Too often, I see congregations tiptoe into property rental. They advertise on a hidden corner of their church website that their fellowship hall is available for rental and ask for a $100 donation in return. In most cases, this donation will not even begin to cover the cost of cleaning the space. They assume there is no demand to rent their space because no one has stumbled across this section of their website. And they get frustrated that the rentals aren't bringing in much income because they didn't do enough research to know the "true cost" of renting their space (cleaning, staffing, etc.) as well as what the market rate for renting this type of space is in their area. Now, don't get me wrong, there are plenty of good reasons to charge below market rate if there is mission alignment. However, that needs to be an intentional financial, not just missional, decision. Another reason that congregations tiptoe into property rental is because of their concerns about tax or insurance implications. That is an important concern that I will address later in the chapter.

One of the key findings of the Funding Forward research project survey is that property rental was the most utilized income source outside of the offering plate. Over 70 percent of the congregations we surveyed had used or were considering using it. One of the more surprising results was that property rental was popular among congregations of any worship size. In fact, it was most common with medium (79 percent) and small (71 percent) congregations. While this income source was popular with congregations in any setting and of any age, it was most popular among 100-year-old or older congregations and urban congregations.[2] It's important to note that First Presbyterian Church of Gulf Shores is a small-town congregation, so this can work well in a variety of settings.

Property rental was the most likely income source to be tapped when a congregation wanted to bring in additional funds. While the income generated from property rental often met or surpassed the congregation's financial goal (60 percent), I was surprised at how often no financial goal had been set (19 percent). While we did not ask this directly in the survey, I've often found in my conversations with congregations that those who tiptoe into property rental often have done little research and have no specific goal in mind except to earn a little extra income. It's challenging to make property rental sustainable without assessing the community need, market rate, and true cost of renting, as well as creating a business plan to achieve a specific financial goal.

Almost all the congregations who had rented property said they used it to provide a consistent income stream for the congregation. In most cases, rental income was used to cover a small portion of the budget: For a little over a third of congregations who had used or were currently renting church property, it covered 0–9 percent of their congregation's budget, and for another third it covered 10–24 percent of the budget. While those numbers may seem small, let's do the math. If your congregation's annual budget is $150,000 and your congregation earned an extra 9 percent each year through rental income, that would be an additional $13,500. Imagine what ministry might be possible with that additional income!

While the financial data is incredibly helpful, I was surprised to see that, like in the First Presbyterian Church of Gulf Shores example, 87 percent of those congregations who had rented property said they had evidence that renting property was successful at creating relationships with people outside of the church. As one of the survey participants said,

> We used to be a black box in the middle of our neighborhood. Nobody inside knew what was going on outside, nobody outside knew what was going on inside. Today we're a focal point of our neighborhood, everyone knows us, everyone comes to activities that we host, some of our services are considered essential.

Nearly 80 percent of those who were currently renting or had rented church property said it was "connected" or "very connected" to their church's mission. Property rental can be a deeply missional move.

This finding reminded me of Mark DeYmaz's concept of "benevolent ownership" that he shares about in his books *Disruption* and *The Coming Revolution in Church Economics.* DeYmaz writes,

> Rather than asking small business owners to pay top dollar for rent, we can lease space to them for much less than they would otherwise expect to pay. In return, we can ask them to pass on the savings to their customers, who might now be able to buy the coffee at a cheaper price, creating a win for us (generating income), a win for the small business owner (lowering overhead), and a win for the community (paying lower prices).[3]

This model is a plus not only for the church but also for the small business owners and the community.

DeYmaz put this idea of benevolent ownership into action in his own congregation, Mosaic, in Little Rock, Arkansas. In December 2012, Mosaic purchased a nearly 100,000-square-foot abandoned Kmart building. They secured their first tenant, 10 Fitness, who rented out over half of the space, before the building was even renovated. As part of the long-term lease agreement, the business owner agreed to pay for the renovations to his area of the space. The lease payments not only covered the building's mortgage but the renovations improved the property value and enabled the church to get a construction loan to renovate the rest of the space for the church's and other tenants' use. The church was able to move into the space in January 2016. As DeYmaz and Li put it, "In just over three years, Mosaic had purchased a building, recruited tenants, secured a long-term lease, created $1.1 million in equity, and seen the value of the property increased by more than $2 million! In addition, 6,000 people from the community joined 'our' 10 fitness, some fifteen to twenty new jobs were created," and Part 1 crime incidents (murder, aggravated assault, robbery, motor vehicle theft, burglary, etc.) in a three-mile radius of the church dropped by 19 percent.[4] This wasn't just about creating a bigger building for the church, or even creating more sustainability for the church, it was about revitalizing the community.

I saw this idea of benevolent ownership come to life on a smaller, but no less vibrant, scale in the story of 7400 Woodlawn in Seattle, Washington. On May 15, 2016, Bethany Lutheran Church made the difficult decision to close its doors after struggling financially for many years and uncovering a situation of financial mismanagement. When Bethany closed, its building in the popular Green Lake neighborhood was released back to their regional church body (Northwest Washington Synod). Even though the building could have likely sold for top dollar, the synod decided they didn't want to give up the congregation's valuable investment in the community, so they decided to start something new there. The first mission developer at 7400 Woodlawn realized that one of the biggest problems in that community was loneliness. He worked to dispel loneliness by forming a small worshiping community and offering spaces for people to rent and create community in their building.

Today, 7400 Woodlawn is a center for community, arts, and spirituality. They currently have twenty-three partners who use the space—including two worshiping communities: Emmaus Table (started by the original mission developer) and St. Mary's Tigrayan Orthodox Church. Approximately a third of the space has been remodeled, another third has been refreshed, and 100 percent of the building has been repurposed for shared use. To codirectors, the Rev. Cara Tanis and the Rev. Harriet Platts, the space sharing is just as much a ministry as the worship with Emmaus Table. Their "threads for mission" purpose document says it so well:

> **We inquire about what is possible at this time, in this place.**
> The Center came into being as a result of the closing of Bethany Lutheran Church. Because there was an "ending," there was room for something new to emerge. 7400 Woodlawn is a repurposed sacred center, where neighbors/partners gather in shared spaces to "do what they do." We embrace curiosity, finding new paths, and testing new theories in order to discern direction for future spiritual and community expressions.
>
> **We cultivate a network of partnerships.**
> We value relational vs. transactional partnerships with economies of mutual flourishing and shared responsibility. We aspire to be responsive and flexible with excellent, frequent communication check-ins. We encourage connections across the partnership collective.
>
> **We embody hospitality.**
> Responsive care/regard for one another acknowledges shared vulnerability and resilience during times of significant cultural shifts. Building a culture of inclusion and respect is our starting place. Providing space for programs and opportunities for connecting with others, the Center's habitat allows for a sense of belonging, even home.[5]

As the codirectors would openly share with you, it took three years of their ministry together to discern what God was calling 7400 Woodlawn to do and to be in this time and place. It has taken time to cultivate a network of twenty-three partners that really feel like partnerships, not just rental agreements. They are still in the process of discerning Emmaus Table's role in this broader center. While it was once the overseer of all the partnerships, it may now be one partnership among many that take place in the building.

One of the key stories that illustrates this partnership was the listening circle they called around the use of the sanctuary space, which has now been renamed Woodlawn Hall. They brought together all the folks who currently use the space to discern together the highest, best use for that room. Out of that listening circle, they formed the "Woodlawn Collective." This is a group of partners that come together once a quarter on Zoom to, as the Rev. Tanis put it in her interview, "update one another on what they're doing" and share "in the questions of what does it mean to be embodying the space together . . . we all have our own mission, but what does it mean to be collected in this time and place?" This is so much more than a landlord-tenant relationship; it's an interconnected network of partnerships. Whenever the codirectors discern a new partnership, they talk with the prospective partner about how they can support the partner's work and create a place where the partner feels comfortable, but also the partner's responsibility to help care for and engage with the broader work of the collective.

This partnership approach also takes place at a financial level. While the codirectors inherited a spreadsheet from the initial mission developer with costs for each room for a particular time frame, they see this spreadsheet as just an initial starting place. They have created a model where the income from some of their partners intentionally subsidizes a share of the rent for other partners. They are very transparent about these different levels of investment. For instance, while they might charge a higher rate to rent Woodlawn Hall for a wedding or concert, this rate helps to subsidize a neighbor who uses the space to teach Tai Chi to a few students once a week. Through this partnership model, they hope to create a place for mutual flourishing, an alternate economy.

Given the interconnected network of religious and nonreligious partners, I wondered how the group of partners present for the interview might receive the final interview question: "Where did you see God in the process of creating and/or shifting the financial model?" Surprisingly, it was a partner from a nonreligious organization who spoke up first. He spoke about the way he experienced God through the first Woodlawn Collective meeting with the spiritual meditation ritual they used to start the meeting as well as the conversation as a whole with the partners. He said,

> Being someone who grew up in the church and doesn't attend a church regularly now but tries to stay in touch with spiritual communities, it felt like healing for me. And I think that's a cool thing that happens for the people involved and whether they're in a choir or attending a concert or just coming for a workshop or something. It's the less visible parts. It's not the cross on a building, and it's not a Bible in someone's hand. It's nothing like that. And that's really what most people I know nowadays are connecting to. [It's the spirit of the place.] It's subtle and not labeled.

Going back through the interview, I noticed how this participant named the spirit of welcome and hospitality present at 7400 Woodlawn. The space is not only accessible and centrally located but also quiet and welcoming. He said, "It feels like that warm hug from the auntie that's going to provide you some tea and a biscuit or something. That energy is really important, and most venues, most churches, don't have that actually. It's somewhat rare, unfortunately." He appreciated that 7400 Woodlawn embodies hospitality and a calm spirit without asking every partner to share their same views and beliefs. This partner uses the sanctuary space, Woodlawn Hall, as a concert venue. While his organization is not religious, this is a space where he felt that he and the concert attendees could engage in the spiritual practice of experiencing music together. *In a context where so many are done with or disconnected from religion, what does it look like for the church to be a place of peace and hospitality where people can experience God together in new ways?*

Common Questions about Property Rental

- **How will we pay for the needed repairs and remodeling to make the space rentable?** There are many ways to tackle this issue. *Could there be a long-term renter who might be interested in not only renting out your space but investing in the renovations to make it their own? Is there one space that you could rent out "as is" and use the earnings from that space's rental to fund renovations on the next space? Or, is your congregation a historic landmark?* If so, there may be grant money available to help you renovate the space. We'll talk more about these funding options in chapter 9. However, one of my favorite examples of this comes from First Presbyterian Church of Gulf Shores. One of the "heroes" of their story is a lay member who is retired and skilled at fixing things. He, and some of his friends from inside and outside the church, joined together to give the spaces the care and attention they needed to make them available for rent. And he's continued to tend to ongoing maintenance. This is a service the congregation would not have been able to afford to pay for and was a beautiful way for this member to use his skills. What an asset! *Are there people in your congregation who might never serve on a* *committee or lead worship, who might be very happy to offer their skills in renovation and maintenance?*

- **We want to rent our church's property. Where should we start?** One of the best places to start is by taking inventory of the property to get a clear sense of which spaces you might rent and how much work might be needed. I encourage you to check out the variety of resources named in Appendix C starting with Rooted Good's "How to Rent Well" resource. It's a comprehensive guide to walk you through all the steps of the process in an engaging and manageable way.
- **Will the occasional rental be enough?** In most cases, no. Long-term rental agreements are often the best pathway to sustainability.
- **How much should we rent for?** This can be tricky. I'd encourage you to take your time with this step, determining not only the market rate but also the true cost of renting the space (in other words how much it costs for maintenance, wear/tear on the space, utilities, staff time, etc.), your congregation's missional alignment with the organization, and the organization's ability to pay the rent. The answer to this question is deeply contextual. I really appreciate the process that Rooted Good outlines in their resource "How to Rent Well" (Appendix C). Just because you know the market rate for the space doesn't mean that is what you have to charge, but it is important information to have in the decision-making process. You may also decide to employ a sliding scale like 7400 Woodlawn, where some renters pay more than others. Another church in our interview process also employed a similar model. They have a rental property that is intentionally rented out at market rate; however, they will also be creating affordable housing on their property in the coming year. According to Dave Harder, owner and principal consultant of Parish Properties, it often takes quite a while to see a financial return with affordable housing, but "mixed use," or a combination of affordable and market rate housing, can often produce a financial return while also tending to the social fabric and health of individuals in a community. Imagine the missional impact of having people in multiple socioeconomic brackets living together in community![6]

Remember, this should not be a decision that the church's pastor or other key leaders make alone. Likely you have businesspeople in your congregation and/or community who would love to help you figure out the right price or scale of prices.

- **But it is our church's mission to offer our space for free to the community, is that still OK?** There is nothing wrong with that. Given the mission of your congregation, this isn't the right income source for you. Instead, you'll want to find other ways to bring in income that subsidizes this ministry.
- **Is property rental always mission aligned?** Absolutely not! Galileo Christian Church in Fort Worth, Texas, one of our interview sites, shared in the survey that they stopped renting their property for just this reason. They originally began renting their property because they were one of the few affirming spaces where LGBTQIA+ people could host weddings, receptions, and parties. However, they found that renting their property was a hassle even though it was generating income.
- **What about the tax and insurance implications?** Great question! If you decide to pursue property rental, I encourage you to talk with tax and legal professionals. Depending on your state, municipality, and how the property rental aligns with your mission, you may have to pay UBIT (Unrelated Business Income Tax) on the income you receive from the property rental. Rooted Good has an exceptional resource, "What About Taxes?" (Appendix C), designed to help you think through the tax implications. Sometimes I find that the idea of having to deal with the tax implications stops a congregation from considering property rental at all. As you saw from the survey data, many congregations are engaged in this work and the tax/insurance implications have not stopped them from earning a viable income. Having the right conversations early on can prevent a lot of headaches later.

Tales of Selling Church Property

Over the last few years, I have heard various views on selling church property. Some argue church buildings are needed for the social fabric of society:

Where else can Alcoholics Anonymous (AA) or the struggling yoga instructor afford to meet? Cities would love to have the property tax revenue from the space and are unlikely to allow it to be converted back to sacred (tax-free) space again. On the other hand, I've heard from countless congregations who have found freedom in selling their space to be used for missional purposes like creating affordable housing or providing needed social services. They enjoy the freedom of being renters even in a space they once owned and find they are living even more deeply into their mission through this new arrangement. I've heard stories of property developers that prey on churches and of property developers that opened a congregation's mind to see new ways that a space could be used that they could never have imagined on their own. Obviously, this topic is fraught and we haven't even touched on the grief a congregation experiences before, during, and after the sale process.

So, should a church sell their property? I think that depends first and foremost on God's mission as well as the congregation's property, context, and financial situation. There is no "one-size-fits-all" answer. Plus, it's important to note that property sale often does not mean selling the congregation's entire space. This is not an "all or nothing" proposal.

Looking at the survey data, only fourteen congregations had sold or were in the process of selling church property. The common characteristic in this group is that the majority of them (57 percent) had sold property or began the process of selling property in the last five years. The common reasons why they sold or were in the process of selling church property was to make better use of church property (86 percent), to live out the church's mission in a new way (79 percent), to meet a need in the community (71 percent), and to raise additional funds for the church (71 percent). Over 70 percent of the congregations who had sold or were in the process of selling church property said that the sale would meet/met or would surpass/surpassed their financial goal. Interestingly, nearly 80 percent of the congregations said they had evidence that the sale (or the sale process) was successful at creating relationships with people outside of the church, including neighbors, local government officials, nonprofit organizations, other congregations, and even the media. Some congregations noted in their comments that the sale had increased foot traffic to the congregation and raised the congregation's reputation in the eyes of the community. An overwhelming 71 percent of the congregations who had sold or were in the process of selling their property said this decision was "very connected" to the congregation's mission. This wasn't an act of desperation—it was an intentional move to engage more deeply in God's mission in their community. The income from the sale was sometimes used to fund a specific project (29 percent), but more often it was used to create a stream of regular income (36 percent) or both (36 percent).

In the interviews, we had the chance to hear three very different property sale stories: one where part of the property was sold (River Heights Vineyard Church and La Viña Inver that I mentioned at the beginning of this chapter); one where the whole property was in the process of redevelopment, being sold to an affordable housing developer, and part was being bought back (Clarendon Presbyterian Church in Arlington, Virginia); as well as one where the whole property was sold (Common Ground Church in Lodi, Wisconsin) mentioned in chapter 5. Each of these decisions was deeply thoughtful and aligned with the mission God was calling them to join.

While Clarendon Presbyterian Church had a similar goal as River Heights Vineyard Church of selling the church property to create affordable housing, they have taken an entirely different approach to their building sale. Clarendon Presbyterian Church realized that their building was past the point of repair and the cost to redo everything was more than the congregation could manage on their own. While they had a history of renting their space to the community, particularly to a childcare center, they realized they were called to do more. After hearing of many congregations in Arlington who had sold their spaces to create affordable housing, they decided to do the same. As of the time of our research team's interview, they plan to sell all of their church property to a nonprofit developer, and they will then buy back a small portion of this property to rebuild the church to fit the needs of the current congregation as well as to house the childcare center. The rest of the building will be used to create LGBTQIA+ affirming, affordable, senior housing. They plan to provide light programming for the residents of the senior housing community as well as potentially hire additional church staff to attend to the needs of this community. As part of the building sale, they hope to generate funds that would make this ministry possible and create an endowment for the congregation. They are living out the mission displayed on their website: "Following the spirit's call to go into the world with love, joy, and creativity, we are a community of faith following the way of Jesus in solidarity with marginalized and disenfranchised people doing justice, loving mercy, and walking humbly with God. We seek companions on the journey from all walks of life. All means all: all races, ages, genders, orientations, classes, convictions and questions."[7]

They are intentionally sorting through what they want to preserve from their current space. This is a process they have been through before. They converted their very traditional sanctuary into a more modern one with moveable seating. As they went through the conversion process, they were very thoughtful about what they did with each piece of the space, particularly the pews:

> We kept some of the pews along the sides. So there's removable seating, but there are some moveable, although heavy, pews along the side. We moved some pews down to the social hall. And we took some of the pews and literally the wood from the pews was rebuilt into this gorgeous table that's essentially the altar. And wood in the pews was rebuilt into these beautiful lecterns . . . We took the podium, and it is now in the back of the church. Underneath the podium houses the electronics for our online worship.

They are finding thoughtful ways to honor the past while still moving forward. They are holding together grief and hope. Even within the Spirit's refining and renewal, they are remembering the ways that God has journeyed with them before and will continue to journey with them for years to come.

For Common Ground Church, it was clear after many years of discernment that church closure, selling the building, and being released from the building's maintenance and accessibility issues was the best choice for them. Without the sale of their building, they would not have had the bandwidth to follow God's call to move from a historic, centralized church platform to a distributed network of smaller, micro-communities. In their case, closure and full sale was necessary, but as you can see from the other examples above, that isn't always the case.

Common Questions about Property Sale

- **Where should I start?** One of the best places to start is by taking inventory of the property to get a clear sense of which spaces you might sell and how much work might be needed before the sale can take place. Rooted Good's "How to Develop Well" resource (Appendix C) is a great place to start as you consider the critical questions around property sale and development.

- **Can I really trust a real estate developer?** Yes, there are many real estate developers who have experience working with churches and nonprofits. It's important to do your homework. This is a great opportunity to lean on the gifts of people in your congregation and community who have expertise in this area. They will know the right questions to ask to get to know the developers in your community. I really appreciate the approach Parish Properties takes to property development. They specialize in reimagining church buildings for community impact. They measure their work by what they call a "quadruple bottom line": their "work is driven by concern for the environment, spiritual health of the community, financial sustainability, and social impact."[8] It is a collaborative process between the congregation, the community, and the developer.
- **Is it just about getting as much money as possible?** Going back to Rooted Good's Money and Mission Matrix, just because something generates money doesn't automatically mean you should go in that direction. We have to look at the mission impact as well. The goal is to find opportunities for sale that not only generate income but also further the congregation's mission. Likely this means you aren't going to get the highest possible price for the property and that is OK.
- **If a church closes and sells its property, where does the money go?** This varies by denomination and regional church body, but it's often listed in the church bylaws. For some congregations, this money might return to the regional church body, and for others, the congregation might have the ability to determine where this money might go.

Another Way Forward: Property Sharing

I was first introduced to the idea of property sharing by SpringHouse Ministry Center in Minneapolis, Minnesota. In the words of their mission statement, "Springhouse is an ecumenical ministry center that provides a home and sacred space for three unique ministries united in God's love and spirit.

Together we seek to share God's love by serving and ministering in our community and the world."[9] In other words, SpringHouse is three separate congregations who share one building. While they have separate worship services, they have many shared ministries, and they share the income generated by renting their space.

SpringHouse's story began in the early 2000s as Salem Lutheran Church (Salem) faced the question of church closure. They had a large, unsustainable facility that needed more resources than the small congregation could manage. In 2005, they made the courageous decision to move into a neighboring congregation's, Lyndale United Church of Christ (Lyndale), space four blocks away. Together the two congregations worked with property developers to keep Salem's historic sanctuary space intact and sell the education wing to create Greenleaf—a mixed-use development including sixty-three units of affordable housing, underground parking, and retail. Lyndale eventually sold their space as well, and the two churches moved into Intermedia Arts, an art gallery and theater space in the neighborhood.

During this time, the two congregations began talking with a third congregation in their neighborhood who had also recently sold its building: First Christian Church (Disciples of Christ). In January 2011, these three congregations created a formal partnership and together they renovated Salem's large, historic sanctuary space into SpringHouse Ministry Center. The ministry center includes three flexible worship spaces, education space, a commercial kitchen, offices, and community rooms. The three congregations rotate among the three worship spaces over the course of the church year. While worship may be separate, the congregations share Sunday school, youth ministry, some justice ministries, coffee hours, and even some staff. They also worship together four times a year.

The three congregations take their partnership seriously. They have a signed covenant that guides their shared ministry, and the operations of the ministry are guided by a joint board made up of three members of each congregation, a board chair from each congregation, and the senior pastor from each congregation. The three congregations did not merge but operate as partners: "maintaining our unique identities, ministry and history, and yet sharing resources, together creating a sustainable facility (sustainable because it's green, and sustainable because they can share the costs), and living as a distinct witness of Christians working together in a time when divisions are so prevalent."[10] Each congregation owns one-third of the land and the facility.

While the concept of yoking congregations together to share pastors and staff has been around for a while, SpringHouse has taken a decidedly different approach, choosing to share a building as well as some of the staff and ministries while allowing the congregations to each keep their unique ministry identities and pastoral staff. They were able to create a space that fit each of the congregation's needs, pool their resources together so they did not have a mortgage to support, and share building maintenance costs three ways. They also alleviated the burden of renting out their individual buildings by sharing the cost of two staff members who handle building rental and maintenance.

One of the beautiful blessings of the shared ministry is the way that these congregations' unique identities have influenced each other and opened up new opportunities for members of each of the other congregations. For instance, Lyndale's passion for justice has helped members from Salem get connected with their Center for Sustainable Justice.

I see this same spirit of collaboration and property sharing in River Heights Vineyard Church & La Viña Inver's story. River Heights Vineyard Church's pastors felt a call to serve the Latino community, but they knew this was something they could never do on their own. They sought out pastors who could lead this community and ended up interviewing Pastors Martha and Antione Duran, who were living in Ecuador at the time. River Heights Vineyard Church offered these pastors space as well as a small salary to help them get the ministry started. In the beginning years, Pastors Martha and Antione also worked as hotel cleaners, and their salary rose as their ministry grew. Now, they receive their salary completely out of the tithes and offerings of La Viña Inver. As I noted earlier, the two congregations share children and youth ministries as well as their mission/purpose statement. They also preach the same sermon two-thirds of the time and use a lot of the same training materials. They are, "two languages, one church family."

If your congregation is interested in property sharing, it can be helpful to identify the assets your congregation brings to the table as well as what you are looking for in a partner. Then, begin conversations with other congregations in your community and/or with your regional church body. Remember, you will likely need to have many conversations before you find the right partner.

A Reminder: Does "Our" Property Really Belong to Us?

More than any other asset, congregations often need to be reminded that their property is not really theirs. The property and the land belong to God, and it is imperative that congregations discern how God would have them use these assets to God's glory and not their own. This realization that these resources belong to God, not to us, can help us to release some of our scarcity thinking and begin to open up our doors (literally and figuratively) to new opportunities. We can also begin to release some of the shame that can sometimes accompany conversations around property rental, sale, and partnerships; as these resources were never ours, we can trust that God has something beautiful in store for them. Through careful discernment and stewardship, we can guide these resources toward their highest and best use both missionally and financially.

I also think these pivotal moments where there are shifts in property ownership are a good time to acknowledge the origins of this property and make reparations to the communities who have been harmed. You might do this by donating part of the profits of a land sale, using part of the rental income to pay "real rent"[11] to the indigenous communities in your area, or something else entirely. There are no easy answers, because there is no "one and done" way to repair the indescribable harm that was done (and continues to be done) to black, indigenous, and other communities through colonization, enslavement and systemic oppression.

Transitioning Possibilities into Action

If your imagination was sparked by the ideas discussed in this chapter, I encourage you to begin taking steps forward to see if that spark can become a flame. Most of the projects discussed in this chapter took years, not months, to see the fruits of their labor. The transformation that needs to be done with many congregations' properties requires decisive action. Doing this work well takes time, so it is imperative that the work is started before the financial need is acute. Dave Harder shared in *Crisis and Care*:

> Engaging with neighbors takes time, figuring out property development plans takes time, getting sign off from multiple layers of bureaucracy takes time . . . [congregations] are waiting for all this to pass [hoping] they

> will experience the vitality and growth of years past. Sadly, in moments of crisis, waiting just acknowledges the path of death we are on, a hospice care of sorts, a sense of holding on peacefully until we pass.[12]

There is absolutely a ticking clock when it comes to this work. Now that isn't to say you should rush to bring in renters or sell your property without doing the proper discernment work, but it is good to get the process rolling, since it may take longer than you imagine. When we follow the Spirit into God's future we lose control, and our buildings are often the last vestige of that control. But the good news is that in this process, we are renewed, refreshed, and rebuilt. Giving up control of any part of our property can be as scary as it is liberating. As Harder puts it,

> As I sit and reflect on why so many congregations have started the journey with excitement and then for some reason fizzled out, a catalog of reasons come [sic] to mind. For some it was the financial burden, for others they acted too slowly, for others they made the decision to go back to what they were, and for others it was governance models or the leadership of a few that stifled the momentum. If I was to choose one reason it is fear. Fear of the future, fear of change, fear of losing the past, fear of moving forward into the unknown.[13]

Fear can be the enemy of change, but it can also be a great motivator for change. Throughout the interviews, I saw a consistent pattern that those who shifted their financial models had the courage to take risks. This does not mean they were fearless, but it does mean that they didn't let their fears and concerns stop them from taking the next best step forward in the process.

♦ Practice: Holy Imagining Property ♦

In line with the Spirit's penchant to destroy and rebuild, take some time to imagine what your church might look like if you were able to demolish it and start from square one again. Imagine you could rebuild your congregation's property with your congregation's current mission, neighborhood, and membership in mind. What space might you need? How might it be used throughout the week? What features from the old space would you preserve? Imagine money was not a factor in the rebuilding process. Give the group space to write and/or draw out their vision. Then, share your visions with one another. Notice what common themes emerge.

Reflection Questions

- Which congregation's story from this chapter did you resonate with most? Which story sparked your imagination?
- Do you think God might be calling your congregation to rent, sell, and/or share its property? Why or why not?
- How does property renting/selling/sharing align with your congregation's mission?
- What next step might you take to discern how God might have you steward your congregation's property?

CHAPTER SEVEN

Social Enterprise

Matthew 13:1–9

"That same day Jesus went out of the house and sat beside the lake. Such great crowds gathered around him that he got into a boat and sat there, while the whole crowd stood on the beach. And he told them many things in parables, saying: 'Listen! A sower went out to sow. And as he sowed, some seeds fell on the path, and the birds came and ate them up. Other seeds fell on rocky ground, where they did not have much soil, and they sprang up quickly, since they had no depth of soil. But when the sun rose, they were scorched; and since they had no root, they withered away. Other seeds fell among thorns, and the thorns grew up and choked them. Other seeds fell on good soil and brought forth grain, some a hundredfold, some sixty, some thirty. Let anyone with ears listen!' "

Dwelling Questions

1. What word or phrase jumped out at you as you read the passage?
2. What is one thing your congregation has tried that has failed? What did you learn from that experience? Which seed from the parable does it best represent?
3. What is something your congregation tried that succeeded more than you could have imagined?
4. What might God be saying to you or your congregation through this passage?

Prayer

Eternal sower of seeds, you have called us to sow the seed of your good news far and wide. Teach us to sow with reckless abandon, knowing it is you, not us, who creates the growth. Give us patience as we tend your seedlings and courage to follow your call to farm in new ways. Amen.

In the summer of 1981, the Rev. Nicholas J. Zook (Pastor Zook), a newly minted seminary graduate, and his wife made the pilgrimage from seminary in Gettysburg, Pennsylvania, to Concordia Lutheran Church, a Swedish Lutheran Church on the North Side of Chicago, to begin his first call. When Pastor Zook arrived, the congregation had been without a pastor for two years. It had gone through a process of trying to merge with another congregation in the neighborhood that kept falling apart. So, Concordia Lutheran Church's leadership decided they would do a fundraiser to raise enough money to call a full-time pastor again. As Pastor Zook tells the story, the congregation leaders then reached out to the bishop and said, "Send us the cheapest pastor you've got, which is right out of seminary." But what they didn't tell the bishop, or the newly minted seminary grad they called as their pastor, was that they had only raised enough money for one year.

So, when Pastor Zook arrived, he stepped into a situation in which the church had enough money for one year, an old building with deferred maintenance, and worship attendance of 15 to 20 people. But what struck Pastor Zook was the energy of the congregation's leadership. The leaders told him: "We are excited . . . We know there is no future in our past. We are open to trying something new." This newly minted pastor saw that as an opportunity and leaned into their openness to change.

Three days after he started in his new role, Pastor Zook had an encounter that would change the course of the congregation's ministry:

> I was on my way back home to the parsonage, and three women were outside in the neighborhood talking. And they saw me. I was dressed with my collar, and they said, "Are you the new priest over at that church on the corner?" And I said, "Well, yes." And they introduced themselves. I don't remember their full names, but they all had the first name of Barbara, and they all had one thing in common . . . they were single

> moms. And they said, "We need childcare for our children. They're over at [the neighboring school]. But we can't come home at 3 o'clock from our jobs. Is there anything the church can do?" And I said, "Well, sure. Let's talk." And so I brought them back, and we had a meeting with the [church leadership team] here who had this attitude of, "Yeah, let's see what we can do. Maybe we can start an after-school program." And the argument we made with the [team] and the congregation was we have an empty building which is now a liability. The community has a need. If we put them together, maybe the building gets used, and the need of the community is met.

Two months later, the congregation started their first after-school program. Fast forward forty years, Concordia Lutheran Church now has four care centers. Over the last few decades, the ministry has expanded from serving school-aged children to people of all ages. While this ministry, Concordia Place, is now a separate nonprofit organization, it is still deeply tied to the church community and its mission. As they share on their website, "Concordia Place believes all people deserve to reach their full potential and that it starts with a strong foundation. [They] build well-being through a wide-range of educational, enrichment, and wellness programs for young children, teens and adults, and people no matter their age or circumstance."[1] Tuition at each of the centers is scaled so that no one from the community has to pay more than they can afford. They are building bridges and creating relationships in a way the church never could.

On the surface, this may sound like a shiny success story, and in some ways it is, but that doesn't mean the process of finding financial sustainability hasn't come with its share of challenges. They figured out how to remodel their congregation's space on a shoestring budget using half of the money they had set aside for the pastor's salary and a lot of volunteer support. They made a quick pivot to hire a director when the pastor realized that he could not lead the after-school program all on his own. Once they outgrew the congregation's space, they had to acquire a new space. They ended up remodeling a vacant Catholic school space that wound up costing about twenty times as much as the pastor originally estimated. The process has required them to trust the Spirit's leading, step boldly into the work God has called them to do, and connect with new community partners they never could have imagined working with before.

What Is a Social Enterprise?

According to Mark Elsdon, a social enterprise is "a venture that seeks to engage in social impact while also generating revenue from operations."[2] These ventures are looking for not only a financial return but also a social (or missional) return on their investment. This is referred to as a double bottom line return. In some cases, they may also be seeking a triple bottom line return by factoring in the environmental impact as well.

Social enterprises are businesses. They may be as simple as monetizing an existing service of the congregation, like selling breakfast for people to eat before worship, or they may be as grand as Concordia Lutheran Church's example of a nonprofit overseeing four different care centers. These businesses may be contained within the church or structured as a separate nonprofit or for-profit business entity. They may also have a stream of grant or donation funding that supports their work outside of the revenue generated by the business.

This isn't a church bake sale. This is a business where both the work itself and the way the profit is used generate both a financial and missional return. I really appreciated the way that Thad Austin summed this up in his dissertation on "Social Entrepreneurship Among Protestant American Congregations":

> The data suggest that there are at least three main theological tenets of congregational social entrepreneurs, applying across contexts: 1) Work is good, 2) Business can be good, and 3) Business can be ministry. . . . Although anyone engaged in social enterprise could potentially accept the first two theological tenets (work is good and business can be good) from a philosophical standpoint, the third theological tenant is particular to persons of faith. Lay and clergy leaders understand their work as a form of ministry.[3]

Social entrepreneurship is one of the primary places where money and mission come together. The Rev. Chrisy Ennen from First Presbyterian Church of Gulf Shores in Gulf Shores, Alabama put this so well in her interview:

> We are right on that growing edge of this whole idea of social enterprise and how that plays out. And I think this can be transformative for so many churches to turn the focus outward and really—because, I mean,

> I've said it all along and I have people on my [church leadership team] that remind us of it, remember, this is a ministry. Yes, it's helping our bottom line, but this is a ministry and the bottom line is not the end goal. The end goal is providing this service for our community.

For them, the "Hand-in-Hand Business Center" isn't just a business, it's a ministry. While finances may have been the catalyst to start the social enterprise, it is the enterprise's mission and ministry that encouraged them to move forward with the idea.

Many of these businesses take time to become revenue-generating, and some are intentionally self-sustaining rather than profit-generating. As I listen to the story of Concordia Place, and so many other social enterprises, I am continually reminded of the parable of the sower. There is a lot of trial and error, learning from failure, and watching closely to see what actually grows. The failure rate among small businesses is high. Half of businesses survive five years and less than a third will last ten years.[4] Faith-based social enterprises are no exceptions to this. While Concordia Place's ministry may have lasted forty or more years, there are many faith-based social enterprises that are just around for a season and maybe that's just what God has called them to do. I hope to expand your imagination about the variety of congregational social enterprises, offer guidance on how you might get started, and answer a few common questions. Ready to start a social enterprise? You can find an abundance of resources in Appendix D.

Social Enterprise Data

In the survey we captured data about social enterprises using a few different categories since I've noticed that many congregation leaders aren't as familiar with this term and thus would not necessarily classify their ventures as social enterprises. We asked people about "starting and maintaining a social enterprise or business," "selling products or services," as well as "forming a nonprofit organization." I also found that some congregations classified some of their social enterprises as "self-sustaining ministries." We found that twenty congregations had started a social enterprise or business (fourteen were considering it in the future), seventeen were currently selling products or services (six were considering it, two had done it in the past), and twenty-six congregations were forming/had formed a nonprofit organization (sixteen were considering it). Looking at the defining characteristics of these congregations, starting social enterprises was most popular with suburban congregations, forming nonprofits tended to be most popular with urban congregations, and selling products and services tended to be most popular with younger congregations (0–59 years old). Overwhelmingly, most social enterprises had been started less than five years ago (65 percent).

Given that these are all business ventures, I was surprised by the substantial percentage of congregations (20–30 percent) who did not set a financial goal for their ventures. However, for those that did set a goal, their ventures generally met or surpassed their financial goal with an 85 percent or more success rate. For the most part, these ventures funded 0–9 percent of the church's budget. However, there were two outliers. For about a third of those who had formed a nonprofit, it funded 10–24 percent of the church's budget. And, surprisingly, for about a third of those who had started a social enterprise, it funded 60 percent or more of the church's budget. Interestingly, these congregations were not large; they had three hundred or fewer people in average worship attendance each Sunday.

These ventures weren't just successful financially, they were also successful missionally. For each of these ventures 85 percent or more of those who started them said they were successful at creating relationships with people outside of the congregation and "connected" or "very connected" to their congregation's mission. This quote from one of the congregations who had started a social enterprise captures this connection well:

> [Our church] makes and sells soup at our local farmers market. We always say it's not about selling soup at the market as much as it is about meeting our neighbors. We have built a loyal customer base. These customers talk at length at our booth every Sunday; we hear stories of their and their family's health, their job transitions, what's going on in their kids' lives . . . we really know our customers and our customers know us. We regularly hear that while our soup is delish it's how we show up in public that grabs people's attention and loyalty. [Furthermore,] we locally source our soup's vegetables. This ethical business choice [has] helped us gain credibility among the local farming community. They know they can count on us to help them move their product and introduce our followers to their craft as well as their passion

[for] sustainable agriculture and eating locally. Our soup is designed to share as a way to make friends and fight off loneliness so, additionally, our customers are also taking the soup to nurture relationships beyond the farmers market.

Soup is just one medium in which they live out their mission. It is the entry point to creating relationships and dispelling loneliness. Since this congregation is a "dinner church," where the church service takes place around the evening meal, it only makes sense that food would be a connection point with their community.

Experimenting with Social Entrepreneurship

After property rental, social enterprise was the second most common income source discussed in the interviews coming up in two-thirds of the interviews my research team and I completed. I shared a few stories of property rental that double as social enterprise in the last chapter: 7400 Woodlawn and First Presbyterian Church of Gulf Shores. I'll begin by sharing a few more stories of property-based social enterprises since this is often one of the most popular avenues for congregations.

I'll begin with the story of Peace Lutheran Church, a medium-sized, urban congregation located in the Hilltop neighborhood in Tacoma, Washington. I first connected with the Rev. John Stroeh (Pastor John) as part of Luther Seminary's Vibrant Congregations project in the early 2010s. In spring of 2012, I had the opportunity to visit the congregation along with a team of faculty and staff from Luther Seminary. One of the first things that Pastor John did upon our arrival at the congregation was take us on a walking tour of the neighborhood. As we walked, he described to us the history of the drug trade and gang activity in the neighborhood in the eighties and nineties, as well as the history of gentrification in this racially diverse, working-class neighborhood. While there were a few different Lutheran churches in the neighborhood when the church began in 1909, Peace was the only one to stay in the Hilltop neighborhood through it all. By the 1970s it was on the verge of closure, but through the leadership of the Rev. Holle Plaehn (Pastor Plaehn) the church opened its doors to people of other denominations and cultural backgrounds. As Pastor John put it, "Through the leadership of Pastor Plaehn and the welcoming in and the invitation of African American neighbors to serve and use their gifts in ministry in the church, the church became a diverse place, a flourishing, small, urban congregation." Pastor Plaehn knew everyone in the neighborhood by name and visited one-on-one with each neighbor. That legacy lives on today through Pastor John's leadership. I can't tell you how many times people stopped us on our walk around the neighborhood to have a conversation with Pastor John. He not only knew their names but they knew his. It was clear that he was seen as a pastor to the neighborhood, not just the congregation.

Peace Lutheran Church's social enterprises have flowed out of the congregation's deep and abiding relationships with the community and clear understanding of its needs. Over thirty years ago, Peace Lutheran Church began serving meals to neighbors. Another Hilltop congregation had been serving meals to the community every weeknight all year round. Peace Lutheran Church asked, "Can we host the meals two months out of the year so your people can take a break?" Pastor Plaehn invited a woman who lived across the street from the church to become the meal coordinator, and they began to develop a relationship with other local congregations who each took turns providing a meal to the community at Peace Lutheran Church. Through the meal program they developed relationships with other congregations, who, in the words of Pastor John, "saw both the need and the gift of this congregation and the ministry in the Hilltop." Shortly after the meal program began, some teachers in the church began tutoring some kids from the neighborhood at Peace Lutheran Church. Then in the nineties the church leadership team met to do some visioning and said, "What can we do beyond the feeding and the little bit of tutoring to really come alongside folks to make a difference in their lives?" They decided to raise money to expand their church building to start the Peace Community Center. Because of the relationships Peace Lutheran Church had started with other congregations through the meal program, they were able to build the $1.5 million addition to their building by 2000 and have it entirely paid off by 2003.

Peace Community Center's mission has grown over time. What began with high school tutoring eventually expanded to include tutoring in a local elementary school and middle school as well as accompanying Hilltop students through post-secondary education. These students are often the first in their families to graduate from high school and/or college. Peace Community Center is focused on the academic growth, enrichment, and support of the students so they can graduate and then go on to college, trade school, or a living wage job.

While the connection with the Peace Community Center has certainly been missionally beneficial for the congregation, it has also been financially beneficial. Even though the community center is a separate 501(c)3 nonprofit, since the two ministries share space, the church has been able to use the amazing facility. Over time the space has been expanded and remodeled to include a gym, gathering place, commercial kitchen, and, most recently, new office space with the community center paying for the remodels through its own capital campaigns and partnerships. The church would never have been able to create this space on its own without incurring significant debt. While the church leases the space to the community center for just $1 per year, through a shared cost agreement, the community center pays for 75 percent of the building expenses, including operating expenses, utilities, office supplies, custodial costs, and more. The church is also able to rent the space out to other groups, sharing the profits 25/75 with the community center according to the shared agreement.

Peace Lutheran Church's continued investment in the community has also led them to expand their ministry to include housing. They realized that many of the church's neighbors, particularly long-term neighbors of color, could no longer afford to live in the neighborhood and were being displaced because of the impact of gentrification on the community. So, in 2014, the congregation started to buy up homes around the congregation to create an affordable housing ministry. For Peace, this is an issue of racial and economic justice. As Pastor John put it in his interview,

> Everything comes out of vision and mission. So we're not going to buy a couple of houses just because we think it's a cool thing. We're also not going to buy houses, rent them out at market rate, and whatever we make off the rent, put into our worship and our faith education [budget] like we're just doing the housing thing as a way to make money for the church's other ministries, because that would be disingenuous to our [mission]. The forces of gentrification are doing that all the time in our neighborhood—people buying houses, renting them out at higher rates, making money for themselves at the cost of people who have lived here for decades.
>
> We learned we've got to communicate exactly what we're about, why this is part of our church's ministry. Because some of our members

> asked, "Why should a church own houses? That's not the church's work." And we had to build a case and communicate, "Yes, this is the church's work. This is God's work. Here's the history. Here's the reality in our neighborhood. It's a justice issue. And it is part of our calling being in relationship in our community, serving Jesus in this place. We deeply care about people displaced." We communicate that the people living in these houses are going to be people who have been displaced from our neighborhood who are also people of color so that everybody understands what we're trying to do and how it flows out of our overall mission, given to us by God, that has an anti-racism emphasis, seeking a just and reconciled community.

Out of this mission and vision, the congregation now stewards four homes, providing affordable housing and support for four families of color with ties to the Hilltop neighborhood who would not otherwise be able to afford to live there. In the future they hope to expand this ministry to include denser housing (four-plex, eight-plex, or even larger).

Since families living in these homes need more services than just affordable housing, Peace has recently hired a part-time Resource Navigator who helps the families acquire the basic goods and services needed as they move into their new home. Housing is just the starting point to the work God is doing in and through Peace with the families who live in these homes. They have seen how affordable housing has been a gateway for these families to find more financial stability, receive job training, connect their children with local schools, and share their gifts with the church and/or community center's ministry.

One of my favorite parts of this story is how partnerships have played a significant role in making these social enterprises possible. As Pastor John and Peace Lutheran Church member Carol Watson put it in a recent article for Faith+Lead,

> Peace Lutheran, by itself, could not do this. We have partnered with local organizations to help sustain our ministry, including the City of Tacoma (providing new roofs), Metropolitan Development Corporation (providing weatherization), other congregations (sweat labor, maintenance materials, and solar panels), Associated Ministries, Housing Connector, Spinnaker property management, and church members who have volunteered their time. We received a major Big Dream grant from ELCA Hunger to provide the down payment to build the fourth housing

> unit, a two-bedroom DADU (detached accessible dwelling unit) in the backyard of one of the houses we steward. Peace also contributes a portion of monthly offerings to this ministry.[5]

This enterprise was not created in a silo. They brought all their network assets to the table to make this ministry possible.

Peace Lutheran Church's story shares many common themes with the story of The Emory Fellowship in Washington, DC shared in chapter 3. Like Peace Lutheran Church, The Emory Fellowship's affordable housing ministry emerged out of its deep connection with its neighborhood and decades of ministry with the unhoused. What began with a ministry feeding and housing people within their church, continued to renovating their old parsonage to begin a transitional housing program, and has now expanded to include the Beacon Center that provides affordable and transitional housing, a food pantry, weekend backpack program, immigration clinic, small business assistance, and more—all under the church's roof. This project, like Peace Lutheran Church's, was motivated by community need and flowed out of the congregation's mission and ministry.

Similarly, it took many hands coming together to make the vision of remodeling The Emory Fellowship's space to include the Beacon Center a reality. They raised $1.4 million through their own campaign efforts in the congregation and partnered with the city to receive housing production trust fund monies, tax credits, along with other low-income housing monies. They also received support from their denomination to make this vision a reality. Outside of the financial element, they also received invitations from other houses of worship to use their space while their facility was being renovated.

The Emory Fellowship's story is a great example of how a mission-focused project can also help the congregation financially. While the needs of their community were the primary motivation, the pastor also realized that their building was falling apart, and with all of the development happening in their neighborhood, there was a real possibility that the church would be priced out of the neighborhood as well. Through this project, the church was able to create a new, right-sized space for the congregation, and eventually it will generate income from the affordable housing units.

For both Galileo Christian Church in Fort Worth, Texas, and The Table UMC in Sacramento, California, property played a key role in getting their social enterprises off the ground; however, the property in question was not theirs to begin with. Galileo Christian Church, "a quirky church for spiritual refugees,"[6] intentionally does not own their space but rent it. While it took them some time to find a good landlord who supported their mission, they have found financial freedom by not having to budget for ongoing building maintenance. However, when they felt called to start a social enterprise for the transgender community, they did not have space of their own that they could use for that endeavor.

Like The Emory Fellowship and Peace Lutheran Church, Galileo Christian Church is deeply connected and invested in its community. Their first missional priority is to "do justice for LGBTQ+ humans and support the people who love them."[7] Given the increase in laws threatening the rights of transgender people in their community, they felt called to do more. Their landlord had an open space right next door to the barn they currently rent out. In the fall of 2021, Galileo Christian Church tried to find a tenant for this space that could help them live out this mission, but it did not work out. After months of not being able to rent the space, in early 2022, Galileo Christian Church's pastor, the Rev. Dr. Katie Hays (Pastor Katie) was talking to the president of her congregation's missional logistics team and they had joked that the landlord should just give them the space. They both understood that the landlord rented out the space to make money: Why would he give the space to them and forgo the income?

And yet, miraculously, two hours later the landlord called Pastor Katie and said, "If you can figure out something to do for the trans community in that space, I'm just going to give it to you." Out of this phone call, the social enterprise, Finn's Place, was born.

Pastor Katie began by gathering a group of people from the church and the community to discern what they would do with the space. They decided to create a community center "for trans and gender-diverse people to gather, grow, and flourish."[8] As Pastor Katie mentioned during her interview, the goal is that "no trans or gender-diverse person will ever be charged for anything that's happening there. If you are a trans or gender-diverse service provider, we will pay you for what you're doing there, even if you're offering it free to people." Similarly, no one from the trans or gender-diverse community who attends an event, gathering, or meeting can be charged, but others can be. They received $25,000 in funding from their denomination, which they used to renovate the space. The church hosts the space, holds the 501(c)3, and will provide all the funding for the first three to five years until Finn's Place becomes self-sustaining. They are also seeking outside grants and funding to make this ministry happen. They feel called to help launch this ministry and serve as a legacy funder.

For some social enterprises, the goal is income-generation, for others, it's finding a self-sustaining model. Galileo Christian Church is using the variety of assets God has entrusted to their care to make this ministry self-sustaining. Yes, they provide financial support, but their biggest gift to the project was their network capital. This project was possible due to their relationship with the landlord and access to denominational funding and grants. Galileo Christian Church could have chosen to make Finn's Place a ministry of the congregation, run by people from the congregation, and funded by the people of the congregation in perpetuity. Instead, they created a separate board with members of the community who oversee the operation of Finn's Place and are committed to help the social enterprise launch well, which will free up space for Galileo Christian Church, financially and missionally, to launch other ministries once Finn's Place is on its feet.

The Table UMC's story also includes miraculous provision of space, this time a small plot of land from a neighboring Catholic school. In 2018, during a time of transition in youth ministry leadership, The Table UMC had a desire to reimagine what their youth ministry might look like. Around that time, they were accepted into an innovation accelerator at The Institute for Youth Ministry at Princeton Theological Seminary. Through short, design thinking activities they discerned together their values, their mission, what they were called to do, why they wanted to focus on youth, and what the youth needed.

Through this process of listening to the needs of young people, particularly young people in the transgender community, they honed in on a desire to address the issue of isolation and loneliness. The team decided they would transform the congregation's 1959 kitchen into a bakery where young people could come together to not only bake but break bread together. They were just getting ready to move forward with the kitchen remodel when COVID hit and they decided to hit "pause" on the project until the community could be back indoors together.

A month after they decided to hit "pause," one staff member at The Table UMC had a brilliant idea: what if they took over the operations of a local farm? Farming, like bread baking, could help to dispel loneliness. It was outdoors. They could grow food alongside their neighbors and give food away through an interfaith food bank. A Catholic elementary school offered to lease out their small farm space to The Table UMC for $1/year. Quickly, they decided to pivot. This new enterprise became Table Farm. In the first year they gave away over two thousand pounds of food and offered produce and flower subscriptions as a way to bring in income.

In December of 2022, they finally finished the kitchen renovation and started Table Bread. They are helping to fund this ministry with bread subscriptions. For $40/month, one loaf is given away through the interfaith food bank and the subscriber receives one loaf of bread each week throughout the month. The proceeds go to support Table Farm & Table Bread. In the future, they hope to expand these subscription offerings.

On the surface, some might wonder how these social enterprises are connected to the congregation's broader mission "to create a community of faith in Sacramento that is rooted in grace, growing in faith, and reaching in love."[9] Co-Pastor of the Table UMC, the Rev. Matt Smith described it so well in his interview:

> We think that Jesus was kind of serious when he invited people to break bread. And so we're trying to live that out. And then to grow food alongside neighbors and to give that away through an interfaith food bank. To us, that's what it looks like to align with or try to be connected to the way that God's healing is moving in the world. So it's trying to tend to this backyard of a school that was mostly neglected and abandoned and to practice regenerative farming there in ways that bring life to that space. And so for us, that's what it means to follow Jesus or to root our lives in grace and grow in faith and reach in love.

Again, The Table UMC's ministry illustrates how these enterprises are much more about the mission than the money. It takes immense courage to take such a faithful risk amid a pandemic, after you already had your heart set in one direction. Like the farmer scattering seeds, they were willing to try another idea, experiment, and see what would take root.

The last social enterprise I want to showcase is Church Anew, a ministry of St. Andrew Lutheran Church in Eden Prairie, Minnesota, mentioned in chapters 1 and 3. Like many of the social enterprises that I discussed in this chapter, I think their story really encapsulates the balance between money and mission, financial sustainability and social impact. As with so many of the stories in this chapter, Church Anew's story began long before the ministry's launch in 2018. St. Andrew Lutheran Church started in 1977. The congregation grew quicker than anyone had anticipated, becoming one of the fastest growing churches in the ELCA. However, after a period of rapid growth, they then experienced a time of rapid decline, becoming one of the fastest declining churches in the ELCA. After this season of growth and decline, they experienced a season of renewal and revitalization under new pastoral leadership that has allowed the congregation to flourish.

The pastoral staff knew that the congregation had learned a lot from this season of rapid growth, rapid decline, and revitalization that they could share with other congregations. They also realized that they were a resource-rich congregation. As of the time of the congregation's interview with my research team, they had five pastors, about thirty full-time and part-time staff, a multi-million-dollar budget, and a congregation full of generous people eager to serve and to give. They knew that this was not the norm in Minneapolis or other areas of the country. They wanted to share some of this abundance with under-resourced congregations. They started by reaching out to congregations with a solo pastor to provide them with secretarial support, preaching materials, marketing for church programs, and a pastor from St. Andrew Lutheran Church to preach when the solo pastor was away. St. Andrew Lutheran Church did this work at a financial loss to help these congregations in need, but the venture never saw the growth or connection the leadership had hoped for.

They decided that they wanted to take this venture a step further by creating a space where congregations of all varieties could learn together. As the Rev. Matthew Fleming (Pastor Matthew), St. Andrew Lutheran Church's Teaching Pastor and Director of Church Anew, shared in my research team's interview with him, they weren't just eager to share their stories of success but also to learn from others. They wanted to create a level table where congregations of all sizes could learn together.

After their first in-person event they realized they were gaining traction. They continued to offer in-person events, learning from their success and failures along the way and beginning to right-size their staffing to make these events possible. Then the pandemic hit, and they had to put the brakes on any in-person events. They went through the stages of grief and denial that so many of us experienced at the beginning of the pandemic, postponing the events for one week, then one month, and finally realizing that in-person gatherings of this magnitude might be on hold for a long time.

During this time, Church Anew pivoted their ministry to focus on a blog and online events. They saw incredible growth throughout 2020, growing their audience to "150,000 unique users [from] 83 countries [and] every state in the nation [from] countless denominations." But the growth didn't stop there. By the end of 2021, they had nearly 300,000 unique users and "had hosted these virtual gatherings for 6,000 people [with] somewhere around 1,500 congregations participating." They began to realize that their online presence was allowing them to reach many more people than their local in-person events could ever have reached on their own.

Their success has come from leaning into the Spirit's leading, being attentive to how their events and blog posts are being received, and learning from their successes and their failures. As Pastor Matthew shared in the interview,

> Discernment, when I heard about it in seminary, was this extensive, long, kind of stretched-out process that got overly complicated. And sometimes, discernment is just saying, "Yep. Let's go," right? Sometimes, discernment is saying, "Yes," is listening carefully, is having an immediacy of response. Sometimes, it's not stepping back. Sometimes, it's actually like falling forward.

Currently Church Anew is made possible because of a gift from a generous donor, the financial support of the congregation through donations and the funding of the Church Anew staff, as well as the profits from the events. Their goal is that this ministry will eventually become self-sustaining and be able to support the salaries of the staff members. In my interview with two of the lay members from St. Andrew Lutheran Church who are connected with Church Anew, I was excited to hear about the ways they see this ministry fulfilling their congregation's mission to live out faith in daily life. It sounds like they have a bevy of people from the congregation who are eager to offer their time and financial support to make this ministry happen. The congregation members are eager to brainstorm ideas, offer feedback, volunteer to staff the in-person events held at the congregation, and share the mission and ministry of Church Anew. There are many hands involved in making this venture possible.

Common Questions about Social Enterprise

- **Where should I start?** Check out the resources listed in Appendix D. This is a great time to look back at the assets you identified in chapter 3, particularly the skills/time assets. Where might there be untapped potential? What's an asset that makes your congregation unique?

- **I have an idea. How do I put it into action?** In chapter 10 of *We Aren't Broke,* Mark Elsdon shares five key ingredients for any social enterprise and walks through each step in detail: "focus on the core mission," "measure and manage impact outcomes" (this can include both hard data and stories), "make it work–attend to the business model," "align money and mission," and "embrace risk and failure."[10] Once you're ready to craft a business plan, the Small Business Association offers a lot of great resources and free business consulting should you need it.
- **What if the social enterprise isn't specifically mission oriented?** I see this sometimes with congregations who generate income from a cell phone tower, church parking lot, even selling candy to raise money for a youth trip. Often these activities are justified because of the outcome: the money will be used to send kids to camp, maintain the building, or support a new staff position. While these outcomes are great, it's important that the actual income-generating activity has a mission focus as well. Looking at the Money & Mission Matrix, Mark Elsdon invites us to proceed with caution even if the activity is "mission neutral" and certainly stop if it detracts from the congregation's mission. *Does the activity itself align with the congregation's mission? What's the case to be made?* You saw this in the EV charging station example I shared earlier. While it initially seemed mission neutral, they eventually discerned it was indeed mission aligned. If you find the activity is just "mission neutral," I'd then ask how much time, effort, and money the church needs to put in to make it happen. If the phone company will do the installation of the tower with minimal staff supervision and will pay for any needed building repairs, maybe it's worthwhile to have the tower in your building. If it does require an investment from the congregation, then I'd encourage you to seek another more mission-aligned opportunity. If you proceed with it, I'd also encourage you to be very explicit about how much money the church is making from this venture (people in the pews often assume it's much more than it really is) and where that money is going. It's best to put the money towards a related project and preferably one that the congregation would not be as excited to pay for. For instance, revenue earned

from the parking lot or cell phone tower could go towards building maintenance.

- **This sounds like a lot to do on my own. Are all social enterprises clergy-led?**
  Absolutely not! Most of the social enterprises that I have come across are led by lay staff or volunteers and supported by the clergy. Clergy play an important role in keeping the focus on the mission, maintaining the tie to the congregation, telling the story of the social enterprise's ministry, and listening in the community. In most cases, clergy are not the ones running the day-to-day operations. This is a great opportunity for the church to tap business leaders and entrepreneurs from the congregation and/or the community to collaborate (and even lead!) this project. This will likely be a unique moment to engage a group of people who may have been previously disengaged from serving in your congregation's ministry. As Mark DeYmaz and Harry Li share in *The Coming Revolution in Church Economics*, often pastors misplace the gifts of entrepreneurs in their congregations, inviting them to serve as church "employees" (greeters, ushers, Sunday school teachers, offering counters, etc.) or as "managers" (serving on a church leadership team, leading a small group, supervising a ministry, and so on).[11] While these positions are important, entrepreneurs are best suited to join God's mission as "entrepreneurs." As DeYmaz and Li state, "When entrepreneurs are rightly empowered to help the church meet economic challenges and overcome financial obstacles in partnership with pastors, in recognition of their life experience and in the strength of their gifting, they come alive!"[12]
- **Will it generate income?**
  As with any business venture, there are no guarantees. Like the parable at the beginning of this chapter, you are scattering seeds. As you scatter, you're unlikely to know which seeds will fall on rocky soil, which will be choked by the weeds, and which will thrive. However, as I look across the stories of social enterprise that my research team and I had the chance to listen to, I hear a few key themes: the need to consider financial sustainability from the outset as you are crafting the enterprise, the courage to take risks, and the ability to pivot if things aren't going as planned. It's important to remember

that this income may come in a variety of forms: as in Peace Lutheran Church's example, it might help to offset building maintenance costs and give the church a better space to use, whereas in St. Andrew Lutheran Church's example, the enterprise may help to offset pastor and staff salaries, or the venture may be intentionally self-sustaining. Sometimes the income may come from unexpected places; it may not come solely from the profits from the venture but rather from grants, government funds, or other sources.

- **When should we form a nonprofit?**

  In most cases, it makes sense for the church to start a separate nonprofit when it is looking to solicit funding such as government aid or grants that the church might not be eligible for, the social enterprise expands and needs more oversight than the church can provide, and/or the social enterprise's business is not substantially related to the church's tax-exempt purpose and is costing the church quite a bit in taxes. If the church does decide to make the social enterprise into a separate non- or for-profit business this would be a separate entity from the church; however, the church can maintain ownership of it if it chooses. If you are considering this route, I suggest consulting an accountant and tax advisor to see what the best course of action would be for your enterprise. Often churches will resort to creating a separate entity too quickly without thinking through the reasons for creating this entity. As I will discuss in chapter 9, there are many grant opportunities open to congregations and other faith-based organizations, so having a nonprofit is not the only way to secure these funds. As my research team and I talked to the congregations who had decided to shift their enterprises into separate nonprofit entities, I heard a need for clear oversight and policies so that these nonprofits remained connected with the congregation and the mission for which they were originally started. We heard from one lay group in particular that they no longer felt connected to the nonprofit they had started, even though it was located in their building. While the pastor still served on the board, there were no congregation members on staff anymore and there were very limited updates to the congregation about the nonprofit's work. In the past, the congregation had been very engaged in fundraising, volunteering, and telling the story of the nonprofit's work. Now the relationship between the congregation and nonprofit seemed to be in name only.

- **Can for-profit enterprises still be faithful?**
  Absolutely! As I often tell my students, nonprofit vs. for-profit is not about profit as much as it is about the structure of the business. Both types of organizations generate income, but they differ in the ways in which the income is used. According to the National Council of Nonprofits,

  > The term 'nonprofit' is a bit of a misnomer. Nonprofits can make a profit (and should try to have some level of positive revenue to build a reserve fund to ensure sustainability.) The key difference between nonprofits and for-profits is that a nonprofit organization cannot distribute its profits to any private individual (although nonprofits may pay reasonable compensation to those providing services). This prohibition against "private benefit" is because tax-exempt charitable nonprofits are formed to benefit the public, not private interests.[13]

  For-profits are often easier to start than nonprofits, and you can still have a mission-focused for-profit venture, like a B-Corp. However, if you are looking to generate income from grants, donations, or government funding in addition to any profits earned through the enterprise, a nonprofit structure may be a better fit.

I often find people are skeptical of the mixing of church and business. And yet, I think as more and more people become disconnected from the church and unaffiliated from religion, sometimes freshly made bread, a box of produce, a safe and affordable place to live, even a well-written blog article, can tell the story of God's love in a way that opens the door to creating relationships we would have never had otherwise. You never know what seed might fall on good soil and begin to multiply in ways you never could have imagined.

♦ Practice: Holy Imagining Social Enterprise ♦

If your church was invited to start a social enterprise, what would you do? Look back at your congregation's mission and the needs/hopes from your community that you've heard through your listening. Like the sower in the dwelling passage, your job is to do the scattering; don't focus too much on how successful that particular seed might be. Engage in a brainstorming session where you think of as many ideas as you can over the course of ten minutes, then share your ideas as a group. Notice the common themes that emerge. Vote on three ideas that you'd like to examine further as a group. Then, use Mark Elsdon's Money & Mission Matrix to see which ideas have the strongest money and mission alignment.

Reflection Questions

- Which congregation's story from this chapter did you resonate with most? Which story sparked your imagination?
- Do you think God might be calling your congregation to start a social enterprise? Why or why not?
- Are there any ministries of your congregation that might be a fit to become their own social enterprise?
- What next step might you take?

CHAPTER EIGHT

Staffing

Luke 9:1–6

"Then Jesus called the twelve together and gave them power and authority over all demons and to cure diseases, and he sent them out to proclaim the kingdom of God and to heal. He said to them, 'Take nothing for your journey, no staff, nor bag, nor bread, nor money—not even an extra tunic. Whatever house you enter, stay there, and leave from there. Wherever they do not welcome you, as you are leaving that town shake the dust off your feet as a testimony against them.' They departed and went through the villages, bringing the good news and curing diseases everywhere."

Dwelling Questions

1. What word or phrase jumped out at you as you read the passage?
2. What stands out to you about the way that Jesus sent out his disciples in this passage?
3. How are members of your congregation sent out to share the good news with the world?
4. What might God be saying to you or your congregation through this passage?

Prayer

> Commissioning Christ, just as you sent out your disciples, we know that you also send us out to proclaim the kingdom of God. Thank you for reminding us that you have provided us with all that we need to do your work. Grant us the courage to listen to the Spirit's call as we follow you to the people and places where your good news is needed most. Amen.

As I was selecting the congregations to participate in the second phase of the research project, I knew I wanted to interview a congregation that was at the beginning of the process of shifting their financial model. So many of the congregations we were talking to would be in a more settled place: They had sold their church building, they had started the enterprise, they had built a community center, and so on. While these congregations would never say they had "fully arrived," they had made some significant progress. That's why I was so excited when First Congregational Church of Kensington United Church of Christ (KCC) in Kensington, New Hampshire, agreed to be a part of the interview process. Their interim pastor, the Rev. G. Jeffrey MacDonald (Rev. Jeff), is well-known for his work as a journalist and part-time minister. He has also done quite a bit of research and writing in the area of part-time ministry. I've shared his book, along with other resources about church staffing, in Appendix E.

Due to financial constraints, KCC decided to move from a full-time to a half-time pastor. At the time the decision was made, it was purely a financial one. The congregation's leadership team didn't give much thought to how moving from a full-time to a part-time pastor might impact the congregation's ministry. The first part-time minister who came essentially fulfilled the duties of a full-time pastor for a half-time salary. She was a second career pastor who was nearing retirement and routinely worked more hours than allotted in her covenant with the church. The only difference the congregation noticed was that she was not present at the congregation as often as their previous full-time pastors had been.

However, when the Rev. Jeff came to the congregation in the middle of the pandemic, the congregation experienced a wake-up call to what part-time ministry actually looks like. The Rev. Jeff is present on Sunday mornings for worship, has time blocked off to prepare for Sunday, and has one day in the office. The Rev. Jeff has been very firm with the congregation about when he is available and what he can commit to. As he has been instilling these boundaries, he has also been trying to actively lift up lay leaders in the congregation to fill in some of the roles that had generally been led by a pastor in the past.

During the interim pastoral search process, the Rev. Jeff gave the search team a copy of his book, so they had a clear sense of his approach to part-time ministry and what he had learned through his research. The congregation agreed that they wanted to learn how to thrive in part-time ministry. However, the process of figuring out what that looks like at KCC has been challenging for both the Rev. Jeff and the lay leaders. The congregation members were very eager to support the pastor's work but very nervous about leading some of this work themselves.

The congregation decided to get started by clarifying their mission. The lay leaders of the congregation led a small group process where they discerned that they are called to foster a loving, Christian community in Kensington and share God's hope and peace by serving others in the name of Christ. During this small group conversation process, they learned that there was broad congregational support to open up their building to be used for other purposes. They also learned that the congregation agreed that even though their pastor was part-time, they still expected him to lead worship each week. During this process, the Rev. Jeff checked in about the lay members' openness to trying on different congregational roles: leading worship, Bible study, adult education, among others. There was some openness to leading conversations in the adult education hour centered around a video, which was a big step for them to take. There was also openness to having a lay group (affectionately called the "Space Force") take the lead on the conversation around creative ways to use the building.

However, it became obvious to the Rev. Jeff that a broader cultural shift was needed. The congregation hasn't authorized lay ministry. As he shared with me during his interview, "The lay leaders need to know that the congregation is behind them." They need to hear "we're going to be with you in the places that you lead, and we'll support you. And we'll give you feedback, and it needs to be a partnership." They haven't given that level of trust and support to anyone except the pastor. The Rev. Jeff has pushed the congregation on this and explored the idea of commissioning lay leaders with the ritual of laying on of hands.

However, he believes the pushback is about more than just commissioning. Some of the church leaders have "this concept of the church as having a religious side and a secular side, and that the religious side belongs to the pastor and the secular side belongs to the rest of the congregation." This idea "has contributed to a culture in which the people feel like the religious domain of the church is not theirs except to show up and support that which the pastor creates. But it's really not theirs to create." Whereas the Rev. Jeff has a wider view of ministry and has pushed the congregation to expand their view: "The ministry is for all of us. We have different roles within it, but it's a shared ministry. And it's all religious enterprise. There is no sort of domain in which God is absent in the church, whether you're washing dishes or sweeping floors, or either giving sermons or running video discussions. God's in every part of it."

The Rev. Jeff is working to change the culture and it is slowly catching on. During the lay interview, I had the opportunity to connect with two people from the congregation who were taking on new roles in its ministry. They were both members of the "Space Force" team. One was also leading "Messy Moments" for children during worship. When children are present in worship, they leave during the sermon to do a thematic craft, and then during prayer time the children come up front to show the congregation what they made and what it means. The other interviewee, currently serving as the moderator of the congregation's leadership team, was looking for new ways to reach out to the community. She was making new inroads in the neighborhood that she hoped would lead to partnerships. The Rev. Jeff had encouraged the church to read, *Sharing Leadership: A United Church of Christ Way of Being Community*. The moderator shared how both the book and the Rev. Jeff's guidance had changed the way she saw part-time ministry and encouraged her, and others, to engage in ministry roles that she thought only the pastor could do.

This lay member's energy was contagious throughout the interview. It was clear the Spirit was at work in her, helping her to see her role and her community in new ways and giving her the courage to take risks. I noticed that the fellow members on the call had seen this transformation in her as well. It filled me with hope and made me wonder if KCC just might be able to embrace this move from a full-time to a part-time minister.

In my faith tradition growing up, the line between lay and clergy leadership was permeable. There wasn't much that a clergy person could do that a lay person could not. In high school, I watched my peers preach, lead worship, and even preside over and serve communion. However, at the majority of mainline churches that I have attended since then, I've noticed a very clear distinction between the clergy/church staff and the laity. Instead of being invited to lead the work of ministry, lay members are invited to support it by singing in the choir, reading scripture, serving communion, greeting at the door, and bringing treats for the fellowship hour. The only real way to lead is to serve on a committee that makes decisions about how ministry happens but often doesn't play a role in making it happen.

In this chapter, we'll look at a few different models of part-time ministry staffing, a growing trend across denominations. Often when these different options are discussed, the focus is on the financial savings of moving from a full-time to part-time pastor, however little time is spent considering how the roles of clergy and laity need to change to make these models work. Even if your congregation does not decide to shift its staffing model, I hope the content in this chapter will still be helpful to you in considering how you might shift the power dynamics in your congregation to invite lay people to not just support but lead in ministry. While this may be helpful from a financial perspective, it will have an even greater missional impact.

The Growth and Gifts of Part-Time Ministry

Of the congregations in the survey who had reduced their budget by 5 percent or more to better align with their congregation's mission, most made changes to staffing. Sixty-five percent reduced the number of paid clergy and/or staff, 55 percent employed bivocational, part-time and/or contract clergy/staff, and 45 percent relied more heavily on volunteer and/or unpaid leaders/staff. This shouldn't be surprising. Most churches spend about half of their budget on salaries, benefits, and payroll expenses for clergy and staff.[1] It only makes sense from a financial perspective that a congregation looking to cut its budget would start with the largest category.

Bivocational ministry is becoming more and more of a ministry norm. Bivocational ministry (sometimes referred to as co- or multi-vocational ministry) is where a minister holds two different vocations at once. This may mean working two jobs, for instance being a part-time journalist and a part-time pastor, or it might look like being a part-time pastor and stay-at-home parent or serving on contract as a pastor a few hours a week during retirement. According to the 2021 report of the National Congregations Study, "one in three congregational leaders (35%) is bivocational, and one in five (18%) serves multiple congregations. And the number is growing as congregations shrink."[2] Looking specifically at two of the denominations represented in the survey data, "Fully one-fourth of the congregations in the Evangelical Lutheran Church in America (ELCA) can no longer afford a full-time pastor with full benefits. . . . Almost half of Episcopal parishes are led by part-time priests, supply priests, or lay people."[3] As Rev. Jeff shared in an article for *The Presbyterian Outlook,* part-time ministry is "very normal. This is not a fringe phenomenon."[4] While this has been a growing trend in rural churches in recent decades, in many traditions this has been the norm for a very long time:

> [Churches] that are predominantly Black or predominantly Latino . . . (as well as) immigrant churches and Asian churches are much more familiar with this (part-time) model. Some of them have been doing it for generations. . . . They would be surprised if their pastor didn't have a secular job or something outside the church.[5]

These churches have often, from the very beginning, been "lay-led, clergy-supported" out of financial necessity. *What might we learn from these traditions who have often seen the ministry as the work of the whole people of God?*

The data from Ben Connelly's 2021 study of bivocational ministers can help us answer this question. Connelly surveyed over eighty bivocational ministers who held a ministry position and a non-church job. In most cases the non-church job provided half or more of the minister's income, with 40 percent saying that the non-church job provided all of their income.[6] Most of the ministers (75 percent) pursued bivocational ministry intentionally. While church and personal finances were a common motivation for pursuing this ministry path, there was often missional motivation as well: "Fully 90% of respondents cited 'missional living' as at least 'somewhat a factor' in their consideration of bivocational ministry, with 33% claiming 'missional living' as 'the primary factor' for bivocationality. This was the highest reported 'primary factor' of the eight categories on the survey."[7]

Beyond these missional motivations, I was surprised to see the ways bivocational ministry created new avenues for collaboration and even spiritual growth:

- **Ministry as a Team:** 95 percent of participants said bivocational ministry has somewhat or greatly enhanced their view of "ministry as a team."[8]
- **Dependence on God:** 90 percent indicated it has greatly or somewhat enhanced their dependence on God.[9]
- **Priesthood of All Believers:** 90 percent said bivocational ministry has somewhat or greatly enhanced their view of "activating 'the priesthood of all believers'"[10] The priesthood of all believers means that all people of faith have equal access to God whether they are a pastor or a lay member of a congregation. Everyone is responsible to minister to other believers and proclaim God's word. There is no spiritual divide between the clergy and the laity.
- **Embracing Others' Giftings:** 85 percent of participants indicated that bivocational ministry had somewhat or greatly enhanced their view of "embracing others' giftings."[11]
- **Humility:** 80 percent responded that their humility was greatly or somewhat enhanced by being bivocational.[12]
- **Spiritual Growth:** 75 percent or more of respondents indicated that it had somewhat or greatly enhanced their view of God, "God's care and provision," "Christian community," and their "personal spiritual thriving."[13]

Rather than simply being a financial necessity, when entered into intentionally, bivocational ministry could be a gift to both the congregation and the minister.

Free Range Priest

The Rev. Catherine Caimano, the Free Range Priest, intentionally chose part-time congregational ministry. She had heard stories of peers whose congregations paid them a part-time salary but generally expected them to work full-time. She wondered what it might look like to work on contract with a congregation, paid by the hour, where there was a specific agreement with the congregation about what they might need and what she was responsible for providing. A minister could potentially have multiple contracts at once, adding up to one full-time call. Or, in the Rev. Catherine Caimano's case, serving just one congregation on contract frees up the rest of her time to do coaching, teaching, and consulting.

For instance, the Rev. Catherine Caimano serves one congregation part-time for ten hours a month and is paid by the hour. She leads worship two Sundays a month. She isn't "in charge" of the congregation. She doesn't have keys to the building, attend meetings (unless she is specifically invited), and she doesn't represent them to the larger church. She walks alongside the congregation, helping them discern where God is in all they do. She leads worship and prayer when scheduled. When asked, she offers pastoral care and supports members as they care for each other. She trains and supports lay members in their ministry roles, and she is there for theological interpretation and counsel when requested.[14]

This model places the leadership of the ministry into the hands of lay people. It empowers them to not only support ministry but take an active role in it. She helps to train lay people to preach, offer pastoral care and support, lead Bible studies, and more. The Rev. Catherine Caimano only partners with congregations who are willing to work within this model. It has to be the right relationship both for her and for them. This is a shared ministry, one where the laity and the contracted pastor have a clear understanding of their roles. She is willing to train lay people who are willing to learn and serve in churches that are ready to take ownership of their ministry, but she is not called to lead in congregations that are pastor-centric. You can find out more about this training in Appendix E.

From Generalist to Specialist

In the fall of 2022, I had the chance to connect with the Rev. Drew Peterson (Pastor Drew), Pastor of Knox Presbyterian Church in Spokane, Washington. Pastor Drew shared with me a bit about his church's model, which includes multiple part-time ministers and staff who each play a specific role in making the church's ministry happen. As I looked at the leadership page on their website, I was drawn in by this language at the top of the page:

> Knox does not practice a hierarchical or top-down leadership model. We purposefully invite all members of the Knox family to participate in shared ministry, as we seek to serve our community and follow the ways of Jesus. We share in preaching, teaching, worship facilitation, hospitality, and administration. However God has gifted and wired you, there is a place for you within the shared leadership of our church.[15]

After this statement, they list the members of the church's leadership teams as well as their ministry teams. Only after reading through this list will you find the names and bios of the church pastors and staff. For Pastor Drew, being a part-time minister has freed him up to serve as the Land Stewardship Guide and Co-Director of Cyclical Ministries for the Presbytery of the Inland Northwest. While it is clear that he is passionate about Knox and its ministry, he is not the primary person making it happen. He is free to share his specific gifts both with his congregation and the presbytery rather than having to be a "jack-of-all-trades" to his congregation.

The Rev. Dr. Rosario Picardo (Pastor Roz) follows a similar model at his church, Mosaic, in Beavercreek, OH. Pastor Roz is one of twelve church staff, including three co-pastors. In addition to his part-time work at the church, he writes, consults, and teaches at United Theological Seminary. In an interview on the Pivot podcast, Pastor Roz mentioned that having multiple part-time pastors has allowed him and his colleagues to move from being generalists to specialists.[16] Each pastor is able to focus on their unique gifts for ministry.

This model isn't only for larger congregations. I've seen a similar model at a church I attended online in Seattle, Church of the Apostles (COTA), that had about forty people in worship each Sunday evening. This part-time co-pastor model offers the congregation a variety of voices and ministry gifts. While both pastors share in presiding in worship, one is more focused on pastoral care and the other is more focused on church leadership and administration. Like the example from Knox, this type of leadership model with part-time pastors as well as a handful of part-time staff has helped to flatten the church hierarchy and lift up the gifts of laity. At COTA, you are just as likely to hear a lay person preaching as you are to hear one of the pastors preaching during the Sunday night service.

How to Engage Lay Leadership

One of the most fascinating findings of the entire research project was that shifting a financial model was not something that pastors could do on their own. They needed community partnerships and a strong network of lay leaders to make it happen. Pastoral leadership came up in the interviews just as often as lay leadership. While lay leadership often referred to the congregation's leadership team, it came in many forms. It was the group of handy people (some church members, some not) who showed up at the church to make repairs to the building, so it was suitable to rent. It was all the people who came together to imagine what the future of youth ministry might be for their congregation. It was the person who had a connection on the zoning board and helped to expedite the process. It was the couple who led four capital campaigns. It was the people who stopped to pray twice a day at 6:10 to make the project a reality. While the pastors may be the catalyst of many of these shifts, it is the support and energy of the lay leadership that has sustained the congregations throughout the change process.

Cultivating this type of lay leadership in congregations today is more of an adaptive challenge than a technical one since it requires not only changes in behavior but also the fundamental attitudes and beliefs about how ministry is done and, ultimately, what it means to "be" the church. The behaviors that many of the pastors we talked to used to cultivate this type of leadership appeared more passive than active. It was more about "making space" and "stepping out of the way" than it was about dragging people along or forcing people to take on roles they didn't feel called to. Like my experience in my church growing up, it was about affirming people's gifts, setting them loose, and offering support where it was needed.

If your congregation has a very clergy-centric approach, it can be challenging to know where to start. The Rev. Jeff from KCC as well as the Rev. Joe Daniels and the lay leaders of The Emory Fellowship in Washington, DC, have used a few key practices to help their congregations make the shift to a shared ministry model:

- **Outlining Responsibilities:** One of the first things that the Rev. Jeff did was talk through expectations for both clergy and lay members. He identified areas that the congregation was not willing to budge on as well as areas they might be willing to take a risk and experiment with taking leadership. If the congregation continues on this trajectory, it's likely these expectations and responsibilities might change over time as they continue to grow their lay leadership.
- **Everyone is Called to Serve:** This is a central part of the ethos of these churches. They don't just profess that there is a "priesthood of all believers," they live it. They not only know the mission, they own it. As one member from The Emory Fellowship shared, we are

"all called to serve, and we are all encouraged to serve. Whatever gifts we may have, we're expected to share those gifts, and God blesses us in return" Similarly, once a new idea emerges, if it's an idea that is shared and owned by the congregation, it's amazing to see the variety of ways that people offer their assets to support it. Sometimes that's financial support, but often it was with their time, their skills, and their networks.

- **Forming Lay-Led Teams:** The "Space Force" at KCC is a lay-led team. While the Rev. Jeff supports this work when asked, the leadership and decision-making ultimately belongs to the people on the team. I sensed that the lay members present at the interview appreciated the Rev. Jeff's guidance, but they also felt that they had ownership over this initiative.
- **Sharing Resources, Not Giving Direction:** The Rev. Jeff mentioned that on many occasions the congregation had asked him, "What should we do?" and he refrained from giving them an answer. Instead, he gave them options and equipped them with resources (about part-time ministry, use of church space, etc.) so the lay leaders could expand their knowledge and discern next steps on their own. He even created a resource library the Space Force team could draw from. While the congregation has sometimes found this approach frustrating, this is an important step in moving ministry from "clergy-led, lay-supported" to "lay-led, clergy-supported." If pastors are the only ones with the answers, they will continue to be seen as the only authority.
- **Permission Giving and Encouragement:** When members do have ideas that align with the mission instead of having the staff take and run with the idea, we saw many examples of pastors encouraging the member to take the initiative to pursue it or taking the time to brainstorm together before making a decision. For instance, when a lay member approached the Rev. Joe Daniels at The Emory Fellowship about starting the immigration clinic, he was supportive and invited these leaders to go for it. While this may feel a little odd for lay members to come to the pastor for "permission" to pursue these types of projects, I think many lay people, including me, need that permission at least at the outset. We want to know our project

> fits with the vision, and we need to be encouraged and supported in doing this work. We also want to be sure we aren't stepping on any toes.

As I heard countless times during the interviews, these practices and others cannot guarantee that any congregation can make the shift. Some congregations simply will not be able to make this move. For some larger congregations who have enough money to support a larger staff, that may be alright. But, for many of those smaller congregations, their inability to make this shift will likely lead to hospice ministry and the eventual closure of the congregation.

Staffing for the Church Season

While I do believe that lay-led, clergy-supported ministry led by a part-time pastor(s) will be the future for many small- to medium-sized congregations, it's important that each congregation's staff is right-sized for its particular season of ministry. In some of the congregations that we interviewed, that meant growing not contracting their church staff. For instance, Clarendon Presbyterian Church in Arlington, Virginia, had shifted its model to have many part-time pastors and staff rather than one full-time pastor under the lineage of the previous pastor. This model worked for a season, but after a new pastor came in, it was no longer a good fit. So, the church's leadership team and the Rev. Alice Tewell (Pastor Alice) decided to make some changes to staffing that worked within the congregation's current budget. About six months into the pandemic, the church administrator desired fewer hours and the music director was not needed as much for online church. For a period, the pastor and second pastor, who was the Director of Mission, split additional administrative hours, bringing Pastor Alice to full-time and the Director of Mission to thirty hours a week. After the Director of Mission's contract came to an end after three years, the position was not renewed. Given Pastor Alice's passion for building projects (this will be her third redevelopment project) and the large project that the congregation is about to embark on to renovate their entire space to include senior housing, this is the right step for this season of the congregation's ministry. While the staffing configuration may have changed, I was struck by the ways the congregation has maintained its dependence on lay leadership and encouragement of lay ministry.

I heard similar right-sizing stories from other congregations. Galileo Christian Church in Fort Worth, Texas, had previously contracted with a few different people to do particular projects on a very part-time basis (five to ten hours per week). In many cases this work was performed as a side job in addition to their work or studies. They decided to cluster three of these roles together, with the full support of the people in them, to create a second full-time role at the congregation. This role will be an associate pastor position and allow for more coordination between the two full-time roles, since these positions will be working similar schedules rather than having to coordinate with the sometimes opposing schedules of those working on contract. Similarly, the pastors from both River Heights Vineyard Church and its sister congregation, La Viña Inver, in Inver Grove Heights, Minnesota, started out as bivocational ministers with the knowledge that their positions could grow into full-time paid ministry roles as the congregation grew. This has been the case for pastors at both congregations.

Depending on the ministry God is calling your congregation to engage in, your staff may need to grow or contract. However, what I hear in each of these stories about staffing is that these staffing changes were made to fit within the current congregational budget as it grew, contracted, or stayed the same. It was also guided by the congregation's mission and vision. Many congregations who are engaging in new uses of property often find they need to add a new staff member to manage the building; if that cost can be rolled into the building rental fees, then it can be cost neutral to the congregation's budget.

♦ Practice: Holy Imagining Lay Ministry ♦

Create a job description for a lay person in your congregation. This isn't designed to connect with a particular leadership position or committee role; instead think more broadly. What is expected of a lay person in the congregation today and what might you expect in the future? Are there roles and responsibilities that the pastor has that might be filled by lay people? Are there ideas from this chapter you could put into that job description? If it's helpful, you might write a job description for the pastor as well so you can compare the two. You may also want to add a line or two to the pastor's job description about cultivating lay leadership.

Reflection Questions

- Which congregation's story from this chapter did you resonate with most? Which story sparked your imagination?
- On the continuum from "entirely clergy-led" to "entirely lay-led" where do you think your congregation falls?
- Might God be calling your congregation to move towards a "lay-led, clergy-supported" model? Why or why not?
- Do you think God might be calling your congregation to right-size its staffing? Why or why not?
- What next step might you take to cultivate lay leadership and/or right-size staffing?

CHAPTER NINE

How Might We Fund What God Is Calling Us to Do?

Luke 10:25–37

"Just then a lawyer stood up to test Jesus. 'Teacher,' he said, 'what must I do to inherit eternal life?' He said to him, 'What is written in the law? What do you read there?' He answered, 'You shall love the Lord your God with all your heart, and with all your soul, and with all your strength, and with all your mind; and your neighbour as yourself.' And he said to him, 'You have given the right answer; do this, and you will live.'

But wanting to justify himself, he asked Jesus, 'And who is my neighbour?' Jesus replied, 'A man was going down from Jerusalem to Jericho, and fell into the hands of robbers, who stripped him, beat him, and went away, leaving him half dead. Now by chance a priest was going down that road; and when he saw him, he passed by on the other side. So likewise, a Levite, when he came to the place and saw him, passed by on the other side. But a Samaritan while travelling came near him; and when he saw him, he was moved with pity. He went to him and bandaged his wounds, having poured oil and wine on them. Then he put him on his own animal, brought him to an inn, and took care of him. The next day he took out two denarii, gave them to the innkeeper, and said, "Take care of him; and when I come back, I will repay you whatever more you spend." Which of these three, do you think, was a neighbour to the man who fell into the hands of the robbers?' He said, 'The one who showed him mercy.' Jesus said to him, 'Go and do likewise.' "

Dwelling Questions

1. What word or phrase jumped out at you as you read the passage?
2. When did you receive generosity from an unexpected giver?
3. When did you share generosity in a way that surprised the recipient?
4. What might God be saying to you or your congregation through this passage?

Prayer

God of surprise, we give thanks for the ways that you cross chasms to show us your love again and again. You confound us with your generosity. Even in the direst circumstances, you provide us with all we need to follow your call. May your Spirit guide us as we forge new partnerships and renew dormant relationships so that we might live into your mission together. Amen.

Believe it or not, The Emory Fellowship in Washington, DC, started their ministry to the unhoused with lunch money. One lay member, who was particularly passionate about this issue, asked if she could invite every congregation member to give up one day's worth of lunch money to help get the program off the ground. The pastor said "yes". So, they placed a basket on either side of the altar and this special offering was used to fund this work. This story is a humbling reminder that sometimes it doesn't take much funding to join in the work God is doing in our community. Like the Samaritan in this passage, those present at The Emory Fellowship that Sunday were invited to give from what little they had on them. Having everyone pitch in one day's lunch money was enough to get it started, and it was this generosity that paved the way for The Emory Fellowship's robust ministry today.

The Good Samaritan is far and away my favorite biblical parable. It is one of the Bible's purest embodiments of stewardship as love of God and neighbor. When I first started learning about and preaching on this passage, I was drawn in by the Samaritan's "superheroic" version of generosity. The Samaritan stops at nothing to care for this beaten man, his cultural enemy. Despite being on the road, he offers him everything in his saddle bag. *Don't we all wish we could be as generous and magnanimous as the Good Samaritan?* What a stewardship idol to live up to!

Then I heard a different reading of this passage by David Lose that entirely shifted my perspective. In his "Dear Working Preacher" letter for July 8, 2013, Lose drew attention to Jesus's question after the parable, which is markedly different from the one the lawyer originally asked. Instead of asking, "Who is my neighbor?" Jesus is asking "Who acted as a neighbor?" whether they would have been included in that original list or not. The obvious answer is the Samaritan who crossed societal boundaries to care for his cultural enemy: the beaten Israelite man. Which leads us to a few uncomfortable questions: *Who has been a neighbor to us of late? When have we been a recipient of someone else's generosity?* As Lose writes, these questions are uncomfortable for us "because we spend so much of our time, energy, and money trying to be invulnerable, trying precisely to need as little as possible from those around us . . . so many of us are absolutely mortified by the idea of showing our deepest needs to others and have a hard time receiving a compliment let alone serious aid or help."[1]

I could never read the passage the same way again. Instead of striving to be the Samaritan, I now see myself through the eyes of the beaten man, the person most in need of care, the person at the whim of others' generosity. This passage invites us to remember the times that we have received God's love, grace, mercy, and even generosity at the hands of those we would least expect or want to help us, no matter how uncomfortable the exchange might have been.

My research team and I heard echoes of this story over and over again in the interviews. We heard about landlords who rented out their space free of charge, politicians who advocated for government funding for a church's child-care center, secular land developers who partnered with churches to reclaim their property and use it in new ways, and so many more large and small miracles that came from unexpected partnerships. The most predominant theme across all the interviews was partnerships/community relationships; it came up a whopping 148 times across all of the interviews. The second most predominant themes were lay leadership and pastoral leadership, which each came up 111 times. If you're hoping to do this work alone, or even just with the people in your congregation, think again. This work is never done in isolation. None, not even one, of the twelve congregations we interviewed engaged in this process without connecting with outside partners.

In this chapter, I'm going to explore the intersection between what I call "inside funding" (funding from those inside your congregation) and "outside funding" (funding from partners or other community members). I often saw a pattern of these two forms of generosity coming together to help a congregation to take bold steps to follow God's call. Between the "inside funding" and "outside funding" sections, I'll be sharing data on congregations with self-sustaining ministries so we can explore the inside and outside funding sources congregations used to make those ministries sustainable.

While the funding sections below are mainly designed to help you think through ways you might fund the new work God might be calling you to do, it's possible you may also find new ways to fund the work you are already doing. While I share many ideas in the sections below, it is not designed to be a complete or exhaustive list. There are certainly other forms of funding, but based on our research project and my conversations with congregations, these seem to be the most critical ones.

Inside Funding[2]

Once you have a clear sense of what God is calling the congregation to do, there is often a need for startup funding. Usually, a church will start with their own internal means before they move out to talk to outside funders. This is a good practice since many outside funders will want to know that the congregation has made a significant financial investment in the project before they are willing to jump in. In some cases, you may find that internal funding is enough to get the first phase of the project off the ground. As the project grows, you may find that external funding is needed.

Here are some key options for inside funding:

Budget Realignment

Budget realignment is a key, and often necessary, strategy to help the congregation focus its energy on the mission God is calling them to join. It may be tempting to look at other forms of funding that I'll discuss below, which may seem easier to attain, but don't be lured in by this temptation. Pruning and reallocating congregational budget dollars is often the best first step to gain broader mission alignment and make more effective use of the dollars the congregation is already receiving. Plus, what a great story to tell those giving to the congregation! Their regular contributions are getting in on the ground floor of a new and exciting project. However, the biggest win for budget realignment is that it can often produce a more sustainable income stream that the congregation can use for years to come. Given that many of these projects end up taking more time than anticipated, it's nice to have a funding source that has an indefinite timeline attached to it.

Benevolence Funds

While benevolence funds are often considered for projects outside of the congregation, this can be a great resource for startup capital for new projects as well, particularly when it is a project that pushes the congregation outside of its walls. You might commit benevolence funds for a certain number of years to get the project off the ground or you might designate a specific fund for new projects.

Endowment Funds

Similarly, most congregational endowment funds were created with just this purpose in mind. Each year's draw was designed to go towards new missional projects in the congregation or the community that the church's regular budget could not cover. Many congregations are letting their annual draws languish or using them to fund the congregation's regular budget, which is outside of many endowment funds' intended purposes. This is a good time to revisit the endowment fund bylaws to see how this money was intended to be used and see if any new or current congregational projects might be a good fit.

Restricted Funds

If your congregation has been holding on to funds for a restricted purpose and that purpose no longer aligns with the church's mission, this is a great time to go back to the original donors to propose a new use for those funds. This generally works best when there is some alignment between the new project and original project. If you cannot reach the original donor, you may be able to go to your state's Attorney General's office to apply for a change in the donor restriction.

Individual Fundraising

Depending on the financial capital of your congregation's membership, it's possible you may have members who are particularly passionate about this project and have the financial means to get the project off the ground. This was the case with Church Anew, the social enterprise ministry of St. Andrew Lutheran Church in Eden Prairie, Minnesota, where a significant portion of their startup capital came from one anonymous donor. Before approaching a high-capacity donor, it's important to have a clear sense of the mission and vision for this project as well as how much money you will need and why. While your congregation may not have one wealthy member who can fund all of the startup capital, you may have a few families who can come together and pool their resources to make this project happen. This was the case for The Table UMC in Sacramento, California, where one family gave $100,000 and several other families committed $25,000 gifts. These gifts were key in making their kitchen renovation possible.

Special Offering

Depending on the amount of startup funds required, one or two special offerings from the congregation may be enough. As I mentioned, The Emory Fellowship's ministry to the unhoused was funded by a lay leader's request that everyone in their congregation contribute one day's worth of lunch money. If you decide to do a special offering, it's important that you are very clear about what the special offering is for and how much money needs to be raised. People may wonder why the money for this project isn't coming out of the regular budget, so you'll need to be prepared to answer that question.

Capital Campaign

Many of the congregations we talked to used capital campaigns to get their more major projects off the ground. A capital campaign is a fundraising campaign focused on a specific project or goal, often seeking significant gifts over the course of a multi-year period. While some people will give to a capital campaign out of their regular income, usually capital campaigns will seek gifts from invested assets. Capital campaigns can be a great tool to help the congregation get to know the project and allow them to get in on the ground floor before other funding comes in. The Emory Fellowship raised $1.4 million dollars to build the Beacon Center through a capital campaign. This campaign happened early on in the project, so it made the congregation feel like they were a part of it and had something at stake. Many people made significant personal pledges. These financial gifts early on and the consistent communication throughout the eleven-year process to make the project happen made the congregation members feel "vested in it."

Self-Sustaining Ministries

I was surprised to see that nearly 50 percent of the surveyed congregations currently had at least one individual ministry that was self-sustaining, and an additional 20 percent who did not have one now hoped to in the future. These congregations were more likely to be urban and medium- or large-size congregations. They were also more likely to have sold (or considered selling) church property, sold (or considered selling) products or services, or started (or considered starting) a social enterprise. Surprisingly, three-quarters of these self-sustaining ministries became self-sustaining in under ten years and nearly half in less than four years. While just over half of the surveyed congregations with self-sustaining ministries set the intention for the ministry to be self-sustaining early on (55 percent), others set it shortly after it began (18 percent), later in the program's life (16 percent), and for others this was never their intention (11 percent). As you might expect, the sooner the intention was set, the sooner the ministry became self-sustaining.

We asked what tools they used to help these ministries become self-sustaining. I've bolded the items from the list above that relate to outside funding and italicized the inside ones. Note the percentages do not add up to 100 percent because many congregations used more than one funding source:

- **Community partnerships (70%)**
- Clarifying the program's mission (66%)
- **Fundraising outside the congregation (66%)**
- **Grants from outside of the church judicatory [regional church body] or denominational bodies (58%)**
- *Fundraising inside the congregation (51%)*
- **Grants from church judicatory [regional church body] or denominational bodies (38%)**
- *Repurposing property (37%)*
- *Selling products or services (29%)*

- Rethinking program staffing (26%)
- *Social enterprise (25%)*
- *Seed funding from the congregation (22%)*
- **Corporate sponsorships (18%)**
- **Crowdfunding (15%)**

You can clearly see the interplay between inside and outside fundraising in making these ministries self-sustaining. Self-sustaining ministry does not happen in a silo! It often takes both inside and outside funding to get these projects off the ground.

Outside Funding

Outside funding needs to be a win not only for the congregation but for the funder as well; mission alignment and partnership matter. You have to be very clear, even clearer than with inside funding, about why this project matters to you both. This may mean that you have to share the church's mission in a different language or that you may focus on one small area where there is alignment. It's imperative that the "why" is clear and compelling for both parties. While many churches assume that their outside funding efforts fail because "secular institutions don't give to churches" or "the community won't support a church project even if they will benefit from it," this often isn't the real reason for the failure. The failure is rooted in not doing the necessary front-end work to tell a clear and compelling story in a way that sparks the curiosity and generosity of those outside the congregation. In this section, I'll explore different options for outside funding, paying close attention to when they are most helpful and what amount of work is required.

Grants

Far and away, grants are the outside funding source I get asked about the most. As one regional church body leader recently described it to me, grants are often seen as a "pot of gold" that can make sustainability possible again. While grants can be incredibly helpful in getting projects off the ground, they are not free money, they can be very time-consuming, and they are often designed with specific projects in mind.

Depending on the project, grants can be a great source of startup funding and in some very specific cases may provide longer-term funding for a project. Often congregations assume that there are no grant opportunities that will be open to them because of their faith-based status. However, there are many funders that are open to working with faith-based organizations if they have a project that aligns with the funder's goals. Many of the congregations we connected with during the interview process received grants from their regional church bodies or denominations—these grants, while smaller, are often easier to access. I have often heard of congregations receiving grants from other local organizations or foundations and occasionally from larger, national foundations.

Some of the congregations in the interview process, particularly those with affordable housing projects, received funding from the city and other governmental bodies. Depending on the grant, a congregation may need to start a separate nonprofit to gain access to these funds. However, it's important to do your research and make sure that your congregation actually needs this status to receive these funds and that this organizational structure makes sense for your congregation and your specific project.

In the survey we asked specifically about grants the congregation received from outside of denominational or regional church bodies so that we could get a sense of how many congregations were getting grants from these sources. Those are the types of grants we'll be talking about in this section. Looking at the survey data, grants were the second most common income source used by the surveyed congregations. Over half of the congregations in the survey had utilized (or were considering utilizing) this income source. Congregations of any size utilized grants. However, the most popular demographic for those using grants tended to be newer (0–59 years old), urban congregations. Interestingly, most congregations had received grants in the last ten years, so this is a relatively new income source compared to others on the survey. This is also a good reminder that if your congregation has searched for grant funds in the past and hasn't had any luck, it may be a good time to check again. Generally, grant funds met or surpassed the congregation's financial goal (69 percent). Grant funds were also helpful in creating relationships with people outside the church (67 percent) whether with the funders or beneficiaries of the project.

Often congregations ask me how to solicit grant funding. I've put together a small grant funding guide in Appendix F based on an interview with fundraising expert Kristal Frazier, who has coached and trained thousands across North America, Europe, and Africa to collectively raise $200 million from funders and individual donors over the past decade. Most importantly for this conversation, she has been on every side of the "grants table." She has not only been a grant writer, but she has also been a grant evaluator for federal grant programs.

Crowdfunding

Crowdfunding can be an exceptional fundraising tool if the project might be of interest to an audience outside of the congregation's traditional fundraising base. Crowdfunding is a type of fundraising, generally done through an online platform (like Kickstarter or GoFundMe), that solicits micro gifts for macro impact. Like grants, it's important to tell a compelling story that can reach outside the walls of the congregation to a new audience. Most often the external backers of a crowdfunding project might come from a congregation's local community, other community partners, or people who might be impacted by the project. While there are certainly crowdfunding projects that go viral and reach people around the world, those projects are few and far between. It's important to have a clear sense of the external audience for your crowdfunding campaign so you can tailor the project description and any rewards to fit their interests. Having a crowdfunding campaign on a public platform doesn't necessarily mean that people will find and support your project; you have to specifically direct people to it and invite them to share the project in their networks as well.

In the survey, we asked if the congregations had used a crowdfunding campaign to solicit donations. Only 21 percent had done so. Of those who had, most said that it met or surpassed their financial goal (62 percent). For 90 percent of those who had used a crowdfunding campaign, it led to new donor relationships. And, over half said the crowdfunding campaign helped to create relationships outside of the congregation. As one congregation shared, "We've used crowdfunding for specific programs: literary program, food pantry, community garden.

Crowdfunding helped us launch or expand these ministries and getting the word out was part of the strategy. We have retained donors who still contribute regularly to these programs." Crowdfunding is a great opportunity to bridge the gap between congregational fundraising and broadening the congregation's donor base as both those in the congregation and those outside of it may appreciate the opportunity to donate to the campaign.

Considering starting a crowdfunding campaign? I recommend looking at Adam Copeland's guidebook "Crowdfunding for Congregations and Faith-Related Nonprofits."[3] Copeland walks through the various types of campaigns, shares examples of faith-based crowdfunding campaigns, and outlines the ingredients to a successful campaign. While the guidebook is a bit dated, the material can help your congregation get a successful start and avoid common pitfalls.

Partnerships

Throughout the interviews, we saw countless examples of raising money from and with partners. Sometimes the congregation asked directly for these funds and other times these funds were simply offered by nature of the relationships. One of the key outside fundraising partners was other congregations. As the Rev. Katie Hays was getting Galileo Christian Church in Fort Worth, Texas, off the ground she went to individual congregations in her denomination, the Disciples of Christ, and asked them for donations. She summarized the message she shared during her interview, "Your kids and grandkids are not in church. . . . What if there were a church around here that was for them? . . . What if you could think of this as kind of a missional outpost . . . here reaching the people that your church doesn't?" This request garnered congregational sponsors as well as individual donations; some donors have continued funding the congregation even a decade later. Church Anew received $12,000 from another congregation's endowment fund as seed funding for one of their events when it was first offered. The success of both the Peace Community Center in Tacoma, Washington, and their current affordable housing initiative is due in large part to the network of relationships that Peace Lutheran Church has created with other congregations. These relationships often started with local congregations coming to help serve meals at Peace Lutheran Church. This service eventually led to generous financial support of the community center, and now to bringing time, labor, donations, and expertise to their affordable housing project. Similarly, the rich partnership between River Heights Vineyard Church and La Viña Inver not only involves an exchange of funds, but it has also brought so much more through shared services, shared staff, shared resources, and an expansive cultural perspective.

Looking beyond congregational partnerships, many of the interviewees mentioned nonprofits and local government officials helped them to get their projects off the ground, grow them, and/or sustain them over the long term. Sometimes these partners brought their own funding, but most often they opened up doors to new partnerships by helping the congregations connect with grants or other funding sources they would not have been aware of or had access to on their own.

Too often congregations assume that outside partners will not be interested in supporting their causes. They wonder if these partners might be willing to sponsor a church, when in reality they are helping to support a specific project that may be aligned with their own interests as well. It's important to offer an avenue where these partners can give a designated gift to support this specific project.

Impact Investing

Impact investing is one of the newest and most underutilized resources. This is often the case because people don't quite understand what impact investing is. According to the Global Impact Investing Network (GIIN), impact investments "are investments made with the intention to generate positive, measurable social and environmental impact alongside a financial return."[4] This is a form of investment, not charity, so there is an expectation that the original investment will return to the investor and that there will be a financial return as well. What separates impact investing from other, more traditional forms of investing, is that financial return is not the only measurement of success. For impact investors, the social impact of that investment is just as important, if not more important, than the financial return.

Often the amount that congregations give away each year is only a fraction of what's available in their endowment fund or savings account. *What if it was possible to magnify the support of causes your congregation cares about by investing some of the congregation's endowment/savings in a different way?* The good news is that it doesn't have to be an "all or nothing" proposal. A congregation might begin by investing just a portion of their assets in this way and growing that amount over time, if they choose.

Mark Elsdon utilized impact investing as he was getting the student apartments at his campus ministry, Pres House, off the ground. In addition to grants and traditional loans, he sought out an impact investment of $2.5 million from his regional church body (Synod of Lakes and Prairies PCUSA). This allowed Pres House to access funding with more lenient terms than what they had received from a traditional bank loan, and it was a win for the synod because they could tell an amazing story about the ways their endowment principal was providing a welcoming and supportive community on the University of Wisconsin-Madison campus.

In so many communities, there are congregations that are rich in assets but struggle to know what God is calling them to do, and congregations who are struggling financially but have a clear sense of what God is calling them to do. Bringing these assets together for the purpose of investment, not just donations, could make an exceptional difference and release large amounts of capital to make many of the projects we discussed in these chapters possible.

If you found ideas in this chapter to fund your church's ministry, absolutely pursue these. This can be a great first step that can free up assets for a larger process. This single technical change can make way for a larger adaptive change. However, this is also a great opportunity to dream bigger and cross chasms to connect with partners you never might have considered before.

♦ Practice: Mapping Your Congregation's Network ♦

Since partnerships are such a primary part of the funding work, take some time to map your congregation's network of partners. I encourage you to create a visual map, so you know how your congregation is connected to those different partners (through members, through community connections, through other partners, etc.). While you can certainly put individuals on the map, most of the partners on the list will likely be other organizations, businesses, community groups, or congregations. Here are some questions to get you started:

1. Who are some of your congregation's current partners? This might include partners who have supported the congregation, used congregational space, partnered on projects, received support from the congregation, and others.
2. Who has your congregation partnered with in the past? Going back in history a bit, these don't have to be recent connections.
3. What potential partners are present in your congregation's neighborhood that someone in the congregation has a connection with who might be interested in joining in what God is calling you to do?
4. What potential partners are present outside of your congregation's neighborhood that someone in the congregation has a connection with who might be interested in joining in what God is calling you to do?

You can start by doing this activity with your Funding Forward group or church leadership team, but I encourage you to expand the circle wider to include others in your congregation. For instance, you could send out a survey, invite people in the congregation to fill out a card during worship to put in the offering basket, or write their responses on sticky notes to put up on the walls of the narthex as they enter/exit worship. Invite the congregation to respond to these questions:

1. What organizations, businesses, community groups, and/or other congregations in our neighborhood are you connected with that might be interested in joining us in this work?
2. What organizations, businesses, community groups, and/or other congregations outside our neighborhood are you connected with that might be interested in joining us in this work?

Have people put their name along with the potential partner's name so you know who to tap if you decide to explore the partnership. Put that connection on your network map. This web of partnerships should help you see that you're not alone in this work and you already have connections in place to lean on. No need to make any cold calls!

Reflection Questions

- Which funding source(s) from this chapter is your congregation already using?
- Which funding source(s) from this chapter has your congregation used in the past? Why did you stop using it/them?
- Which funding source(s) from this chapter might be a fit for the ministry your congregation is already doing?
- Which funding source(s) from this chapter might be a good fit for the work God is calling you to do?
- What next step might you take to tap these new funding sources?

CHAPTER TEN

How Can We Shift Our Congregation's Financial Model?

Luke 19:1–10

"He entered Jericho and was passing through it. A man was there named Zacchaeus; he was a chief tax-collector and was rich. He was trying to see who Jesus was, but on account of the crowd he could not, because he was short in stature. So he ran ahead and climbed a sycamore tree to see him, because he was going to pass that way. When Jesus came to the place, he looked up and said to him, 'Zacchaeus, hurry and come down; for I must stay at your house today.' So he hurried down and was happy to welcome him. All who saw it began to grumble and said, 'He has gone to be the guest of one who is a sinner.' Zacchaeus stood there and said to the Lord, 'Look, half of my possessions, Lord, I will give to the poor; and if I have defrauded anyone of anything, I will pay back four times as much.' Then Jesus said to him, 'Today salvation has come to this house, because he too is a son of Abraham. For the Son of Man came to seek out and to save the lost.'"

Dwelling Questions

1. What word or phrase jumped out at you as you read the passage?
2. What stands out to you about the way Jesus approaches Zacchaeus? What stands out to you about Zaccheaus's response?

3. What's one way God is inviting your congregation into new life? How might your congregation respond?
4. What might God's Spirit be saying to you or your congregation through the passage?

Prayer

God of spirit and truth. Thank you for meeting us where we are and inviting us into new life with you. Accompany us as we take faithful risks to follow your call. Give us grace when we fail and strength to try again. Amen.

In the early 2000s, St. Andrew Lutheran Church in Eden Prairie, Minnesota, purchased a struggling, neighboring congregation and made it into a satellite site: St. Andrew West. They maintained the site for about eight years before letting it go. As one lay leader explained, "I think we failed [and] we're stronger for it. We know we can fail and stay together as a congregation. And we know that we, along the way, helped some people." This was a hard experience for all involved, particularly those who were a part of the satellite site. And yet, I was curious to see the ways that this failure and the lessons they learned through the experience set the congregation up for success as they approached other new ventures like Church Anew. This failure made them more cognizant of possible pitfalls and created space for something new to emerge. Instead of causing the congregation to be more cautious about change, this failure and others from other congregations in the research project seemed to build the congregations' resilience and open them up even further to try new things.

What failures from your congregation's past might you recognize, learn from, and even celebrate as you walk into this new future?

Recently, I heard Michael Beck share his "failure fest" practice on the Pivot Podcast:

> We have a commitment that if anybody names a failure, we will stop the meeting and we will stand up and . . . we will clap and celebrate that. Because . . . if we're not failing, we're not really trying. And are we learning from our failures? . . . When you get stuck in imaginative gridlock, you just keep doing the same stuff, trying harder that it just

> keeps feeling more and more pressure and nothing's working. And what teams really have to do in that is play and experiment and get out of that gridlock . . . you fail your way out of it.[1]

What would it look like for your congregation to not only learn from but celebrate your failures? How might honoring our failures encourage more faithful risk-taking and maintain our openness to change? We clam up after failure because of fear, and yet, Beck reminds us that even failure can be an act of faith.

As my team in the Stewardship Leaders Program and I worked with the nine learning community congregations in 2021, I noticed something interesting. They were quick to understand "why" they needed to pursue alternative options outside of the offering plate, eager to determine "what" they might be called to do, but often got stalled on the "how". How would they bring this work back to their congregation? How would they get them on board with these ideas? How would they recover if the idea failed? It was these questions that drove us to lean in and learn more about the practices the congregations in the research project used as they engaged the Funding Forward process to shift their financial model. The Funding Forward process isn't a small tweak; this is a large cultural shift. I hope these practices will help you move this process from ideation to transformation, bringing your whole congregation along for the ride.

Rocket Fuel

Of the forty or more practices identified in the interviews, there were six practices that came up consistently: partnerships/community relationships, pastoral leadership, lay leadership, focus on mission, generosity, and openness to change. These six practices appeared in the conversations with all twelve of the congregations, except for generosity, which only appeared in eleven of the twelve sites. When I put the data from how many times these individual practices appeared in the transcripts into the software I use to help me visualize the data, I was surprised to see that it formed a rocket ship. The more that I sat with this image in the figure, the more I liked it (see figure 3 on page 166). These six practices were the fuel that the congregations needed to get this process off the ground and to endure as they created cultural change.

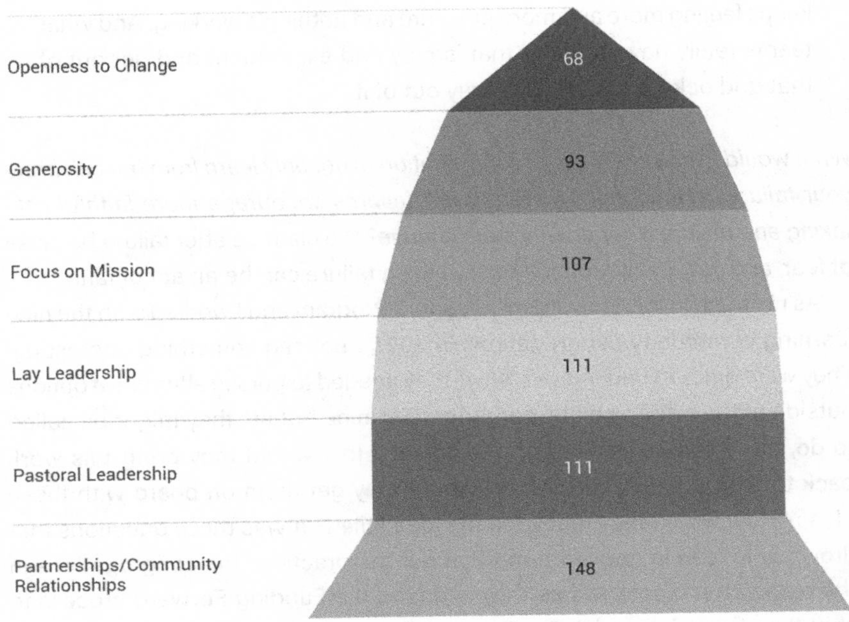

Figure 3. Top six practices that came up most consistently in the interviews.

Often, congregations assume that pastoral leadership is the singular driving force behind these changes. I remember the pastors in the learning community saying, "I don't know if I have the skills to do this work. I'm not sure how I'll be able to manage this on top of everything else on my plate." There seemed to be a perceived expectation that they would be the main driver of the work. While pastoral leadership was certainly a key element, it's just one part of the rocket ship. Partnerships and community relationships were the foundation for this work—no one was able to accomplish this alone. Similarly, lay and pastoral leadership came up the same number of times. Decisive and active lay leadership was essential to getting this process off the ground. While the pastors often had a role in the Funding Forward project(s), the most important role they played in the process was the identifying, empowering, and encouraging the lay leaders. The pastor functioned more as coach than solo artist. Dwight Zscheile, Michael Binder, and Tessa Pinkstaff found a similar trend in their faithful innovation work, writing,

> Most people do not like to do things they haven't done before. People get uncomfortable when they aren't sure what the end result is going to be. This is why it's vital to create an environment where people feel safe enough to try new things together. The leader must cheer people on as their capacity for this work increases. When people begin to try new things, they need to be celebrated and affirmed no matter how it turns out. That's why the role of the ministry leader is essential in this journey. In faithful innovation, the pastor serves as a coach—someone who helps the other participants find the courage to try things that put them outside of their comfort zones.[2]

In addition to partnerships and leadership, a single-minded focus on the congregation's mission, financial generosity, and openness to change made all of the difference in making this transformation possible. I had assumed, as I'll discuss more below, that keeping an eye both on the money and the mission would be key in this process, but it turned out that focus on mission was much more important. This often came out in two ways. First, the mission was the lifeblood of the congregation. Not only the pastors but the lay members of these congregations were able to immediately articulate, explain, and give examples of the church's mission. For instance, River Heights Vineyard Church and La Viña Inver's in Inver Grove Heights, Minnesota's mission to "love God, love people, and change the world" is something not only everyone in the church knows, but as Pastor Peter Benedict put it "Everyone in the church can articulate at least three ways that we're doing ministries that plug into that mission . . . the church mission is pretty central to why people come." Second, the mission was used as a litmus test when considering new ideas. For instance, Galileo Christian Church in Fort Worth, Texas has five missional priorities that guide all of their decision-making. If an idea doesn't fit under one of those five, it's a "no" from the church side to actively staff and support the work. However, they do invite the member to do this on their own.

Generosity from the congregation and other outside funders was key to making this work possible. It's more than just tithes and offerings. We were stunned by the stories of sacrificial generosity: The Emory Fellowship in Washington, DC raising over a million dollars to fund its building project,

Galileo Christian Church's landlord simply giving them the space to build Finn's Place, the anonymous donor who gave the startup funds for Church Anew, and many more. Generosity doesn't live outside of the Funding Forward process; it's an integral part of it. As we see in the story of Zaccheaus, God invites us and our congregations into generous, faithful risk-taking.

Finally, I was intrigued by the way that openness to change formed the point of entry for the rocket. It was the openness to change that allowed these congregations to soar and break into new atmospheres. Openness to change was a prerequisite (and often a litmus test) for doing this work. It's important to note that while some of the congregations we interviewed were radically open to change in all areas of their congregational life, some were open to change just in one area of their church's life. So, if your congregation is not generally open to change, you may be able to find a small opening. You might start with a smaller project and grow as you learn to trust the process and one another. The key to this practice is not as much "change" as "openness." There was enough trust in the system that the people in these congregations were willing to go on this journey together. They were prepared to have hard conversations, ask tough questions, and take the time to discern where God was calling them to go. Their openness to change didn't always mean the change process was easy—some of the congregations experienced conflict, and almost all experienced roadblocks along the way—however, their openness helped them to stay in the conversation and explore new ideas when things got tough.

Tools for the Journey

My research team and I gathered a robust list of over forty practices organized around these key themes: change, connection, focus, leadership, learning, spiritual practices, and support. I realize a list of this size can feel overwhelming. The goal is not for you to adopt all of the practices but instead to pick up a few to focus on throughout the change process. Like Jesus in the story of Zaccheaus, I hope to meet you where you are. There are likely some practices your congregation is already engaged in—great! *How might you dig deeper into those practices as you move through the Funding Forward process?* There are also some new practices that God might be inviting you to try. Consider one or two practices from each category that you might focus on—these are important tools to bring along on your Funding Forward journey. I'll explore each theme area individually and share the full list of the practices associated with that theme.

Spiritual practices

Spiritual Practices

(326 total mentions in the interviews, 20 total practices)

Generosity (93)

Discernment (47)

Identifying assets in the congregation (36)

Listening (36)

Naming God's action (31)

Prayer (22)

Faith (14)

Bible reading and study (13)

Hospitality (8)

Retreat (4)

Sabbatical (4)

Spiritual direction (4)

Meditation (3)

Wesleyan table practice (3)

Anti-racism (2)

Compassion (2)

Anointing (1)

Fasting (1)

Laying on of hands (1)

Money autobiography[3] (1)

While I had expected leadership to play a key role in making change happen, I was amazed at the integral role that spiritual practices played. Spiritual practices were mentioned over three hundred times across the interviews—more than any other theme. While each congregation had their own specific practices they leaned on, it was clear that these were the glue that held the congregation together throughout the process. While these practices were often initiated by the pastoral leadership, people at every level of the congregation took part in the practices and brought them outside of congregational gatherings and into their everyday lives.

A great example of this is the prayer practice I described earlier that The Emory Fellowship used as they were building the Beacon Center. It was so powerful, it's worth sharing again. As one of my research assistants described,

> The congregation prays regularly when making big decisions. As an example, they had a church wide '6:10' prayer time (their address is 6100 Georgia Ave in Washington DC.). Every church member was asked to pray daily for the affordable housing project, and to do so at 6:10am and 6:10pm. . . . When they had evening meetings, everyone's alarms would go off at 6:10, and people would stop, pray together, and then resume their meetings.

This practice helped to keep the congregation focused on and invested in the project, reminding them that this is a project that God was calling them to complete.

Another great example is The Table UMC in Sacramento, California's "Kitchen Tables." These are groups of six to eight people who meet weekly for ninety minutes to walk through John Wesley's key questions for spiritual formation: "How are you doing good? How are you not? And how are you staying in love with God?" This faith formation practice is the heartbeat of The Table UMC. It's a way in which they hold their lives in conversation with the gospel and reflect together on how they are loving God and neighbor in everyday life. As Pastor Matt Smith put it,

> Without the faith formation process of our Wesleyan tradition, without centering that or keeping that at the heart of how we're trying to do this, I don't think [Table Farm & Table Bread] would have happened because . . . all of these enterprises grow out of a living out of theological commitments and living into the messiness of what it means to love God and love neighbor. Not in theory but in a practical way . . . without that faith formation process coming to life . . . I think it wouldn't have happened.

I was particularly impressed by Common Ground Church in Lodi, Wisconsin's approach to cultivating lay leadership using spiritual practices. They encouraged their church leadership team to be not only church leaders but spiritual leaders. They started an early morning mid-week Bible study for the leadership team that any congregation member is welcome to join. They also engaged in spiritual direction and prayed together. It was clear that these practices helped them to be grounded in Scripture, the Spirit's direction, and offer each other mutual support as they discerned God's leading amid deep conflict.

I intentionally took a wide view of spiritual practices, including more traditional practices like Bible study, retreats, and prayer, in addition to less commonly recognized spiritual practices like asset-identification, listening, meditation, anti-racism training, and working through a money autobiography. Looking back through the list, the diversity of practices fills me with hope. There isn't just one spiritual practice that works for every congregation. Each had their own unique set of practices that kept them going through the process. What binds the practices together is the way in which they connect the congregation members to God and one another.

Leadership

I was astonished to see that pastoral and lay leadership came up the exact same number of times in the interviews. It was clear that both forms of leadership were required to make this process happen. I was intrigued by how little other staff, outside of the pastoral leader, were mentioned.[4] For churches that have them, staff may be an underutilized asset. They are often the "worker bees" behind the scenes that make these projects possible. *What might it look like to invite them to be more involved in the entire process, from discernment to execution? How might these staff members be ambassadors of the congregation's mission as they go about the business of making these ministries possible?*

Leadership
(254 total mentions in the interviews, 3 total practices)

Lay leadership (111)

Pastoral leadership (111)

Staff leadership (32)

Whether it's pastoral, lay, or staff leadership, people support what they help to create. As CEO and Serial Entrepreneur Ty Bennet put it, "if we want the commitment of our people at the point of implementation then we need to involve them at the point of creation."[5] This is countercultural for many congregations and yet it will be imperative for making this process possible.

As the Rev. Chrisy Ennen, Pastor of First Presbyterian Church of Gulf Shores in Gulf Shores, Alabama, shared during her interview,

> A pastor that I worked for [told me], "If I have a brick wall that needs to come down, I can get in my truck and I can drive through that brick wall, and then I can try to get people to follow me through it. But that doesn't mean they're going to follow." He said, "But by inviting them to help me take that brick wall down piece by piece, they're going to be in the bed of

> the truck when you drive through it." . . . You've got to build that collateral with people before you just say, "Hey, we're going to change things." And I didn't come in saying, "Oh, we're going to change everything." I came in saying, "Okay. There are some issues that we have here. How do we solve them?" And asking for help. And I think that made a whole lot of difference in people's willingness to be a part of change.

I went into the interview process wondering if pastoral tenure would be a huge factor in making this process possible. It takes time to build up trust and credibility to make these types of changes. However, I was amazed to see that a quarter of the pastors we spoke with, including the Rev. Chrisy Ennen, had been there for three years or just shy of it, and much of those years had been during the pandemic where they had limited opportunities to form relationships in person. So, even if you (or your pastor) are fairly new to a congregation, there is still a possibility to create change as long as the other key elements of the "rocket" are in place.

Support

It's not just about the leaders; support from people inside and outside of the congregation is required to make this process possible. External partnerships are the foundation that makes this shift possible. These partners might be other nonprofits, city officials, other congregations, and/or neighbors in the community, and they might offer financial support, verbal support, expertise, experience, or connections to other partners/resources. One key partner for many of the congregations was their regional church body and/or denomination. They offered financial support, grants, and staff support.

> **Support**
> (224 total mentions in the interviews, 3 total practices)
>
> Partnership/community relationships (148)
> Congregational support (56)
> Judicatory/denominational support (17)

Congregational support was a key component, coming in as the seventh most mentioned practice. During the lay interviews, we heard a theme of joint ownership; these were projects of the whole congregation, not just one particular leader. It can feel tempting to want to create these changes on your own or with a very small team without bringing the broader congregation along. However, we consistently heard that it was worth it to invest the time and effort to reach a consensus. It didn't happen immediately, but it was a process they entered into over time.

I appreciate Zscheile, Binder, and Pinkstaff's reminder:

> Many people think they must get one hundred percent of people—everyone—to accept an innovation in order for it to be adopted into their congregation. This isn't true. Studies on leading change in organizations suggest that if just twenty percent of a group begins to adopt a new way of doing things, that innovation has a good chance of being accepted by the whole group over time. This means that if an innovation can gain early support among just a few people, it has a good chance of becoming part of the life of the congregation over the long term. Sharing stories about the listening work [practices and experiments] is one way to help people join the work and adopt an innovation in a congregation. Stories help people who are more resistant to change see the tangible impact these new ways of doing things are having on people like them in the congregation.[6]

Often people don't support change because they don't fully understand who it benefits or why it matters. Stories can convey this message in a way that facts never will. If you believe that many people in your congregation might be opposed to making this shift, start small. *Maybe you begin by listening together to the needs of your neighbors or discerning your mission?* Once there is a shared understanding of community needs and God's mission for your congregation, it might be easier to take these other steps forward.

Change

My research team and I anticipated change would be a key challenge for many congregations, so we asked about it specifically in the interviews in order to break down which aspects of change were most important in making this process work. One of the key practices that emerged was the "courage to take risks." Bold, faithful risk-taking seemed to be an important piece of the puzzle. *Don't we all wish that change could come without risk?* But change takes bravery, stepping into the unknown, a place most of our congregations don't

Change
(177 total mentions in the interviews, 7 total practices)

Openness to change (68)
Courage to take risks (34)
Exploring options (29)
Approaching the shift like an experiment (18)
Letting go (11)
Endurance (10)
Timing (7)

like to go and yet, this is a very biblical place to be. This courage and faithful risk-taking is necessary to follow God's call and shape the church of the future. As one lay participant from St. Andrew Lutheran Church, put it, "It takes [bravery] to embrace innovation, recognizing that that is going to come with some gains and some losses and believing that, in the end, it helps us frame a living, breathing church that serves multiple generations."

COVID, in many of the congregations we talked to, was a catalyst for change. It was a time where the congregation was already in the midst of so much upheaval that they were often open to additional changes and more ready to take up the posture of faithful risk-taking. *Might there be a season or event in your congregation's life (like an anniversary, staffing transition, etc.) where your congregation might be more open to change?*

These congregations also recognized a need to explore a variety of options in the decision-making process and approach the shift like an experiment, so they had the freedom to make small changes as they went. We also heard a need to prune and let go of what is no longer serving the congregation. Sometimes this letting go was about specific buildings, programs, or partners, but it was also about closely held ideas about mission and ministry. This release created space for new life to flourish.

Similarly, timing was a key factor. Sometimes this meant jumping in when an opportunity presented itself and other times this meant pivoting direction to a different project when the timing wasn't right for the original project they had in mind. Like explorers, these congregations constantly had their compass out to discern that they were headed in the right direction. Discernment is not a "one and done" practice. For many of these congregations, change did not happen overnight. They needed endurance to stay in the change process when things got tough.

Focus

Focus

(138 total mentions in the interviews, 2 total practices)

Focus on mission (107)

Focus on financial sustainability (31)

Going into the interviews, I had assumed that focus on financial sustainability and focus on mission would be of equal importance. However, it became clear that focus on mission was the primary practice that sustained the congregation. While focus on financial sustainability was certainly a key piece in making the individual projects successful, it played much less of a role in making the congregation's shift to a new model possible. This is good news! While the whole congregation should care about the mission, only some in the congregation need to be focused on the congregation's financial sustainability. That is an important task that a small group can tend to. However, in thinking about the makeup of the congregation's lay leadership, a mix of both can be really helpful. As the Rev. Nicholas Zook, Pastor of Concordia Lutheran Church in Chicago, Illinois, shared, "To have the money person and the visionary sitting next to each other at a table is the only way a project like this works. Because you have to be smart about the money part of it because it's real. But you also have to be willing to take the risk and dream, too. So a great combination of people to have altogether."

Connection

Connection

(89 total mentions in the interviews, 4 total practices)

Clear communication (38)

Trust (27)

Transparency (17)

Sharing food and eating together (7)

It was important to the ministry leaders (both lay and clergy) to bring the entire congregation along. This required helping them stay connected during the change. One of the key ways they did this was through clear, consistent communication.

As a lay leader from Clarendon Presbyterian Church in Arlington, Virginia, explained,

> I think the most important thing . . . is communication, getting the buy-in [throughout], and really making sure people understand why you're doing it, what's at stake . . . And for us to approve spending $1.2 million on a piece of property, that's a huge decision. But we had all these professionals in the room explaining, "Okay, here's how this works. Here's what this means." And everybody's questions got answered . . . [we were] as transparent as we could be.

But the communication did not just start and stop at the project approval phase, it continued into implementation and beyond. Regular updates from the ministry leaders (about both successes and struggles) were a key part of the work. Similarly, as I look at the stories of Concordia Lutheran Church and Peace Lutheran Church in Tacoma, Washington, the two congregations with the longest-running nonprofit ministries in the interview dataset, this communication needs to continue even after the project is up and running. It can be challenging to keep mission alignment between a church and a separate nonprofit entity. It requires regular updates and interactions between the two entities, as well as participation and leadership from the congregation in the nonprofit.

Learning
(64 total mentions in the interviews, 5 total practices)

From failure (22)

From books/articles (16)

From other congregations/organizations (11)

Innovation accelerator (8)

From past success (7)

Learning

Paired with the posture of openness to change, there was also a posture of learning. Congregations learned from books, articles, other congregations, partner organizations, innovation accelerators, and even their own past successes. But the most prominent fodder for learning was their own past failures.

Will Every Ministry Be Able to Shift Its Financial Model by Completing the Funding Forward Process?

No, they won't. Change is difficult. The projects that we have talked about in this book take all of the assets God has entrusted to your congregation's care, and sometimes there just isn't enough energy in the congregation to make the shift happen. As I was working on the second half of this book, I heard that Tree of Life had made the difficult decision to close. My heart broke that no one else would be able to experience the genuine love and life that this congregation had offered those who had been burned by church. At the same time, I was not surprised by this news.

Before I left Minneapolis, I decided to put together a sustainability plan for Tree of Life. I presented them with a variety of paths forward: including cultivating lay leadership, shifting their staffing model, soliciting outside funding, and leaning into social enterprise. Given my interest in Funding Forward, it felt like the best "goodbye" present I could leave them with, particularly since their founding pastor was leaving right around the same time I left. That being said, after COVID cut Tree of Life's membership in half and a season of pastoral transition, there just wasn't enough energy left in the congregation to explore these options. While "openness to change" was baked into Tree of Life's DNA from the very beginning, they lacked the other five factors in the rocket ship to get change off the ground. Ultimately, Tree of Life's roots were not strong enough to make the changes needed to thrive in the next season of its ministry.

The good news is that death does not have the final word for Tree of Life. Even as I write this chapter one week after its closing worship service, small seeds are beginning to sprout. Since Tree of Life decided to close when it still had money in the bank, it was able to cover the candidacy fees of two new seminarians from the congregation, and they are in conversations with their regional church body (Minneapolis Area Synod) about using the funds the synod had budgeted for Tree of Life as seed money to start a new ministry. For more than a third of the congregations my research team and I interviewed, it was the decline and/or closure of another congregation that paved the way for their ministry to find new life. There was a distinct pattern of death and resurrection. Letting go laid the foundation for the work God was inviting them to join, even if they weren't the ones to carry that mission forward.

♦ Practice: Celebrating Failure ♦

One of the most difficult shifts for congregations is changing the way they view failure. If we are afraid of failure, we will never give ourselves permission to experiment and try new things. We will want to perfect an idea to death before it is rolled out. But no matter how much talking we do, failure is inevitable and the process is too urgent to wait. It is only when we step out onto the edge and take courage in God's strength that we will find the places God is calling us to go.

Begin the process of celebrating failure together and learning from it. Consider: What are some ways your congregation has failed throughout its history? If you don't have a congregational example, use a personal example. Then go around the room sharing your failures. After each failure is shared, clap, cheer, and give it a standing ovation. I realize this may feel awkward, but this practice will help you to "act your way into a new way of thinking." After the celebration, ask: What did you learn from the experience and what did/will you try next? The worst outcome is to let the failure leave you mired in guilt and shame rather than letting it propel you forward into a new, better idea.

Reflection Questions

- Which of these practices is your congregation already using today?
- How open is your congregation to change? What types of change might they be open to?
- Looking at the rocket ship, which of the practices are strong for your congregation and which might be growth areas?
- What spiritual practices might your congregation use to sustain it through the change process? These might be practices from your congregation's history or current tradition; they might also be new practices you'd like to try.

Afterword

From Sustainable to Sustained

When my seminary students first started doing case studies with congregations who were experimenting with Funding Forward, I invited them to ask, "Is the ministry currently sustainable? What vision of sustainability is this ministry striving toward?" The most common response my students seemed to receive to this question was laughter. Next to no congregation they talked to thought that their ministry was sustainable. The word "sustainable" seemed to conjure up an image of a ministry that would stay in its current form forever, standing the test of time. This was not the end goal for the ministries we talked to. They knew that each season of ministry would bring its own challenges as their communities change and God invited them to take new risks to follow God's mission.

While sustainability may be a helpful word to describe the financial side of this process, it presents an incomplete picture of this work. I wonder if the move we need to make is from "sustainable" to "sustained." We are not looking to shore up a congregation's finances so that it can remain the same forever. Instead, we hope to be a community that is sustained by God's Spirit, leaning into God's leading, and using the resources God has entrusted to our care to the best of our ability. This doesn't mean that we forget the finances. Good stewardship is a key part of this process, but God's leading is even more important. We can find sustainability by focusing just on the finances, but we will never be sustained.

Throughout the process of writing and research, I have experienced this shift in myself as well. As a financial educator, I was curious about the financial elements that would make this process work. I was eager to see models that worked on paper and in practice, and I'm pleased to say we found them. But there was so much more to this story. At every turn, I was reminded that God is the primary agent of this process, not us. It is God's resources, God's direction, and God's work that sustains this process. I was slapped in the face by this realization as I looked through the survey and saw that the richest data was from one of the last questions about where they had seen God at work in the process. I was reminded of this again when "spiritual practices" emerged as the primary theme among the practices. God makes this work happen, not us. It is by focusing more on God and less on the numbers that the shift is possible.

It wouldn't be overstating to say that this research was a spiritual awakening for me. This research not only changed the way I see finances in the church but expanded and deepened my personal relationship with God. I realized as I sat in meetings at the seminary where people were bemoaning the decline of the church and grieving all that we had lost, that I no longer felt this way. I had spent a season bearing witness to a different story. God is alive, active, and on the move in the church today. Yes, there are churches that are declining, but there are many who are thriving as they live into God's mission. I felt called to share this message of hope with my colleagues.

Similarly, in my personal life, I felt drawn to dig into my spiritual practices of morning prayer, Bible reading, Prayer of Examen, and weekly worship more than I ever had before. I felt compelled to ask God for guidance and direction as I wrote this book. I approached God with confidence that my prayers would be heard and answered, but also that God might speak through me. I was stretched in my theological thinking as I heard stories that went outside of my own experiences of God. I was moving from a season of searching to a season of being sustained by God's Spirit.

For those of you who are mired in grief over what the church was, and fear of what God has in store for the future, I hope that this book leaves you with glimmers of hope. God has not left us. God is present with us in our grief and shaping us for a new future. It is in leaning into God's direction, not away, that we can find our way forward. This does not mean that churches will not close, or that budgets will not be in the red. For more than a third of the congregations we talked to it was the decline and/or closure of another congregation that paved the way for their ministry to find new life. There was a distinct pattern of death and resurrection.

As a financial educator, I have often struggled when students responded to important financial questions with the pat answer of "God will provide." As if God would magically meet all their needs if they just waited long enough. I heard this answer so often that I became jaded, sometimes focusing so much on our need to provide for ourselves that I left God out of the equation.

As I have walked through the research, I have been continually reminded of the tagline that first led me to the Evangelical Lutheran Church in America (ELCA): "God's work. Our hands." It is God's work, not ours, and we have the privilege of being the agents of God's work in the world. God does provide in abundance, and we have a key role in being stewards of that abundance and directing that abundance to where it is needed most.

This research has helped me to trust that God is at work, even when we cannot see it. It has reminded me that the arc of God's mission is long. This process took months, years, and sometimes even decades for the congregations we interviewed. Sometimes our own impatience can lead us to lean on our own understanding rather than trusting God's work and waiting on the Spirit's direction. May we have the patience to wait on God's guidance and the courage to act when new and often unexpected opportunities arise.

I end this book with a blessing that I wrote for my students. It is based on a blessing first spoken by Bishop Woodie White at the 1996 General Conference:

> And now, may the Spirit awaken you with dreams of God's kingdom on earth.
>
> May Christ keep ever before you: your congregation's wealth, your community's needs, and the mission that binds them together.
>
> May God grant you the humility to ask for help when you need it and the discernment to choose good partners.
>
> May the Spirit breathe new life into you as you encounter scarcity thinking, reminiscences of the church's "good old days," differences of opinion on what church leaders "should" be doing, and desires to keep the church safe and comfortable for those inside it ignoring those who need it most.
>
> May Christ afflict you with a burning thirst for justice and the strength to advocate for it in your corner of God's world.
>
> May God equip you with affirmation of your call, courage to speak truth, and compassion for all of God's creation as you seek to: make your church more sustainable, deepen your engagement in the community, and follow the Spirit to the places where God is already present making all things new.

Acknowledgments

It feels a bit cliché to say it took a village to write this book, but it's true. Like the congregations in this book, I could never have done this work alone, nor would I have wanted to. The stories from my research project are the heartbeat of this book. I am eternally grateful to the twelve congregations who shared their stories in the interview process and the 101 congregations who completed the survey. I have learned so much from all of you, and I'm so appreciative of the time you gave to this process.

This work would never have been possible without my exceptional research team. Deb Coe trained me on how to do qualitative and quantitative research, got the survey up and running, and was available for any question that came up along the way. You were an invaluable resource to the research process, and your support of this work kept me going on the days when the process felt too arduous. Peter Benedict, Melissa Pickering, and Jaz Waring served as research assistants offering suggestions of congregations to participate in the survey, reviewing the survey questions and data, shaping the interview questions and process, conducting many of the interviews, and assisting in the interview coding. Your honest feedback, insightful analysis, and eagerness to learn and care for the congregations doing this work made this research possible on such a short timeline. Melissa Pickering and Lexy Steinle assisted me in culling the list of suggested congregations for the survey: a monumental task. I'm so grateful for the curiosity you brought to each of these congregations' stories and your hard work in helping me reach the goal of two hundred congregations for the survey invite list. Throughout the research process, I reached out to hundreds of people for suggestions of congregations to include. Thank you to everyone who took the time to offer suggestions. This research was funded and supported by the Villanova Center for Church Management, the Lilly Endowment's National Initiative to Address Economic Challenges

Facing Pastoral Leaders, and Luther Seminary's generous donors. I'm so grateful for your investment in this work.

To my students, past and present, who have journeyed with me since the idea of Funding Forward was just an inkling on the horizon. Your stories, questions, and comments have shaped, grounded, and fueled this work in ways I could never have imagined. It is a privilege to teach you and to learn alongside you. I continue to believe that I learn much more from you than you could ever learn from me.

This work stands on a foundation that was laid by so many others. To Adam Copeland, thank you for planting the seed of this work during your time at Luther Seminary. It has been my pleasure to tend to this seedling and watch it grow. To Mark DeYmaz and Harry Li, thank you for inviting us to think about church funding in new ways. Your work has transformed the way I approach this topic. To Mark Elsdon and Rooted Good, your work, writing, and interactive resources have helped bring this work to life in creative ways. Thank you for accompanying me and so many congregations through this process. To the nine congregations who participated in our learning community, I'm so grateful for your willingness to journey with us. Your questions, comments, and stories have had a profound impact on my research and writing.

I have been blessed by the support of so many people who encouraged me to write this book and held my hand (metaphorically and physically) through the writing process. I am especially grateful to Dwight Zscheile who invited me to write this book, to Arlene Flancher who has been my partner every step of the way as we developed the Funding Forward process, engaged in the research, and began to tell the story of our learnings, to Catherine Malotky who served as the Funding Forward coach for our learning community congregations, to Mary Lindberg whose expertise and encouragement got me through the toughest moments of the writing process, to Chick Lane who has served as sounding board, mentor, and friend, to Jessi LeClear Vachta and Michelle Boss whose support has buoyed me throughout the writing process, and finally to all of my colleagues on the Faith+Lead team who helped to sharpen the ideas in this book and supported me throughout the research and writing process. Thanks also to Dawn Alitz, Jon Anderson, Thad Austin, Peter Benedict, Tim Brown, David Cleaver-Bartholomew, Chick Lane, Tim Larson, Mary Lindberg, Meggan Manlove, Dee Marinnie, Melissa Pickering, Kathryn Pomroy, Barb Portouw, Lexy Steinle, Jaz Waring, Jennifer Wojciechowski, and Dwight Zscheile who reviewed my draft manuscript and shared their honest feedback and support.

Finally, my deepest gratitude to my partner, Tyler Pomroy. It is one thing to support your spouse's dream; it's another thing to shoulder additional responsibilities to create space to make that dream a reality. You alone know the anxiety, tears, frustration, and passion that went into completing this research and writing this book. I can't imagine a better partner to walk with me through all of life's twists and turns. Thanks for always having bigger dreams for me than I have for myself.

Faith+Lead Resources for the Journey

Ready to dive deeper?

Funding Forward is a key resource from Faith+Lead's Stewardship Leaders Program at Luther Seminary, which empowers ministry leaders to foster generous, innovative, and sustainable faith communities.

Explore more at
faithlead.org/stewardship

About Faith+Lead

Faith+Lead is an ecosystem of theological resources and training designed to equip Christian disciples and leaders to follow God into a faithful future. Our platform offers courses, coaching, learning communities, and digital tools that align with trusted theological insights, helping individuals deepen their relationship with Jesus and discover their divine purpose. Embracing diverse Christian traditions, we unite clergy, lay leaders, and ministry innovators, facilitating transformative experiences that resonate with Jesus's teachings.

At Faith+Lead, we are committed to experiential, transformational learning. Genuine transformation happens in community, often with coaching, and over time. We want to help people move beyond simply gaining more knowledge and help them transform into people who love and lead in the way of Jesus.

Learn more at
faithlead.org

More Online Resources from Faith+Lead

Dive into Luther Seminary's Faith+Lead—a digital hub of resources tailored for spiritual learners and leaders just like you. Our diverse ecosystem offers on-demand and live-learning courses, workshops, coaching, and complimentary digital tools. Designed for the evolving spiritual landscape, we hope our resources fortify your ministry endeavors.

- **Faith+Lead Academy:** An online learning platform that fosters multi-dimensional learning experiences. Whether you're seeking growth in daily faith, a deeper grasp of Christian traditions, or leadership capabilities, Faith+Lead Academy bridges you with esteemed theologians, seasoned ministry practitioners, and real-world examples of God's active presence.
- **Faith+Lead Workshops:** Experience our expert-led virtual sessions, packed with practical insights. Each workshop is crafted to impart immediately actionable skills and knowledge for real-world ministry.
- **Learning Communities:** Go beyond conventional learning. Engage in a progressive journey spanning three to twelve months, with on-demand modules complemented by regular live interactions. Between sessions, immerse yourself in hands-on practices, enhancing your ability to resonate with the spiritual pulse of your community and harmonize with the Holy Spirit's guidance.
- **Coaching:** Benefit from bespoke, cost-effective coaching sessions. Our adept coaches, deeply aware of ministry nuances, offer holistic guidance—from personal well-being to leadership acumen, all at an investment akin to your daily coffee.

Learn more at
faithlead.org

More Books from Faith+Lead

 	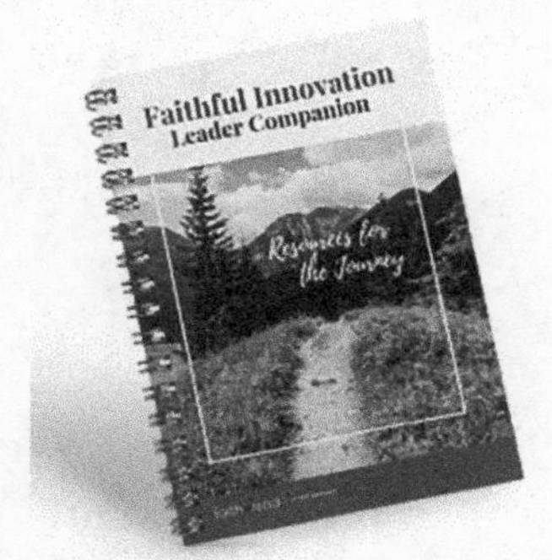
Leading Faith Innovation: Following God into a Hopeful Future	**Faithful Innovation Leader Companion Workbook**
If you feel as if your faith community is going through the motions, you're not alone. Churches are navigating seismic changes. This book offers a grounded yet optimistic blueprint for navigating significant shifts in today's church and societal landscapes. Immerse in real-life narratives and adopt spiritual practices that render each transformative step tangible and achievable.	Designed for ministry leaders, this hands-on workbook emphasizes honing skills in active listening, reconnection, and championing innovation grounded in faith. Prioritizing tangible applications equips you and your leadership teams to discern God's call and navigate confidently to follow God into a faithful future.

Appendix A

Where Have You Seen God at Work?

In the Funding Forward survey, we asked: "As you think back on the work your church has done to add income sources, reduce the budget, and/or rethink staffing, where have you seen God at work?" Below, you'll find the complete list of unedited responses. The identities of the churches and respondents are intentionally kept anonymous.

"In our newest venture that serves Christian leaders, God has been present blazing a trail of relationship and community. In the height of the pandemic, we were poised to gather thousands of congregational leaders and people of faith around the pressing topics of our time. When George Floyd was murdered, during the insurrection at the capitol, following the tragic killings of Asian Americans in Atlanta and the heartwrenching school shooting in Uvalde, we provided inspiration to preachers hours after news broke. God provided protection and invitation to bold proclamation. And has even blazed a trail for our congregation to support and celebrate this vibrant ministry, whose impact goes far beyond the walls of our congregation to every continent on the globe and countless expressions of Christian witness. It has felt more like following and riding the Spirit's wave than leading it at times. God continues to show up now as we reach toward financial sustainability in connecting us with the right partners and organizations who are providing capacity building support and catching the vision for our mission."

"Where do I begin? There have been so many 'God winks' in this process—everything from unexpected financial gifts just when they were needed most, to doors being opened to find the perfect renters for the business center, to relationships being built with various people and organizations in the community, to a sense of purpose and anticipation about how God is leading and providing for the church. Last year at this time, I wasn't sure we would even be here, and the ways God is providing is amazing."

"This has all been A LOT of work for us. The leadership of our church is burned out. And yet, God still finds a way to energize us with curiosity at what is next. We also continue to experience a sense of peace. Though [it] surpasses all our understanding at times, peace at the edge of a financial and ecclesial cliff is like feeling calm and content on hospice care. We don't yet know if death is the next journey for our church, but in that uncertainty, God's peace abounds."

"Our church has 5 very clear missional priorities that guide our decision-making about all our resources. We have never *not* had enough money to fulfill those priorities, and we choose to say that God gives us everything we need to do what God has asked us to do. We consistently pass deficit budgets (expenses outpace income), and the church doesn't panic. They just respond with generous enthusiasm, because they trust that their gifts are carving out a highway for God."

"Grants have been a life-giving source of inspiration and experimentation for our congregation. Since this is a new way of being church that I introduced, I give God 100% of the credit for easing the conflict that this [paradigm] shift would have caused. Grants take up a lot of my time. The congregation just seemed to accept that there would be fewer staff working here due to budgetary constraints, and the rector would be less available to do other church duties."

"God sent (and sends) us the people and connections that made (and make) changes possible."

"Finding a second part time call for pastor so we could drop him to half time at this church"

"The continued ways that we utilize our facility for the community connects our church with organizations and people that we probably never would have encountered otherwise. It is a unique opportunity to have so many people come through our building without being here for a church-related program. As people learn more about our theology of hospitality and welcome, they can feel comfortable in a church building that they possibly wouldn't have entered except for a community event."

"We saw God working His more from our less. We downsized to a Sunday only location and our relationships are deeper and more meaningful."

"There has not been fear in the process, we have seen God provide generously through leaders who give of their time and talents and through a large memorial gift that helps us dream of a future. I know that God is present in all of those things."

"These questions seem to assume our budget has been decreasing. In fact, we have experienced an increase in giving each year now for the last 12 years (our church was planted 12 years ago). We moved into a social enterprise (Table Farm) because we experienced a need and thought our community was well positioned to join with God & neighbors in tending to soil in ways that would allow us to give away food through an interfaith food bank. We raised funds to transform our dated kitchen into a commercial bakery (Table Bread) because we experienced a need among young people who were feeling isolated & disconnected and we believe the bakery aligns with our sense of gathering community to bake and break bread. We hope Table Bread will be fully self-sustaining within 2 years and we anticipate [it] becoming both a job training opportunity and also a way to fund the expansion of Table Farm."

"The discernment in what our community and congregation needed guided our pivoting. This power in listening to those often disempowered has led to new insights and programs that are borne out of the desires from our unhoused Bostonian congregation.

They wanted a way to educate young people, they wanted a way to create and produce beauty. They desired to be fulfilled in this mission and work in the same way the staff and supporters want to see the work fulfilled."

"From the beginning we have recognized that this ministry belongs primarily to God, and we are invited into it (rather than us owning it and bearing the full burden of responsibility). This has freed us to take courageous moves in adding serving days, hiring staff, etc. God is present every time someone comes to volunteer or share lunch. The relationships we have in the kitchen and at the serving window are God's presence among us."

"God using creative gifts to share the radically inclusive gospel"

"The early years of our church, when it was a mission congregation heavily reliant on grant funding from the ELCA and The Episcopal Church, was a bit of a financial mess with not enough transparency. We decided to put every single part of our financial situation in the open and begin to think more practically about income, expenses and fundraising—we also approached it with much more playfulness and courage. Through this process, God brought our community closer together and we started to feel less like our building and expenses were getting in the way of what God was calling us to do."

"God's work was critical throughout the process of selling our land for [long-term] homeless family housing. There were SO MANY hurdles, primarily with the city. Some examples of what felt like God moments:

1. A good number of community leaders (executive director of a community service organization, etc.) came to testify on our behalf, without telling us they were coming, at city planning and city council meetings.
2. Property neighbors who objected to the development met with us, and decided not to show up to protest the project at the city council.
3. As we engaged in community discernment at critical junctures, people reported hearing clear direction from God on quite a few occasions. This happened on several occasions from people who were the least expected. An example: the estimate for building our second sanctuary was beyond our means, but we raised the funds by a hair. Then the company increased the estimate by 40%, due to market changes. A highly risk averse

lay leader was the first to speak after we told the church we could either reduce the features of the new space (e.g., dropping kids' space, dropping disability access to the lower level, etc.), shrink the entire new space, or move forward with trust that God would provide. I can't emphasize enough this leader's risk aversion! He said: 'there isn't even a question. God wants us to move forward.'

4. We met a couple former Vineyard pastors from Ecuador, and five different Vineyards around the nation were hoping they'd come start ministries with them. They chose us! And they are stunningly gifted pastors. They've grown a Latino congregation from zero to 300ish in five years, in a community with very few Latinos, and this despite there being another 5 Latino churches in our area (all with 10–30 members).
5. Our work to help the [long-term] homeless family housing happen took forever, and felt pretty bad at times (e.g., when the project was scuttled by the city due to water drainage issues, at one point). We were gratefully surprised when many of the leaders from the developer, city, county, etc., took time to publicly praise our commitment to God and to community service.

I forgot to mention in another section: the reason we chose to shoot for long term homeless family housing is that our county did a self-study and determined it was the greatest need in our county."

"Everywhere. Seriously, we make shifts to programs and suspend some effort but the next thing we know there's new need clear as can be asking for our attention. The generosity of folks to respond has been something we emphasize and it pays off when ministry opportunities arise. We need to keep working at a model of sustainability, in terms of finance and human resource, but God has given more than we imagined and somehow we keep on, grateful for the call."

"God was at work in the vision to relaunch our church to be relevant to our changing community. This involved selling 6 of 7 acres of property and partnering with a developer to build a mixed-use campus with apartments, hotel, shops, and restaurants—with the new church in the center. Like the woman at the well who went to do an everyday activity (get water) and instead found Jesus, our goal is to offer Jesus to people doing everyday activities on our campus. We dug a huge well!"

"We believe that we live in where the future of the church is headed. Not only do coffee shop operations generate additional income, but it also introduces us to new people every single day. We continue to work so that we are financially sustainable, and God continues to show up, and we continue to look for God . . . working in and through all things."

"We have found that when there is a good vision, with clear communication that [satisfies] a need, the funding will follow."

"God provides people, resources, and energy for us to be in our mission."

"All our staff are part-time employees. Some have [full-time] jobs as well or [full-time] life callings such as caring for family members. The multi-staff part-time ministry model has worked really well for us for the past 10 years and we have seen the church grow."

"We're a fairly recent church plant (12 years old), and have never really been saddled with expectations to do things a particular way. God has been deeply present in the [ever-unfolding] conversations about how we can creatively experiment and adapt to meet needs in our broader community while also sustaining and growing our own congregational capacity and mission."

"Our church rents one of our buildings to the school district's developmental preschool. We receive income from the school district, and unlike other locations, we provide a big and usable space."

"We have received grant funding from ELCA World Hunger to expand our Housing and Community Resources ministries, and we've seen God building and blessing these ministries and our community."

"The relationship of hosting another church in our facility within the past year on Sunday mornings has stretched our faith and built new friendships. This has allowed us to remain in a facility too large for us while we search for a new ministry home."

"Our ministry partners have breathed life into our congregation and where we see God at work as we collaborate together."

"God helped us discern which staff departures not only would be helpful for the budget, but also would be helpful for the health of the congregation."

"While funding has decreased, creativity has increased. It is a challenge to answer this question because it seems like God guides us in small ways to trust and serve. In this time, God has shown us partners in ministry in our community that can work alongside us and move us beyond our church walls."

"The past decade has been an intense trip filled with twists and turns. Collaborating with Trellis to build a funding model that could support the development of not-for-profit workforce housing combined with a for-profit parking ramp was extremely complex and came close to collapse numerous times—it took a lot of faith and grit to push through and achieve this. The parking ramp was intended to be an ongoing source of funding for the church, but by the time it opened we were in the middle of COVID so it ended up being a drain on cash. It is now in the process of being converted to a non-profit operating model affiliated with East Town Apartments. Removing that financial burden, combined with our ability to lease the building's office space to missional tenants, has allowed us to establish a viable financial model going forward: we are a small congregation building a new model of church relevant to our time and space in the midst of a large building. Every Sunday is a step of faith for us as we develop new patterns and practices while we work towards deepening our relationships within the community and with God."

"One church member said that Trinity New Hope affordable housing allowed us to put our money where our gospel is. God has also used TNH as a witness to how the gospel can transform a community of faith to love neighbors with our actions. Hosting the Apostolic Hispanic congregation helped us practice hospitality and meet new people. God has worked through Idaho Gives Day by encouraging us to tell our ministry stories in new ways."

"The congregation has been mostly open to adopting and implementing the new mission and vision."

"Had we had two major givers die in one congregation and had started to reduce budget & staff time in the other, both of our congregations would have been more likely to keep our old models for financially sustainability which were on their last leg anyway. The losses were catalysts for innovation and change—new life—resurrection. One of our congregations wouldn't have thought about selling their building, neither congregation would have thought about collaborating with another congregation (of another denomination) and one of our congregations would never have thought about reducing staff to half time, which actually freed up time, and denominational support, to have a community ministry role be developed. God's activity called us [to] 'de-center' the church needs to meet the needs of the community. In doing that, we have found God alive and well and working in the community. And now we are joining in that work, not just focusing on our own survival."

"We feel that our church is in active relationship with our community, which enables us to see how God is working in the world around us. For example, we began offering space to an AA group, which meets every day. They are helping persons struggling with substance abuse live free from alcohol and drugs, with God's help. We know that God is in this work and that we are fulfilling our mission of "building hope and proclaiming peace" by working with AA. We are participating in God's reign of justice by partnering with (renting to) our local Fight for Fifteen chapter, which works to advocate for low wage workers."

"Ha! Everywhere! God opened doors during the pandemic for a new use for a building that had been empty for almost 12 years. God opened the hearts of the congregation as we listened to each other, God and the community. We heard who God was calling us to be and were open to wherever that might take us. God has restored joy, energy, and excitement in the congregation and deepened our faith. We are continually be[ing] shaped and reshaped as we learn about true radical hospitality and welcome on the behalf of the other. The storehouses have been opened as we step further along the path God has laid out for us. I could go on and on. :)"

"God has been all over this process. Shifting to renting space has seen an increase of the active use of gifting for one of our pastors. Another of our pastors took up teaching high school geometry to help with the financial shift, and that move has also been a place where God is at work. And God has been at work blessing all those we've shared space. As tight as things have been and are, it's clear to us that the Lord is using all these pressures to bring the Kingdom in among us."

"We had a vision of becoming more than a church, but rather a community center that was also a home to a church, and in our cases churches. As we focused in on providing services, community partnerships were formed, other churches and agencies joined us. In this work, in this shift the church has been able to more fully live out [its] primary mission—serving our neighbors in need."

"We were able to create funding sources for a new baking kitchen, new partners, rental income, fund shifting for racial healing, community support for unhoused neighbors, children, arts. Our shifted financing model has allowed for more freedom in following the Spirit's lead in this time of change."

"In August 2021 our [church leadership team] was demoralized over the loss of income. I even went without pay for 2 weeks to help. We set out to refinance our mortgage through a capital campaign that ended up exceeding our goals, and increased our general giving in 2022. It has been a joyful transformation from despair to hope. We reduced our mortgage payments by $2000/mo and that has been the largest factor in financial stability. We also sold an acre of land to the foodshelf and those funds sit in Mission Investment Fund as a float account to help with any rainy day needs."

"Thousands of students have been impacted by living in our housing and participating in our programs each year. Some who have been a part of our sober living program are only still in school because of our ministry with them."

"I'm [struggling] for the words to adequately express how amazing it is to think of all of the children, families, staff, faith community, and broader community that are impacting—or being impacted by—the very real efforts of the NPO, first envisioned and nurtured by the church. Children are safe and learning, parents can work, staff are encouraged to grow, faith community members get to live out their faith when they support these efforts. God is working in all of this—people are being blessed and/or being a blessing to others. (I'm happy to discuss or write more, if needed.)"

"A church cannot be closed to the community if it is going to survive. Allowing our property to be used in different ways by the community has allowed us to spread God's message without being too aggressive about it. To approach people on a level they are at now, in a world that has de-emphasized church membership. Allowing space for recovery groups and seeing that mission become [self-sustaining] while people are healing, has been a joy to watch and something that feels like what Jesus would do."

"We have grown financially over the past 8+ years, with a more than one hundred percent increase in giving. God is in that—because the people giving are new to us, younger, and believe in the mission of the congregation."

"Through receiving a state grant which will help us to build a new building to house our mission partner (a childcare center serving underserved and special needs families.) In more people considering new ways to reach out in mission which may or may not necessarily bring in more income. In rethinking how we do church by offering youth ministry resources to a neighboring church who has no called pastor."

"We had a strong sense that selling our property (traditional [church] building) and building a space that would be designed for 7-day/week business and community engagement that the church would use was God's plan for our church."

"It has been clear that the church is built on the individuals who comprise it. We have seen God through the varied perspective we have been able to glean from talking to our community openly about finances."

"This church has always been devoted and connected to the community. All we have really done is to bring the church back to where it was, a center for community. By having a campus that is more active we better utilize what God has blessed us with. The activity also spurs interest in who we are as a church. While the rentals themselves have not shown much fruit as far as attendance or growth, the sheer fact that [there] are cars in the parking lot 7 days a week has provoked much more community interest and visitors."

"First and foremost, God has been active in the relationships—both new and rekindled. We've been forced to rely on God's faithfulness rather than a budgetary cushion. We've also learned that we can continue to be who God has made us to be (and is shaping us into) even if we stop or change some of the ministries of the church."

"I see God opening up doors for our social enterprise to become a co-op. A worker owned coop for the future."

"In opening the congregation to new partnerships with non-profits now on-site. In expanding camping programs for children in low-income neighborhoods of the city. In helping several smaller congregations find new life. In supporting leadership development, affordable housing, and other justice-focused initiatives."

"I've seen a shift in the congregation's relationship to our surrounding community that I attribute to God's work among us. Often we've viewed our neighbors only as potential members or as competitors for space and attention, but we've really begun to see our neighbors as potential partners. We look for opportunities to join our neighbors in their efforts for the common good and when we begin projects we often ask 'who can we partner with this time?' God has opened up vision in this regard, and we've built relationships with several groups, businesses, and individuals in the process. I also believe God has provided us with the right people and the right gifts at the right time. As we navigated developing lease for our parking lots, the right people seemed to come forward to help us find a way and discern."

"In shifts (both in terms of circumstances of our logistics and the energy levels of our congregation) that radically benefited our ministries—we know God was in them, because they weren't planned or even predictable."

"We believe these new ventures have allowed our physical assets to be used in a way that supports and strengthens families in our community. We have been intentional to partner with groups that connect with a broad segment of the socio-economic spectrum and believe that this work, while not explicitly Christian in nature, is well in line with the person and work of Jesus."

"Some members of congregational leadership are beginning to recognize that the current model of ministry simply is not sustainable, but they find the shift away from a 'Father knows best' mind set to one of shared ministry and leadership. It is a very slow process of conversion, however. God keeps inviting us into opportunities to collaborate with other programs in the community. In other words, God keeps inviting us to deepen our relationships with community partners as an expression of lived gospel. Previously, church leadership cut the administrator's job to half time and then only 15 hours per week, along with other staff. That decision ultimately placed an untenable burden on me as rector to compensate for the work needed to be done. Along with the added workload, pastoral attention waned considerably. Volunteers were not reliable, nor could they provide the continuity needed by parishioners. After 5 or so years we have just returned to having a fulltime administrator on staff."

"Our congregation is incredibly generous and I see god moving in the midst of that. We are also an outward looking congregation that is thinking about the needs of our neighbors. We have a community park, community garden, playground, and more that we consider our gift to the neighborhood and God is clearly at work in the way that our space brings people together."

"God is always at work. When we have faith enough to quiet down, listen and then courage to follow, God works through us including our development projects and financial modeling."

"WHU is a theologically barrier-free spiritual community so we do not often use the word ['god'] without a larger discussion about what that means."

"All over. St. John's has made significant budget cuts, we've also become more strategic about viewing our building as an asset, and leveraging our relationships with building partners to enhance the congregation's [sustainability]—both from a missional / energy / vitality way and financially. It is good for everyone when the building is a hive of activity—as it increases the positive energy, opportunities for synchronicity (aka Holy Spirit moments), and builds real community. In the same way, many of the budget cuts we've made, while significant in terms of dollar amounts have been cutting away unnecessary expenses. Reducing or eliminating those costs have made us a leaner, more efficient operation and forced us to evaluate staffing to truly address the needs of the world now. Building on our congregation's long history—and historic mission of being a welcoming presence in the heart of the city, God has also led us to our current and most audacious building project yet—tearing down our existing building (including sanctuary) to build a ten story high-rise with 100+ units of affordable housing for people who work in restaurants, retail, and service-sector jobs in downtown Madison. This is [a] huge win for the neighborhood as there is a significant need for moderately priced housing, and has generated tremendous neighborhood enthusiasm and support (even & particularly by people who aren't religious or have been hurt by religion—which are many folks in our downtown state capitol / college town neighborhood) because they love that the church is, 'putting your money where your mouth is' and willing to sacrifice its building to do something good for the neighborhood. It is also good for the congregation, because it allows us to age gracefully, and while the overall building will be significantly larger, the congregation specific part will be smaller and easier to maintain."

"The shift came for us as we were trying to purchase our first building. We really believed that we were called to get something for the benefit of the greater community and not just build something for us. At the same time, there is a shift in the community where people don't feel comfortable with mission dollars going to maintain a facility and infrastructure. So, this has become an [opportunity] and a shift all at once. We can say that the [facilities] pay for themselves while at the same time connecting and serving the greater community outside of membership."

"I am grateful that in the middle of the pandemic, when we have to close our door, for a long time, through our non-profit, we were able to see many doors open to serve the community. We were very active serving the community, and God gave us favor with community leader, and stakeholders, such as elected official, and foundations with funding and our income from the non-profit triple during this time. [With] this funding, we continue to finance many of the church services."

"The focus of our congregation mission partners and leadership is more centered on its sense of vocation and rooted in the great commandment. By not owning a religiously designed building, we are forced to ask better questions and less prone to wonder about how others might join the church to support it. Instead, we've been much more reliant on prayer and practicing Christian community in our context and beyond."

"Inspiring the congregation to adopt a part-time pastor model, which has energized our lay leadership, increased the revenue we have to use for ministry, and afforded the pastor with a more sustainable model for small/medium sized congregational life."

"We have spent the last five years in major transition (leadership plus COVID), and we have seen all the challenges that every congregation has—yet our people have largely remained faithful and connected to God and one another."

"We love the idea of holy imagination, we love dreaming about how we can better live into God's calling in our context and work to bring those dreams into reality."

"In all of it, especially in our engagement in our neighborhood."

"God has created incredible new income streams we would not have imagined!"

"We are solid in the area of giving and finances. We have paid down/off our debt and people give regularly to our ministry. The biggest shift we made about 5 years ago was to incorporate electronic giving methods. This shift allowed us to navigate the pandemic well."

"Together with God, our congregation has exercised muscles of resilience and creativity. When we made the hard but necessary decision to tear down two of our buildings in 2017–2018, we had to then reimagine what church looked like. How would we fellowship without a Fellowship Hall? How would we learn without Sunday School classrooms? These necessary conversations strengthened our capacity for adaptation, which has served us well in the disruptive years since."

"In the increased giving even through Covid. The increases aren't huge but every year there is an increase. Also, people are excited about [using] our resources for the community outside of the church."

"We transformed a bankrupt, near-empty church into a major community asset with a thriving congregation in only 7 years. God's work is all over this."

"We have seen God at work as we try to participate in justice in our community. We have seen the Spirit stretch us and lead us to grow as we get to know our neighbors. We have seen God transform individuals in our church as they lived into their callings, and then, in turn, God revitalized and reinvigorated our congregation as a whole. There have been challenges, of course, but God has always given greater hope and vision through our work in the community."

"God continues to bring us new folks for us to be in ministry with."

"We have seen God lead us in discernment as to where and what we should do. As we . . . discern this, after planning and observing best practices, we launched out in faith."

"The miracle of a [400-person] worshiping congregation building a $60 million community/church development project."

"God was refining our mission/place in the world. God put the right people in the right places at the right time. God helped us have hard conversations with grace."

"For sure in the 'cloud of witnesses' the Spirit surrounds us with, who believe in what we are doing, and who support our ongoing work. In the surprising neighborhood partnerships and ways we find connections to people who can use our space, and who become friends without any intention of coming to worship."

"We are part of a new ministry that has seen God working from the onset by providing people along our path that have contributed with knowledge and encouragement."

"The lay people have, sometimes reluctantly, discovered they have vocations & gifts for ministry. And the church has found it doesn't have to generate copious programming; it can rent to mission partners in the future & advance God's kingdom via those partnerships."

"We were a resource during the height of COVID-19 pandemic offering vaccines, boosters and testing."

"It has helped us separate the mission from the church from sustaining the institution of the church. This seems to be critical at this historical juncture."

"Every inspiration and idea for anything that became self-sustaining came during prayer. I also want to name that the Holy Spirit moves people to generosity during times of crisis, and the crises of the past several years (pandemic, uprising) has opened new financial opportunities that were not available previously."

"In the congregations care and commitment to each other and the gathering. Change is hard and 4 out of the 6 original soup church launch team members has stayed joyfully constant and present."

"I have not been in my position for very long, but from what I've heard, we've had to switch our financial model several times, for several different reasons. Sometimes it was because the budget was failing; other times it was because it was booming. In each instance, listening and buy-in from the whole community was considered, and I see God at work in this very community-oriented decision-making process."

"We really saw God move in our people when we decided to build our new facility with a focus on 'them' and not 'us.' We were moved and called to meet a few community needs (a third space gathering place and a high-end preschool). When we started to cast this vision, we were immediately met with excitement. The challenge for our people to stop going to church and BE The Church has changed how we view discipleship. God has blessed us with many opportunities with people who possibly would have never stepped into a "church" building are coming into our Community Center, and we build relationships with and share the Gospel in everyday living!"

"The church is just getting to a point where we are thinking about other income sources, reducing the budget, and reconsidering our staffing. This has pushed the congregation to begin thinking about [its] future and how we continue to live out our mission in the community. The congregation has been open to new ideas and new ways of thinking about their faith community and how they live out their mission in the community. God has definitely been at work as we discern how we continue to live out our faith and create God's kingdom on earth."

"We haven't seen anything that approaches a miracle through our changes. God has been faithful through every season in the life of our church and continues to be with us in many ways. We can look back and see how important it was for our church to purchase the homes we bought way back in the 70s. Few people who attend the church now were a part of that decision but the church wouldn't be here if they hadn't done so. More recently, we have opened our facilities for coworking during the week. For a few years it went well, grew consistently and provided a small amount of income. While it was running it helped get far more connected with the broader community around us. We hired staff who could be engaged there but Covid shut that down the ministry [sic] and we had to let the staff go. We've had a difficult time restarting it. Since Covid, it's been more difficult to discern where God is at work. We're struggling to find direction and trusting God will lead when the time is right."

"We purchased a roller rink 5 years ago now that was in poor shape with the focus of turning it into our church facility. Since then we decided to open the rink as a ministry of the church and also a fundraising arm of our church. So many churches do bake sales or car washes to raise funds for missions etc. We run a roller skating rink that is focused on providing a safe and fun place for children and families in our community. It is part of our 501c3 as a fundraiser and it is in line with our mission and our beliefs. We only play music by Christian artists and work with our community to provide mentors for at-risk youth."

"I have been actively working on finding ways to have clergy (myself included) focused on the church's mission rather than staying the way we are or who we used to be. I have looked at different approaches to staffing admin, and how to handle tenants to rent our space. I believe that it has made us [a] more connected church with God's mission and has helped us work together which is God at work."

"When we lost the income from the agency using our building due to the pandemic, we weren't sure that we could continue to meet our operating expenses. But we reduced our expenses where we could and encouraged congregational giving. It turned out that we were able to make it through the pandemic, and became stronger, fiscally and as a congregation. We have continued the reduced budget/staff time, and with the increased congregational giving (along with an ongoing large monthly grant from the Diocese) we have been able to continue and even grow. We've also been able to raise significant funds (although more is needed) toward a much-needed major roof repair. We continue to be amazed and give thanks for God's grace and the faithfulness of His people."

"Our community food pantry and childcare have become self-sustaining. The childcare is focused on the environment and sustainability. Both fulfill our mission to care for the planet and each other. Both have grown and flourished."

Appendix B
Expectations Analysis Tool

Created by Faith+Lead

Naming Current Expectations

What do you think congregations expect from their regional church body leaders, pastors, and from themselves or each other as a community?

Members' expectations of you as a leader	Your expectations of your role as a leader
What does the congregation expect of members?	**What do you expect of congregation members?**

Reflection and Reframing

1. Look back over what you have named above. Take some time to reflect on what you've listed about what others and you expect of you as a leader. Are these expectations fruitful and healthy? Are they what you need to focus on in order to help the congregation take its next faithful step?

   Circle those you feel are most essential and life-giving (for the congregation and for you). Put **brackets** around those that you feel are unfruitful, unhealthy, or unnecessary.

2. Do the same thing with what you've named about expectations for congregation members. What's missing? Are these the things that congregation members should be focused on in order for the congregation to take its next faithful step?

   Circle the things that you find most essential and life-giving. Put **brackets** around those that you feel are unfruitful, unhealthy, or unnecessary.

3. Make a **list** of the top 6–8 things that you think the congregation most needs you to focus on in order to help it take its next faithful step.

4. Make a **list** of the top 6–8 things that you think congregation members most need to focus on in order to take their next faithful step.

5. What are some things you might do as a leader to help reframe unhelpful expectations and refocus the congregation in the direction God is leading?

Appendix C
Property Resources

These are resources that I use as well as ones suggested by congregations during the interview process.

Dominic Dutra and Albert Hung, *Closing Costs: Imagining Real Estate for Missional Purposes*, Eugene, OR: Resource Publications, 2022.

Jill Suzanne Shook, *Making Housing Happen: Faith-Based Affordable Housing Models*, Second Edition, Eugene, OR: Wipf and Stock, 2012.

Mark DeYmaz and Harry Li, *The Coming Revolution in Church Economics: Why Tithes and Offerings Are No Longer Enough and What You Can Do About It*, Grand Rapids, MI: Baker Books, 2019. (See chapter 6: Becoming a Benevolent Owner)

Mark DeYmaz, *Disruption: Repurposing the Church to Redeem the Community*, Nashville, TN: Thomas Nelson, 2017. (See chapter 5: Disrupting Economics)

Mark Elsdon, *We Aren't Broke: Uncovering Hidden Resources for Mission and Ministry*, Grand Rapids, MI: Eerdmans, 2021. (See chapters 7–11)

Parish Properties

Partners for Sacred Places

Rooted Good "How-to Guides":
https://www.rootedgood.org/resources/how-to-guides
How to Rent Well
How to Develop Well
How to Sell Well

Rooted Good "What About Taxes?" https://www.rootedgood.org/post/what-about-taxes-a-guide-for-churches-starting-to-generate-revenue

Partners for Sacred Places, "Before You Rent Church Space, Calculate the Costs," Lewis Center for Leadership, July 25, 2023. https://www.churchleadership.com/leading-ideas/before-you-rent-church-space-calculate-the-costs/?utm_source=CC&utm_medium=email&utm_campaign=LI20230726

Appendix D
Social Enterprise Resources

These are resources that I use as well as ones suggested by congregations during the interview process.

Mark DeYmaz and Harry Li, *The Coming Revolution in Church Economics: Why Tithes and Offerings Are No Longer Enough and What You Can Do About It,* Grand Rapids, MI: Baker Books, 2019. (See chapter 7: Monetize Existing Services and chapter 8: Start New Businesses)

Mark Elsdon, *We Aren't Broke: Uncovering Hidden Resources for Mission and Ministry*, Grand Rapids, MI: Eerdmans, 2021. (See chapters 10–11)

Rooted Good Resources: What about Taxes?

US Small Business Association

Appendix E
Staffing Resources

These are resources that I use as well as ones suggested by congregations during the interview process.

Darryl W. Stephens, ed. *Bivocational and Beyond: Educating for Thriving Multivocational Ministry*, Books@Atla Open Press, 2022.

Rev. Catherine Caimano offers training to congregations, clergy, and denominations for serving in this model. You can find out more about her work at freerangepriest.org.

G. Jeffrey MacDonald, *Part-Time is Plenty: Thriving Without Part-Time Clergy*, Louisville, KY: Westminster John Knox Press, 2020.

Mark DeYmaz and Harry Li, *The Coming Revolution in Church Economics: Why Tithes and Offerings Are No Longer Enough and What You Can Do About It*, Grand Rapids, MI: Baker Books, 2019. (See chapter 5: Leverage Church Assets)

Rosario Picardo, *Ministry Makeover: Recovering a Theology for Bivocational Service in the Church*, Eugene, OR: Wipf and Stock, 2015.

Appendix F

Grants

Often congregations ask me how to solicit grant funding. One of the best resources on grants that I have spoken to is Kristal Frazier. Frazier is an international speaker, trainer, and author. She has coached and trained thousands across North America, Europe, and Africa to collectively raise $200 million from funders and individual donors over the past decade. Most importantly for this conversation, she has been on every side of the "grants table." She has not only been a grant writer, she has also been a grant evaluator for federal grant programs. I had the chance to interview her in October 2021, and here are some of the best tips she shared:

- **Searching for Grants:** While there are certainly grant databases that you can use, if you're on a limited budget Frazier suggested searching for grants using Google keywords. The first keywords she suggested using are "ministry," "faith-based," and "churches." The secondary keywords should be related to the specific program you're looking to fund, so you might use words like "food pantry," "students," "childcare," "affordable housing," etc. These words will help you get past the first few faith-based funders that everyone is using. She suggested signing up for "Google alerts" so you can see these opportunities as they emerge. She noted that within the first week you'll receive quite a few alerts that aren't a fit for you, so stick with it. She also suggested using the keywords on social media to find grant opportunities. She shared an example of finding a faith-based grant opportunity on Twitter. I've also found it helpful to get on the email list of certain faith-based funders that might be a fit for future projects. For instance, I follow the Partners for Sacred

Places, Stewardship of Life Institute, in addition to regional church body and denominational newsletters that have helped me to find new grant opportunities. She stressed that it's important to use your network to find the right grant opportunities for you and share these opportunities with others so you can find funding together. She shared that most common faith-based grants she sees tend to be for community-based projects, disaster funding, technology upgrades, virtual programs, sustainable food programs (community gardens and programs for food deserts), and youth and young adult entrepreneurship programs.

- **What Reviewers Look For:** She peeled back the layers of how grantors review grant applications. She shared that between looking at the budget and sustainability sections she can usually cut the number of applications she needs to review in half since most applicants don't do these sections correctly.[1] I'll walk through section by section. NOTE: Depending on the grant you're applying for, you may not see each of these sections or they may have a different name.
  - **Budget Section:** The first thing that grant reviewers look at is the budget—this often becomes the litmus test for reviewing the rest of the application. She stressed having a clear and understandable line-item budget for the proposal as well as a budget summary (if the grant application provides space to include it). This summary should explain each line item of your budget in narrative form, answering these questions: *What is it? How will you use the money? What's the purpose?* No matter how self-explanatory your budget seems to those inside your congregation, it's important that someone outside of your congregation can easily understand it. This is a great opportunity to have someone outside of your congregation read the budget and budget summary (with no context from the congregation) and offer feedback.
  - **Sustainability Section:** Next, she encourages potential grant recipients to focus on the "sustainability" section, which is often ignored. The goal of this section is to share how sound your congregation currently is, how you're going to use the grant money if you receive it, and how you'll fund this project if you

don't receive the grant. The answer to that last question shouldn't be "we'll look for more grant opportunities." Frazier is looking for your "future funding plan," which should include a description of your internal support/capacity (this may include staff as well as volunteers), leadership (particularly their skills related to that specific project), partnerships (partners, community stakeholders, key donors, etc.). Even if the funder does not ask for them, she encourages sharing letters of support from your partners. These letters might come from co-applicants, community stakeholders, and/or people who have been impacted by the project. If you are applying with other partners, it's important to note who is responsible for what on the grant as well as who is the lead applicant since that is the contact for the funder.[2]

- **Narrative Section:** This should include not only a description of the project, but key statistics related to the project. Depending on the scope of the project, she suggested sharing local, regional, and national statistics related to the issues your project will address. If you're working with a local funder, they may only want local statistics. However, if you are working with a national funder, they will likely want all three, in that particular order.
- **Evaluation Section:** You want to "create, develop, and collect." Create benchmarks for your specific program: *What is your measure of success?* These are the benchmarks that you will share in your report to the grantor after the grant money is used. You want benchmarks that you can not only meet but exceed. Develop a plan for the evaluation: *When will it occur and how will it be done?*[3]

- **Tone Down the Terminology:** Grant applications should be written at an 8th–10th grade reading level. The good news is that Microsoft Word has the Flesch-Kincaid readability test built in. For reference, as I was writing a draft of chapter nine of this book, I ran this test and found out that the chapter is just above the tenth-grade reading level. The only exception to this rule is if you are talking with a funder that is asking for more detailed information with specific terminology. Be careful with acronyms: Make sure you explain and spell out the acronym first before using it.

- **Ask for Feedback:** Share your proposal with someone in your network who is outside of your congregation to get their feedback. She shared that having at least one or two outside reviewers can make a big difference to make sure your grant application is understandable to someone outside of your congregation. I asked Frazier if congregations should hire a grant writer; she said in most cases it's a better use of everyone's time and money to have someone like her step in to review the grant rather than writing the application from scratch.

I will add one last piece of advice from my experience with congregations writing grants. I've found a few congregation leaders who feel they are "entitled" to money from grantors and that entitlement can seep into the application, which leads to a lot of work for no financial reward and potential damage to your relationship with the granting organization. Instead of thinking of grant money as a "pot of gold" that the grantor owes to you, think of it instead as another partnership opportunity. The project needs to be a win/win for both the grantor and the grantee. Granting organizations will have their own mission and cause they are trying to fulfill; make sure your project is in alignment before you proceed.

If you read through the advice above on grants and thought, "That sounds complicated!" You're right! Grants are much more complicated than most people think. And it's not just the application process that's complicated. In addition to completing the project, many grantors have reporting processes that can be time-consuming. While grant funds can certainly be worthwhile for the right project, it's important to approach this funding opportunity with a clear line of sight to the work required.

If you just need a small amount of funding to get a project off the ground, there may be grants available from your regional church body or denomination that will likely be less time-consuming. Often the projects from the interviews that utilized grant funding used some combination of both denominational grant funding and other grant funding. You might try tapping denominational/regional church body grant funding before moving to outside grant funding where there might be more competition for those dollars.

Another great source of startup funding is Thrivent Action Grants.[4] Thrivent will offer a $250 gift card to be used as seed money to fund any project seeking to make a positive impact in your community. It could be a fundraiser, educational event, or a service project that has a volunteer component to it. The applicant must be a Thrivent member and can only apply for two grants per year. While you can only receive one gift card per project, I've heard of congregations using this funding in really strategic ways by breaking down one larger project into smaller pieces and asking Thrivent members in the congregation to apply for grants for that specific piece of the project. These grants have one of the simplest application processes that I have seen.

Notes

Preface

1 In the ELCA, a rostered minister's first ordained ministerial role out of seminary is called a "first call." Instead of referring to a pastoral or deacon role as a "job," it is referred to as a "call."
2 Special thanks to my predecessor Adam Copeland for pointing the Stewardship Leaders Program in this direction.
3 Mark DeYmaz, *Disruption: Repurposing the Church to Redeem the Community* (Nashville: Thomas Nelson, 2017).
4 Mark DeYmaz and Harry Li, *The Coming Revolution in Church Economics: Why Tithes and Offerings Are No Longer Enough and What You Can Do About It* (Grand Rapids, MI: Baker Books, 2019).
5 We used a very wide definition of church. This list included traditional congregations, new faith communities, campus ministries, and more. Many of these churches included social enterprise, nonprofit, or even for-profit ministries.
6 This ministry's name is also its street address.

Chapter 1

1 Attributed to Pastor Eric Milner-White, chaplain at King's College in Cambridge, United Kingdom.
2 ZA Blog, "The 3 'Quests' for the Historical Jesus," *Zondervan Academic*, September 21, 2017, https://zondervanacademic.com/blog/historical-jesus.
3 Friends of Christ Church Lutheran, "FRIENDS," Accessed on July 10, 2023, https://friendsofccl.org/FRIENDS.
4 Barry Randolph, Zoom interview with the author, December 18, 2020.
5 Church Anew, "About Us," Accessed on July 10, 2023, https://churchanew.org/about-us.
6 Mark Allan Powell, *Giving to God: The Bible's Good News About Living a Generous Life* (Grand Rapids, MI: Eerdmans, 2006), 12.

7 Brené Brown, "Listening to shame," TED, March 16, 2012, educational video, 6:00 to 6:05, https://www.youtube.com/watch?v=psN1DORYYV0.
8 Special thanks to Jessi LeClear Vachta who introduced me to this idea and gave me a framework and language for many of the bullet points I shared.

Chapter 2

1 Cameron Howard, "Lessons in Innovation from the Old Testament," *Faith+Lead*, November 14, 2019, https://faithlead.org/blog/lessons-in-innovation-from-the-old-testament/. See also *The Old Testament for a Complex World: How the Bible's Dynamic Testimony Points to New Life for the Church* (Grand Rapids, MI: Baker Academic, 2021).
2 Howard, "Lessons in Innovation."
3 David P. King, Christopher W. Munn, Brad R. Fulton, and Jamie L. Goodwin, "NSCEP: National Study of Congregations' Economic Practices," *Lake Institute on Faith & Giving*, 2019, https://www.nscep.org/wp-content/uploads/2019/09/Lake_NSCEP_09162019-F-LR.pdf, 15.
4 King, Munn, Fulton, and Goodwin, "NSCEP: National Study of Congregations' Economic Practices," 17.
5 The study found that congregations with fifty or fewer attendees were the least likely to have online giving available before or after the pandemic—many (54 percent) still had no option to give online, as of the summer of 2020 when this study was conducted. In this case, these congregations often asked their members to mail in or drop off their checks at the church. "COVID-19 Congregational Study," *Lake Institute on Faith & Giving*, September 2022, https://scholarworks.iupui.edu/bitstream/handle/1805/23791/lake-covid-report2020-2.pdf?_gl=1*14q8mh8*_ga*MTEyNDkxNjU1LjE2Nzg5MTAyOTU.*_ga_61CH0D2DQW*MTY3ODkxMDI5NS4xLjAuMTY3ODkxMDI5NS4wLjAuMA, 4.
6 "COVID-19 Congregational Study," 4.
7 As Dwight Zscheile noted in the foreword to this book, this isn't a uniquely "church issue" as many voluntary associations are experiencing a decline in both attendance and support.
8 Of US adults who attend religious services, those who are younger are more likely than their older peers to attend "once or twice a month/a few times per year" or "seldom/never." Whereas, those who are older are more likely to attend at least once a week. Comparing the youngest (18- to 29-year-olds) and the oldest group (65+), the contrast is stark: 27% of 18- to 29-year-olds attend at least weekly, compared to nearly 50% of those 65+. US Adults ages 18–29 who attend religious services are most likely to attend once or twice a month/a few times per year (37%) followed closely by seldom/never (35%). See Pew Research Center, "Religious Landscape Study: Age Distribution," accessed July 21, 2023, https://www.pewresearch.org/religion/religious-landscape-study/age-distribution/.

9 Dwight Zscheile, "Will the ELCA Be Gone in 30 Years?" *Faith+Lead*, September 5, 2019, https://faithlead.org/blog/decline/.
10 Zscheile, "Will the ELCA Be Gone in 30 Years?"
11 Mark Elsdon, *We Aren't Broke: Uncovering Hidden Resources for Mission and Ministry* (Grand Rapids, MI: Eerdmans, 2021), 40.
12 Marty E. Stevens, *Temples, Tithes, and Taxes: The Temple and the Economic Life of Ancient Israel* (Grand Rapids, MI: Baker Academic, 2006), chapter 4.
13 David M. Gustafson, "A Church History of Bivo: Tentmaking from the beginning until now," *ECFA Today*, Spring 2016, https://www.efcatoday.org/story/church-history-bivo.
14 Jouette M. Bassler, *God & Mammon: Asking for Money in the New Testament* (Nashville: Abingdon Press, 1991), 85.
15 Bassler, *God & Mammon*, 85–86.
16 William O. Avery, "A Brief History of Stewardship," *Lutheran Laity Ministries for Stewardship*, https://www.rmselca.org/sites/rmselca.org/files/resources/a_brief_history_of_stewardship.pdf.
17 Mark Rogers, "Passing the Plate," *Christianity Today*, March 12, 2009, https://www.christianitytoday.com/history/2009/march/passing-plate.html.

Chapter 3

1 Keith Anderson, "Stewardship 2030: The Stewardship of Our Attention," *Faith+Lead,* January 10, 2022, https://faithlead.org/blog/stewardship-2030-the-stewardship-of-our-attention/.
2 Anderson, "Stewardship 2030."
3 Anderson, "Stewardship 2030."
4 Amy Blaschka, "This is Why You Should Embrace Creative Constraints," *Forbes,* April 20, 2020, https://www.forbes.com/sites/amyblaschka/2020/04/20/this-is-why-you-should-embrace-creative-constraints/?sh=73df5a8b7cb7.
5 Blaschka, "This is Why," *Forbes*.

Chapter 4

1 Johnny Baker, *Pivot Podcast*, Season 4, episode 38, "Practicing Fresh Expressions with Jonny Baker," aired April 3, 2023, on Faith+Lead.
2 Rooted Good, "Mission Possible" instructions.
3 DeYmaz, *Disruption*, 19.
4 Emory Fellowship, "Vision + Mission," accessed July 12, 2023, https://emoryfellowship.org/vision-mission.
5 Dwight Zscheile, Michael Binder, and Tessa Pinkstaff, *Leading Faithful Innovation: Following God into a Hopeful Future* (Minneapolis, MN: Fortress Press, 2023), 16.

6 Zscheile, Binder, and Pinkstaff, *Leading Faithful Innovation*, 46.
7 Peter Benedict, "Community Discernment," written as a paper for a class at Luther Seminary shared via email with the author on February 23, 2023.
8 Benedict, "Community Discernment."
9 Ernesto Sirolli, "Want to help someone? Shut up and Listen!" TED, November 26, 2012, educational video, https://www.youtube.com/watch?v=chXsLtHqfdM.
10 Sirolli, "Want to help someone? Shut up and Listen!" 0:52–1:06.
11 Sirolli, "Want to help someone? Shut up and Listen!" 2:33–2:47.
12 Sirolli, "Want to help someone? Shut up and Listen!" 9:30–9:35.
13 Zscheile, Binder, and Pinkstaff, *Leading Faithful Innovation*, 49–50.
14 Travis Norvell, "How One-to-One Conversations Reintroduced a Church to its Neighbors," *Leading Ideas*, March 8, 2022. https://www.churchleadership.com/leading-ideas/how-one-to-one-conversations-reintroduced-a-church-to-its-neighbors/.
15 Zscheile, Binder, and Pinkstaff, *Leading Faithful Innovation*, 38.
16 Zscheile, Binder, and Pinkstaff, *Leading Faithful Innovation*, 39–40.

Chapter 5

1 Janet T. Jamieson and Philip D. Jamieson, *Ministry and Money: A Practical Guide for Pastors* (Louisville, KY: Westminster John Knox Press, 2009), 101.
2 Lynne Twist, *The Soul of Money: Reclaiming the Wealth of Our Inner Resources* (New York: W. W. Norton & Company, 2003), 194.
3 Unsplash: https://unsplash.com/.
4 My Funding Forward class in winter term 2023 made this activity even more fun by choosing GIFs that described their churches' budgets.
5 L. Gregory Jones, "Pruning for sustainable design," *Faith & Leadership*, September 12, 2011, https://faithandleadership.com/l-gregory-jones-pruning-sustainable-design.
6 Jones, "Pruning for sustainable design."
7 Jones, "Pruning for sustainable design."
8 Jones, "Pruning for sustainable design."
9 Luke 12:31.
10 Unsplash: https://unsplash.com/

Part 2

1 Rooted Good, *Money and Mission Matrix.*

Chapter 6

1 Natalia Terfa, *Uplift*, May 28, 2021.
2 Nearly 90 percent of congregations 100 years or older and nearly 90 percent of urban congregations have used or were considering using property rental.
3 DeYmaz, *Disruption*, 123–124.
4 DeYmaz and Li, *The Coming Revolution*, 163.
5 "DRAFT7400 WoodlawnThreadsforMission/Purpose" shared by the Rev. Cara Tanis via email with the author on March 10, 2023.
6 Dave Harder, interview with the author, July 30, 2020.
7 Clarendon Presbyterian Church, "Who We Are," accessed July 14, 2023, http://www.clarendonpresbyterian.org/who-we-are.
8 Parish Properties, "Hybrid Approach," accessed July 18, 2023, https://www.parishproperties.ca/hybrid-approach.
9 SpringHouse Ministry Center, "Mission/Vision/Covenant," accessed July 18, 2023, https://www.springhousemn.org/mission-vision-covenant/.
10 SpringHouse Ministry Center, "How It Came to Be," accessed July 18, 2023, https://www.springhousemn.org/how-it-came-to-be/.
11 Real Rent Duwamish, "Home," accessed July 18, 2023, https://www.realrentduwamish.org/.
12 Dave Harder, "Reimagining Church Buildings: From Liability to Asset," in *Crisis & Care: Meditations on Faith and Philanthropy*, ed. Dustin D. Benac and Erin Weber-Johnson (Eugene, OR: Cascade Books, 2021), 85.
13 Harder, "Reimagining Church Buildings," 82–83.

Chapter 7

1 Concordia Place, "Our Difference," accessed July 18, 2023, https://concordiaplace.org/principles/.
2 Elsdon, *We Aren't Broke*, 190.
3 Thad Stephen Austin, "Social Entrepreneurship Among Protestant American Congregations: The Role, Theology, Motivations, and Experiences of Lay and Clergy Leaders," PhD diss., (Indiana University, 2019), 225–226.
4 Georgia McIntyre, "What Percentage of Small Businesses Fail? (And Other Need-to-Know Stats)," *Fundera by nerdwallet*, November 20, 2020, https://www.fundera.com/blog/what-percentage-of-small-businesses-fail?irclickid=V5WzyJ0mdxyPUXkxnJxgZUcsUkFzboSLESLm1g0&utm_campaign=Skimbit%20Ltd._10078&utm_source=Impact&utm_content=Online%20Tracking%20Link&utm_medium=affiliate&irgwc=1#sources.

5 John Stroeh and Carol Watson, "Stewardship of Land," *Faith+Lead*, March 27, 2023, https://faithlead.org/blog/stewardship-of-land/.
6 Galileo Church, "Home," accessed July 18, 2023, https://www.galileochurch.org/.
7 Galileo Church, "Home."
8 Finn's Place, "Home," accessed July 18, 2023, https://www.finnsplacetx.org/.
9 The Table UMC, "Our Story," accessed July 18, 2023, https://thetableumc.org/im-new/our-story/.
10 Elsdon, *We Aren't Broke*, chapter 10.
11 DeYmaz and Li, *The Coming Revolution*, 134–135
12 DeYmaz and Li, *The Coming Revolution*, 135.
13 National Council of Nonprofits, "Myths about Nonprofits," accessed July 18, 2023, https://www.councilofnonprofits.org/about-americas-nonprofits/myths-about-nonprofits.

Chapter 8

1 Aaron M. Hill, "How Much Does the Average Church Spend on Payroll?" ChurchSalary, July 25, 2022, https://www.churchsalary.com/content/articles/how-much-of-budget-do-churches-spend-on-salaries-payroll.html#:~:text=How%20Many%20Staff%20Members%20Should%20Your%20Church%20Have%3F&text=Churches%20allocate%20an%20average%20of,trending%20higher%20as%20budget%20increases.
2 Leslie Quander Wooldridge, "Bivocationalism has historical roots—and modern benefits," *Faith & Leadership*, October 18, 2022, https://faithandleadership.com/bivocationalism-has-historical-roots-and-modern-benefits.
3 Ted A. Smith, *The End of Theological Education* (Grand Rapids, MI: Eerdmans, 2023), 130–131.
4 Leslie Scanlon, "Jesus won't abandon you if you don't have a full-time pastor," *The Presbyterian Outlook*, September 12, 2022, https://pres-outlook.org/2022/08/jesus-wont-abandon-you-if-you-dont-have-a-full-time-pastor/.
5 Scanlon, "Jesus won't abandon you."
6 Ben Connelly, "Bivocational Ministry as a Path of Unexpected Spiritual Growth," in *Bivocational and Beyond: Educating for Thriving Multivocational Ministry*, ed. Darryl W. Stephens (Chicago: ATLA Open Press, 2022), 165.
7 Connelly, "Bivocational Ministry," 167.
8 Connelly, "Bivocational Ministry," 172.
9 Connelly, "Bivocational Ministry," 171.
10 Connelly, "Bivocational Ministry," 172.
11 Connelly, "Bivocational Ministry," 172.
12 Connelly, "Bivocational Ministry," 171.
13 Connelly, "Bivocational Ministry," 170.

14 Cathie Caimano, "Bye-bye 'Bi-vocational'," *Faith+Lead*, June 20, 2022, https://faithlead.org/blog/bye-bye-bi-vocational/.
15 Knox Pres. "Leadership," accessed July 19, 2023. https://www.spokaneknoxpc.org/leadership.
16 Roz Picardo, *Pivot Podcast*, Season 4, episode 43, "How to Get Started in the Mixed Ecology in a Local Church with Roz Picardo," aired May 9, 2023, on Faith+Lead.

Chapter 9

1 David Lose, "Who is My Neighbor?" *Working Preacher*. July 8, 2013, https://www.workingpreacher.org/dear-working-preacher/who-is-my-neighbor.
2 A few early readers asked me why I didn't use this section to go into more detail about congregational stewardship and fundraising for the church's annual budget, not just Funding Forward projects. I decided not to spend time on that here since that is a longer conversation and not the focus of this particular book. That being said, the book I co-authored with the Rev. Charles R. Lane, *Embracing Stewardship: How to Put Stewardship at the Heart of Your Congregation's Life* as well as the Rev. Charles R. Lane's book, *Ask, Thank, Tell: Improving Stewardship Ministry in Your Congregation* go into this topic in detail. I would recommend both of these books to you.
3 Adam J. Copeland, *Crowdfunding for Congregations and Faith-Related Nonprofits* (May 2016), https://www.adamjcopeland.com/wp-content/uploads/2016/05/Crowdfunding-Guidebook-Version-1.1-May-2016.pdf.
4 GIIN, "What You Need to Know About Impact Investing," accessed July 20, 2023, https://thegiin.org/impact-investing/need-to-know/.

Chapter 10

1 Michael Beck, *Pivot Podcast*, Season 4, episode 36, "The Mixed Ecology in the US with Michael Beck," aired March 21, 2023, on Faith+Lead.
2 Zscheile, Binder, and Pinkstaff, *Leading Faithful Innovation*, 75.
3 Similar to a spiritual autobiography, a money autobiography is a reflection activity used to help people become more aware of the ways in which their nature and nurture impact their attitudes, behaviors, and feelings about money. While this can be done without a faith component, it is often used in faith communities to help people discover the faithful ways God might be calling them to use their money.
4 This may have been because we specifically sought out interviews with a pastor and a group of lay leaders, however there were some staff who participated in these interviews.

5 Ty Bennett, "People Support What They Help to Create," accessed July 21, 2023, https://tybennett.com/people-support-what-they-help-create.
6 Zscheile, Binder, and Pinkstaff, *Leading Faithful Innovation*, 101–102.

Appendix F

1 Frazier also shared that Candid.org has some great grant proposal templates that you can use if you're new to grant writing.
2 Frazier suggested using a memorandum of understanding (MOU) to make this clear.
3 If you receive the grant, you'll need to collect the data and check it against the benchmarks. Frazier stressed that even if you don't meet the benchmarks, it's still important to share the impact and the stories in your grant report. Grantors are looking for how the money is used, not for perfection.
4 https://www.thrivent.com/about-us/membership/thrivent-action-teams.

Bibliography

Anderson, Keith. "Stewardship 2030: The Stewardship of Our Attention." *Faith+Lead.* January 10, 2022. https://faithlead.org/blog/stewardship-2030-the-stewardship-of-our-attention/.

Avery, William O. "A Brief History of Stewardship." *Lutheran Laity Ministries for Stewardship.* https://www.rmselca.org/sites/rmselca.org/files/resources/a_brief_history_of_stewardship.pdf.

Baker, Jonny. *Pivot Podcast.* Season 4, episode 38. "Practicing Fresh Expressions with Jonny Baker." Aired April 3, 2023, on Faith+Lead.

Bassler, Jouette M. *God & Mammon: Asking for Money in the New Testament.* Nashville: Abingdon Press, 1991.

Beck, Michael. *Pivot Podcast.* Season 4, episode 36. "The Mixed Ecology in the US with Michael Beck." Aired March 21, 2023, on Faith+Lead.

Benedict, Peter. "Community Discernment." Written as a paper for a class at Luther Seminary shared via email with the author on February 23, 2023.

Bennett, Ty. "People Support What They Help to Create." Accessed July 21, 2023. https://tybennett.com/people-support-what-they-help-create.

Beuchner, Frederick. *Wishful Thinking: A Seeker's ABC.* San Francisco: Harper One, 1993.

Blaschka, Amy. "This is Why You Should Embrace Creative Constraints." *Forbes.* April 20, 2020. https://www.forbes.com/sites/amyblaschka/2020/04/20/this-is-why-you-should-embrace-creative-constraints/?sh=73df5a8b7cb7.

Brown, Brené. "Listening to shame." TED. March 16, 2012. Educational video. https://www.youtube.com/watch?v=psN1DORYYV0.

Caimano, Cathie. "Bye-bye 'Bi-vocational'." *Faith+Lead.* June 20, 2022. https://faithlead.org/blog/bye-bye-bi-vocational/.

Clarendon Presbyterian Church. "Who We Are." Accessed July 14, 2023. http://www.clarendonpresbyterian.org/who-we-are.

Concordia Place. "Our Difference." Accessed July 18, 2023. https://concordiaplace.org/principles/.

Connelly, Ben. "Bivocational Ministry as a Path of Unexpected Spiritual Growth." In *Bivocational and Beyond: Educating for Thriving Multivocational Ministry*, ed. Darryl W. Stephens, 161–178. Chicago: ATLA Open Press, 2022.

Copeland, Adam J. *Crowdfunding for Congregations and Faith-related Nonprofits*. May 2016. https://www.adamjcopeland.com/wp-content/uploads/2016/05/Crowdfunding-Guidebook-Version-1.1-May-2016.pdf

"COVID-19 Congregational Study." *Lake Institute on Faith & Giving*. September 2022. https://scholarworks.iupui.edu/bitstream/handle/1805/23791/lake-covid-report2020-2.pdf?_gl=1*14q8mh8*_ga*MTEyNDkxNjU1LjE2Nzg5MTAyOTU.*_ga_61CH0D2DQW*MTY3ODkxMDI5NS4xLjAuMTY3ODkxMDI5NS4wLjAuMA.

DeYmaz, Mark. *Disruption: Repurposing the Church to Redeem the Community*. Nashville: Thomas Nelson, 2017.

DeYmaz, Mark, and Harry Li, *The Coming Revolution in Church Economics: Why Tithes and Offerings Are No Longer Enough and What You Can Do About It*. Grand Rapids: Baker Books, 2019.

Elsdon, Mark. *We Aren't Broke: Uncovering Hidden Resources for Mission and Ministry*. Grand Rapids: Eerdmans, 2021.

The Emory Fellowship, "Vision + Mission," accessed July 12, 2023, https://emoryfellowship.org/vision-mission.

Finn's Place. "Home." Accessed July 18, 2023. https://www.finnsplacetx.org/.

Friends of Christ Church Lutheran. "FRIENDS." Accessed on July 10, 2023. https://friendsofccl.org/FRIENDS.

Galileo Church. "Home." Accessed July 18, 2023. https://www.galileochurch.org/.

GIIN. "What You Need to Know About Impact Investing." Accessed July 20, 2023. https://thegiin.org/impact-investing/need-to-know/.

Gustafson, David M. "A Church History Of Bivo: Tentmaking from the beginning until now." *ECFA Today*. Spring 2016. https://www.efcatoday.org/story/church-history-bivo.

Gustavson, Kent. "Prayer of Good Courage." Mountain Vespers. 2006.

Harder, Dave. "Reimagining Church Buildings: From Liability to Asset." In *Crisis & Care: Meditations on Faith and Philanthropy*, edited by Dustin D. Benac and Erin Weber-Johnson, 77–84. Eugene, OR: Cascade Books, 2021.

Howard, Cameron. "Lessons in Innovation from the Old Testament." *Faith+Lead*, November 14, 2019. https://faithlead.org/blog/lessons-in-innovation-from-the-old-testament/.

King, David P., Christopher W. Munn, Brad R. Fulton, and Jamie L. Goodwin. "NSCEP: National Study of Congregations' Economic Practices." *Lake Institute on Faith & Giving*, 2019. https://www.nscep.org/wp-content/uploads/2019/09/Lake_NSCEP_09162019-F-LR.pdf.

Jamieson, Janet T. and Philip D. Jamieson. *Ministry and Money: A Practical Guide for Pastors.* Louisville: Westminster John Knox Press, 2009.

Jones, L. Gregory. "Pruning for sustainable design." *Faith & Leadership.* September 12, 2011. https://faithandleadership.com/l-gregory-jones-pruning-sustainable-design.

Lose, David. "Who is My Neighbor?" *Working Preacher.* July 8, 2013. https://www.workingpreacher.org/dear-working-preacher/who-is-my-neighbor.

McIntyre, Georgia. "What Percentage of Small Businesses Fail? (And Other Need-to-Know Stats)." *Fundera by nerdwallet.* November 20, 2020. https://www.fundera.com/blog/what-percentage-of-small-businesses-fail?irclickid=V5WzyJ0mdxyPUXkxnJxgZUcsUkFzboSLESLm1g0&utm_campaign=Skimbit%20Ltd._10078&utm_source=Impact&utm_content=Online%20Tracking%20Link&utm_medium=affiliate&irgwc=1#sources.

National Council of Nonprofits. "Myths about Nonprofits." Accessed July 18, 2023. https://www.councilofnonprofits.org/about-americas-nonprofits/myths-about-nonprofits.

Norvell, Travis. "How One-to-One Conversations Reintroduced a Church to its Neighbors." *LeadingIdeas.* March 8, 2022, https://www.churchleadership.com/leading-ideas/how-one-to-one-conversations-reintroduced-a-church-to-its-neighbors/.

Parish Properties. "Hybrid Approach." Accessed July 18, 2023. https://www.parishproperties.ca/hybrid-approach.

Peace Community Center. "About Us." Accessed July 18, 2023. https://www.peacecommunitycenter.org/about-us.

Picardo, Roz. *Pivot Podcast.* Season 4, episode 43. "How to Get Started in the Mixed Ecology in a Local Church with Roz Picardo." Aired May 9, 2023, on Faith+Lead.

Powell, Mark Allan. *Giving to God: The Bible's Good News About Living a Generous Life.* Grand Rapids, MI: Eerdmans, 2006.

Real Rent Duwamish. "Home." Accessed July 18, 2023. https://www.realrentduwamish.org/.

Rogers, Mark. "Passing the Plate." *Christianity Today.* March 12, 2009. https://www.christianitytoday.com/history/2009/march/passing-plate.html.

Rooted Good, "Mission Possible" instructions.

Scanlon, Leslie. "Jesus won't abandon you if you don't have a full-time pastor." *The Presbyterian Outlook.* September 12, 2022. https://pres-outlook.org/2022/08/jesus-wont-abandon-you-if-you-dont-have-a-full-time-pastor/.

Sirolli, Ernesto. "Want to help someone? Shut up and Listen!" TED. November 26, 2012. Educational video. https://www.youtube.com/watch?v=chXsLtHqfdM.

Smith, Christian, Michael O. Emerson, and Patricia Snell. *Passing the Plate.* New York: Oxford University Press, 2008.

SpringHouse Ministry Center. "How It Came to Be." Accessed July 18, 2023. https://www.springhousemn.org/how-it-came-to-be/.

SpringHouse Ministry Center. "Mission/Vision/Covenant." Accessed July 18, 2023. https://www.springhousemn.org/mission-vision-covenant/.

Smith, Ted A. *The End of Theological Education.* Grand Rapids, MI: Eerdmans, 2023.

Stevens, Marty E. *Temples, Tithes, and Taxes: The Temple and the Economic Life of Ancient Israel.* Grand Rapids: Baker Academic, 2006.

Stroeh, John and Carol Watson. "Stewardship of Land." *Faith+Lead.* March 27, 2023. https://faithlead.org/blog/stewardship-of-land/.

Terfa, Natalia. *Uplift.* May 28, 2021.

Twist, Lynne. *The Soul of Money: Reclaiming the Wealth of Our Inner Resources.* New York: W. W. Norton & Company, 2003.

Williams, Sidney. *Igniting Imagination: Leadership Ministry.* Season 8, episode 2. "Fishing Differently with Sidney Williams." Aired April 26, 2023, on Apple Podcasts.

Wooldridge, Leslie Quander. "Bivocationalism has historical roots—and modern benefits." *Faith & Leadership.* October 18, 2022. https://faithandleadership.com/bivocationalism-has-historical-roots-and-modern-benefits.

ZA Blog. "The 3 'Quests' for the Historical Jesus." *Zondervan Academic.* September 21, 2017. https://zondervanacademic.com/blog/historical-jesus.

Zscheile, Dwight, Michael Binder, and Tessa Pinkstaff. *Leading Faithful Innovation: Following God into a Hopeful Future.* Minneapolis, MN: Fortress Press, 2023.

Zscheile, Dwight. "Will the ELCA Be Gone in 30 Years?" *Faith+Lead,* September 5, 2019. https://faithlead.org/blog/decline/.

Index